Immigrants Settling in the City

VALERIE MARETT

Immigrants Settling in the City

Leicester University Press
(*A division of Pinter Publishers Ltd*)
London and New York

© Leicester University Press, 1989

First published in 1989 by Leicester University Press
(a division of Pinter Publishers Ltd)

Editorial offices
Fielding Johnson Building, University of Leicester,
University Road, Leicester, LE1 7RH

Trade and other enquiries
25 Floral Street, London, WC2E 9DS

British Library Cataloguing in Publication Data
A CIP cataloguing record for this book is available
from the British Library
ISBN 0-7185-1283-9

Designed by Douglas Martin
Photoset in Linotron 202 Ehrhardt
Printed and bound in Great Britain by
Biddles Ltd, Guildford and King's Lynn

Contents

PART TWO: THE LONGER TERM

Preface and acknowledgments

In telling this story of the Asians who were expelled from Uganda in 1972 it has been my anxious endeavour to use their perspectives, speculations and explanations of what happened to them before and after coming to Leicester. The book is their story as they told it: only their names are not their own. I remain eternally grateful to all the refugee families who made me feel that I was a friend rather than an intruder.

I count it my good fortune that I knew the Leicester Council for Community Relations when it was a true forum for the exchange of ideas and a force in policy-making in Leicester. Much local information incorporated in this book was obtained from various documents freely circulated and discussed by members. I gratefully acknowledge too, the help given to me by local politicians, educationalists and housing officials. I am especially indebted to those people – predominantly female – who worked in the voluntary groups. Whether Asian or indigenous, they shared one characteristic: they were surprised that anyone should think that they were important enough to be consulted.

My sincere thanks go too to my tutors at the School of Social Work at the University of Leicester who sustained me through the doctoral research on which this book is based. Without the good service of the Library staff at Scraptoft Campus, Leicester Polytechnic, this research would never have been possible.

Finally I must thank the staff of Leicester University Press, especially Susan Martin who guided me through the tedious process of preparing this work for publication.

VM
May 1988

Introduction

1. MIGRATION INTO LEICESTER, 1950–1972

The legendary prosperity of Leicester was founded on its hosiery, knitwear and footwear manufacture and its more recent light engineering, printing, adhesive manufacturing and food processing.[1] The years after the Second World War brought increasing affluence to the city. A local industrialist commented: 'We are suffering from a thousand years of prosperity ... there is an acute labour shortage.'[2] By 1967 Leicester was at the height of this boom. The M1 motorway now ran past the outskirts of the city and Leicester had supported the biggest share of building speculation outside London. It became a magnet town for immigrants from the Caribbean, the Indian subcontinent and, by the 1960s, from East and Central Africa; for one feature of Leicester's workforce had for long been the large numbers of females employed both in its factories and as outworkers; the city could provide jobs for both men and women.

A comprehensive history of this post-war settlement of New Commonwealth people has yet to be written. Although there is a growing literature on specific aspects of the settlement such as housing[3] and the reaction of the local newspaper (the *Leicester Mercury*)[4] to Leicester's new citizens, contemporary accounts such as those concerned with Birmingham[5] or Nottingham[6] are lacking, despite the fact that in 1974 the Highfields area (in the city's inner core) was labelled by a visiting researcher as 'a classic transition area'[7] where immigrants, especially first generation immigrants, find accommodation.

Nowhere is this lack of information better illustrated than in figures relating to the actual numbers of people involved. Ironically, it was only after Leicester's traditional industries went into recession in the second half of the 1970s, forcing Leicester's unemployment rate above the national average, that statistical data became available. In 1977, when Leicester was designated one of 15 local authorities to receive aid under the government's Urban Programme, demographic surveys relating to the city's ethnic minorities were finally commissioned.

The 1940s and 1950s formed the period when the city's Afro-Caribbean community began to settle, following those from Eastern Europe. By 1951 some 700 Asians (mostly Punjabi Sikhs from Jullundur and Houshiarpur) were living in Leicester.[8] The early 1960s saw the arrival of people from Pakistan and Gujarat, including the latter's textile city Ahmedabad. The only annual count of Leicester's growing ethnic minority communities at that time was by the Medical Officer of Health, Dr B. Moss. The figures contained in his *Health of the City of Leicester* reports were criticized as being both inaccurate and scaremongering (much emphasis was placed on the incidence of tuberculosis and high birth rates),[9] but his reports were always given a prominent place in the columns of the *Leicester Mercury*. In 1966 the Sample Census[10] gave the numbers of persons in Leicester whose place of birth was in Commonwealth countries, colonies and protectorates as 10,750 out of the city's total population of 279,030. Moss stated that the methods of calculation might be 'inadequate to compensate for the actual changes' that had occurred since the full Census of 1961,[11] and in 1967 estimated the immigrant population as about 25,000, or 8 per cent of the total. Nowhere was the vagueness over numbers better illustrated than in the *Leicester Mercury* of 12 December 1969. The headline read: 'Immigration: The Facts'. But the report was hardly precise, giving the coloured immigrant population of the city as '21,000 to 30,000'. In 1970 the Community Relations officer provided 'a more definite estimate of 26,000 New Commonwealth Immigrants: made up of 11,000 Indians and East Africans; 2,000 Pakistanis; 6,000 West Indians and 7,000 other groups',[12] and the 1971 Census gave the number of those in Leicester who had been born in the New Commonwealth as 23,280 out of a total population of 284,210.[13] In 1970 Dr Moss calculated that births to 'immigrant mothers' amounted to 22.17 per cent of the total births in the city,[14] and in 1971 he estimated that Leicester's immigrant population was 36,000, of which Kenyan Asians made up 8 per cent.[15]

Six years after the expulsion of the Asians from Uganda in 1972, the Leicester Council for Community Relations estimated that there were 50,000 'black' people in the city:[16]

	Number of group	Percentage of black population
Ugandan Asians	10,500	21
Kenyan Asians	7,000	14
Tanzanian Asians	2,000	4
Punjabis (Sikh)	8,000	16
Pakistanis/Bangladeshi	3,000	6
Rest of Indian subcontinent (predominantly Gujarati)	11,500	23
Afro-Caribbean	8,000	16
Total	50,000	100

More than a decade after the expulsion a major survey conducted by both the City and County Councils estimated Leicester's population as:[17]

		Percentage
White	214,350	74.9
Asian	63,200	22.1
West Indian	5,100	1.8
Chinese	550	0.2
Mixed or other	2,850	1.0

The main places of birth for Leicester residents were:

	Percentage
UK	79.9
East Africa	7.8
Indian subcontinent	7.8
Caribbean	0.9

The reasons for the attraction of these groups to Leicester have already been briefly mentioned: prosperity, lack of strikes, range of industry ('a city of a thousand trades') and work for all including women. In 1968 the hosiery industry had a 60 per cent female workforce, and by June 1973 the *Leicester Mercury* was pointing out that there was a shortage of operatives: 'Work is Available. Where are the Women?' There is evidence that these factors influenced the early immigrants to move from other towns such as Coventry and Birmingham, and by the 1960s Leicester was rated by one ethnic group (the Patels) as the most desirable place to live in the provinces.[18] But there were other factors, of which ease of access to the city was one. Situated in the middle of England, Leicester is at the focus of its communications network – a very significant fact for minority groups who wish to visit and be visited by others for personal, social, religious and commercial reasons. (The use of the motorway network by ethnic minorities has yet to be explored by observers of settlement patterns in Britain.)

Finally, there were cheap houses readily available for purchase. The Highfields area of the city, bounded by the main London Road and the old Midland Railway lines on one side and by Spinney Hill Park on the other, contains a mixture of some larger houses of the Victorian professional classes,[19] which had not gone through post-war re-gentrification as well as smaller versions of these with garrets and cellar/basements and most numerous of all, rows of Victorian and Edwardian terraced cottages. Before the Housing Improvement Programmes of the 1970s and 1980s, most of these properties consisted of two rooms and a back kitchen on the ground floor, with the stairs set at right angles to the row of houses, giving access to three bedrooms. This property had tended to be neglected during the war years, and in the 1950s, when private builders developed estates outside the city boundaries, a migration was set in motion. Highfields became less desirable as a residential area. Lodging houses were opened, patronized by Irish and Polish immigrant workers; many of the smaller houses became short-lease and unsaleable and were rented by people who could not afford a mortgage and were awaiting rehousing by the Council. It was to this area that the early immigrants moved. Housing was cheap, it was near the city centre, and more importantly it was near the foundries and yarn mills and to companies like Metal Box and the British Shoe Corporation which offered shift and night work. The Imperial Hotel, an old Victorian temperance house, was licensed to a Sikh; corner shops became Asian-owned and houses 'subtly orientalised by exotic colour schemes'.[20]

By 1972 Highfields still housed the main concentration of West Indians and Asians, but other settlements had taken place along two main routes out of the city: the Belgrave and Melton Road area (already predominantly East African Asian), and along the Narborough Road. From the 1950s Asians, faced with the overall shortage of private rented housing[21] and the hostility of landlords with their 'No Coloured' notices and policies, with little hope of council housing and with a positive desire to purchase housing for independence and as an investment, had begun buying property. In the 1950s terraced houses could be bought for under £1,000, in 1968 an Asian estate agent was advertising this type of house at £1,400, and by 1972 'unmodernised terraced houses of the standard six room type attained a price of about £4,000.'[22] National newspaper reports, intent on emphasizing 'the middle-class exodus' from East Africa in the 1960s, featured accounts of successful businessmen who had moved out to the suburbia of Wigston and Oadby: 'whether Leicester likes it or not, they [i.e. the Ugandan Asians] will have ambitions to settle in pleasant houses in Wigston and send their children off each morning in smart school uniforms.'[23] But the reality of the material circumstances of most immigrants housed in the inner city is indicated by the fact that there only 57 per cent of houses had a fixed bath, an inside toilet and hot water.[24] The fact remains, however, that had the immigrants (especially those from the Indian sub-continent and East Africa) not invested in the inner city areas by becoming owner-occupiers, many streets would have been demolished and redeveloped as happened in other parts of Leicester and other cities.[25] The improvement to both housing stock and the local environment through the designated statutory programmes in the 1970s (Housing Action Areas and General Improvement Areas) would also have been very different in their application, because these immigrant owner-occupiers had a vested interest in the future of the neighbourhoods where they had bought properties.

Although the social forces which cause clustering of newcomers to urban areas are complicated and debatable, in essence it can be seen as the 'effect of two gross forces'. The first is the positive view, that the group wants to segregate itself in order to perpetuate its own beliefs and life styles. The second sees a group having to cluster together because of the 'negative prospective force' of the majority society. In Leicester as in other locations it is difficult to balance out the comparative strengths of these two phenomena.[26] Although Harrison in 1974 found no evidence that by the early 1970s there was in Highfields any 'close knit community ... it is as fragmented as any British settlement',[27] what was already apparent was the emerging communalism which was particularly characteristic of Asian society in East Africa. By 1972 there were already over 40 different clubs, societies and organizations devoted in the main to the social and welfare needs of Asian groups.[28] Although the Federation of Indian Organizations attempted to function as an umbrella organization, much more meaningful to the majority were their own caste or sect associations such as the Brahma Samaj or the Muslim Khojashia. There were three Hindu temples, three Sikh Gurdwaras, two mosques and an Islamic Foundation. Various national sporting and dance competitions, such as the Raas Garba, were already being staged. Perhaps the most visible evidence of Leicester's Asian population was the opening in 1974, two years after the Ugandan exodus, of the luxury cinema and entertainment complex in Belgrave Road, the Natraj, which opened with the 'grand European première' of the latest Rajesh Kanna film *Aap Ki Kasam*. The modern glass and concrete building also housed saree shops and groceries. At an exhibition of Indian culture organized by the Indian National Club in 1973, catalogues were handed out advertising two branches of the Bank of India, and stating that 'inspired by Leicester's own tradition, Indians now own factories, mostly textile, with capital assets around £10,000–£15,000 ... Indians are entering small engineering factory ownership and buying garages.' This claim was not unjustified – though it should, however, be contrasted with more recent research which shows that the majority of Asians work in the unskilled and semi-skilled sectors of the manufacturing sector, and are typically hourly paid in textiles and light engineering trades.[29]

2. LEICESTER AND THE EAST AFRICAN ASIANS, 1968–1972

The single feature which makes Leicester different from other cities which experienced post-war migration is its 'East African connection'. In the 1950s the immigrants came to fill gaps in the labour force in key industries which indigenous workers did not want, and would not or could not perform. In the 1960s East African Asians came because of the 'push' factor from those newly independent African countries intent on Africanizing their economies – a process which coincided with the imposition of much tighter entry controls by successive British governments.

The British Nationality Act of 1948 divided British citizenship into two categories – citizenship of independent countries of the Commonwealth, and citizenship of the United Kingdom and Colonies. Citizens in both categories remained 'British subjects' but were also 'Commonwealth citizens'. The two terms were interchangeable, but it was the status as British subjects which gave right of free entry to the UK.[30] The 1962 Commonwealth Immigrants Act broke with the principle that all citizens of Commonwealth countries, including citizens of the British colonies, had free and unrestricted entry. Although it did not expressly discriminate on grounds of colour or race, its aim and effect were to limit the admission of coloured immigrants, since Commonwealth citizens and United Kingdom citizens whose passports were not issued in the UK had to obtain a Ministry of Labour employment voucher before being allowed entry. The citizens of the 'Old Commonwealth' countries of Canada, Australia and New Zealand, however, retained their right of entry.[31]

Perhaps the most controversial of all the British Immigration Acts was the Commonwealth Immigrants Act passed by the Labour Government in March 1968. This aimed at extending control, and denying right of entry except to those who had substantial connection with the United Kingdom by birth or descent. The main thrust of the legislation was to impose tighter controls on the immigration of UK passport-holders from East Africa, which was regarded as desirable because as African governments began to reduce the granting of trading licences and work permits to non-citizens, and to put time limits on residence in their countries for non-citizens without licences or permits, the numbers entering the UK from East Africa shot up – from 6,000 in 1965 to 31,600 in 1967 after the African governments disclosed their plans for restricting non-citizens.[32] In an attempt to 'beat the ban' before the legislation came into force, a further 12,823 Asians entered in the first two months of 1968. The British government's quota of 1,500 special entry vouchers for heads of families allowed British Asians in at around 7,000 a year, and this was an attempt to return to the numbers seeking entry before the imposition of restrictions on their economic existence in East Africa. Reginald Maudling, then Deputy Leader of the Conservative Party, set aside the argument that the Asians had been given right of entry to the UK 'by default' – because their passports were issued by the UK authorities. A pledge had been given at the time of Kenyan independence of unfettered entry:

> There is no doubt about the rights which these people possess. When they were given these rights it was our intention that they should be able to come to this country when they wanted to do so. We knew it at the time, they knew it and in many cases they have acted and taken decision on this knowledge.[33]

In view of what was actually to happen in 1972, when there was a very urgent need indeed for the Ugandan Asians to exercise their right of entry after General Amin expelled them, it is worthwhile to note that James Callaghan, the Labour Home Secretary, admitted in 1968 that 'mass expulsion' would swamp the whole procedure' provided for in the bill. 'All one can say is that in that kind of situation one would apply measures that seemed appropriate.'[34]

The reactions in Leicester to the influx of Kenyan Asians in 1968, as reflected in debates in the Town Hall (particularly in the Education Committee) and in the columns of the *Leicester Mercury*, were similar in content, if not in volume and intensity, to those in 1972 to the arrival of the Ugandan Asians.[35] Indeed, certain headlines in the *Leicester Mercury* in 1968 appear to have been reused in 1972; that of 24 February 1968, 'Asians Heading for Leicester', bears a strong resemblance to that of 7 August 1972, 'Many of the Expelled Asians May Make for Highfields'. There were the same reports of the reluctance of India to accept British passport-holders: whether they (or their ancestors) had been born in India or not, the Indian government regarded them as Britain's responsibility.

Letters to the *Leicester Mercury* in 1968 pointed to the social exclusiveness of the Asians already in Leicester, the overcrowding of schools and the lack of understanding about the feelings of those having to live in the 'immigrant area of Highfields, on the part of the middle class let-them-come brigade'. The latter, it was frequently pointed out, did not offer to share their homes with those rushing from East Africa. There were also references to the ignoring of the real wishes of the 'ordinary Leicester citizen … this is Human Rights Year … What about our Rights?', and suggestions 'that the only hope is to be found in an English Nationalist Party'.[36] There were, too, forerunners of the cartoons which were to appear at the time of the Uganda exodus such as the depiction of the Clock Tower in the centre of Leicester as a mosque.

There were marches in the city for and against the government's Immigration Act ('the most disgraceful piece of legislation since the war');[37] and a campaign was waged by the Students Union of the University of Leicester against the *Leicester Mercury*, which was called 'the greatest user of half truths'.[38] The statement of one local MP (Mr John Peel) that 'it would be fatal for all concerned, and nobody knows this better than Leicester ... if a situation were to develop when our schools, hospitals, houses and jobs proved inadequate to cope'[39] was to be reiterated by some of the city's politicians four years later.

Forecasts of how many immigrants would come to Leicester were made in 1968, as they were in 1972, mainly by Asian spokesmen. The Secretary of the National Association of Indian Workers forecast that 1,250 Kenyans would settle in the city, but emphasized that this would cause no pressure on the housing stock since the community would provide accommodation. His fellow Sikhs set up a committee of the Khalsa Dall to integrate the work of settlement. The Secretary placed special value on the 'middle-class status and English-speaking characteristics' of the Kenyan migrants: 'This means that the problems of integration will be less difficult than for those who come from the Indian sub-continent.'[40] As to why Leicester attracted the Asians in 1968, a spokesman of the Indian Workers Association said that 'as for many Indians in the past, not only can men and women earn a decent wage and there is less discrimination than elsewhere.'

By June 1968, when the numbers coming from Kenya had dropped drastically, David Ennals, Minister with Responsibility for Immigrants, came to the city. Under the heading 'Journey into Highfields', an editorial in the *Leicester Mercury* commented on how the controlling Conservative group on the City Council were concerned with the practical issues such as how to find extra school places, and wanted a temporary ban on immigration.[41] On his visit Ennals met with the local Anti-Immigrant Society (AIMS), which claimed to have 13,000 supporters; he had 'friendly discussions' with this organization but stated that he regarded it as being 'harmful to the City's race relations'. The *Leicester Mercury* commented in an editorial that it was not surprised by Ennals's statement, but at the same time 'AIMS has released people from the tongue tied fear of expressing opinions that might be condemned as racialist.'[42]

On 17 May 1968 the leader of the Conservative group, Alderman H. Heard, declared that 'this City has reached its limit ... we need a temporary ban on further immigration.' The same protests were also made, as would be made again in 1972, that Central Government did not understand the extent of Leicester's needs, especially in the sphere of education. When the scheme for the replacement of the Catherine Street primary school in Highfields was axed, the Director of Education described this scheme as 'a vital part of the plan to deal with the worsening situation caused by the influx of immigrant children'.[43] The city's Finance Committee stated that the authorization of an extra £60,430 for public spending was inadequate to meet the costs caused by the number of immigrants arriving in the city during the early months of 1968. Labour Councillor Mrs H. Roberts articulated then a view that was to be frequently repeated, especially by the city's Education Officer in 1972:[44]

> The problems are caused because of the concentration in certain areas ... *we have been dealing without undue fuss since 1946* ... but now there have been particularly large arrivals in March. Other cities have made a great play. Leicester has just as big a problem, but we have rather played it down.

This *laissez-faire* policy can be traced to the tradition that Leicester had always lived up to its motto of 'Semper Eadem' ('Always the Same'), able to accommodate to changes without 'fuss', and that 'in politics as in geographical location Leicester belongs to the Centre.'[45] When the British Association had its annual meeting at Leicester University in 1972, the participants were told that 'in spite of the presence of considerable numbers of West Indian and Asian immigrants racial tensions have up to the present been held in check';[46] yet the *Leicester Mercury* almost simultaneously carried the headline 'City: Future at Stake' – a reference to the expected arrival of the Ugandan Asians.[47]

The attitude of local politicians can be explained in part by the characteristics of the East African newcomers. All generalizations are in part falsifications, and it is easy to expose the myth that all members of this group were English-speaking, with middle-class occupations reinforced by capital which they had managed to transfer to this country. But it can be speculated that many did become socially mobile downwards, because they had lost their traditional middlemen roles, particularly in Kenya and Uganda. So they concentrated on regaining status, for example by opening scarcely profitable street corner grocery shops in the inner city areas, and avoided drawing attention to themselves, or any form of confrontation in politics or public, keeping a deliberately low profile. It was only in 1975 that, exasperated by unfair practices and bad management, they took the lead in the strike at the Imperial Typewriters factory. Leicester's *laissez-faire* stance was in brief a mixture of complacency and the belief that good could come by cautious pragmatism rather than from deliberate policies in regard to its immigrants. It did, however, lead to a panic reaction when the numbers coming from Uganda increased sharply in 1972. In Leicester's defence, it must be said that the city had no lead from successive governments at Westminster. It was only after the Ugandan expulsion in 1972 that the possible repetition of a sudden exodus from other states in East Africa (particularly Kenya) was to haunt successive governments, and political announcements in East Africa were closely watched to see if any increased pressure was being put on Asians to leave.[48]

In 1970 Leicester did have an early warning of the arrival of Asians, who were desperate to leave Uganda, and who had made up their minds to do so before the *coup d'etat* in January 1970 which brought Idi Amin to power. Neither the full-time officers nor the elected representatives on the Council appeared to have taken any notice of a report forecasting the number of Ugandan Asians intending to come to Leicester which was produced by the Joint Council for the Welfare of Immigrants in December 1970.[49] On the basis that the government was about to increase the number of vouchers allowing entry to the UK, the JCWI interviewed a selection of 1,047 families in Uganda, all of whom were without funds. Of these, 229 families stated that they would be going to Leicester, 50 were 'considering doing so' and in addition a group of students stated that they intended to make Leicester their base. The reasons they gave were the obvious ones: their destitute situation left them with no choice about where they stayed, at least for the initial months, but in Leicester they would find people of their own community. In addition, the fact that housing was known to be both good and relatively cheap, that the employment situation was also good and that people already settled from Uganda had found no difficulty in getting jobs, was known to the community both in the UK and Uganda. Among these 229 families there were 282 children of school age, the majority of secondary school age. On the estimation that 30,000 Ugandan Asians wished to come to the UK, it was concluded then that it was 'reasonable for the Leicester authorities to expect in 1971 at least some 3,000 heads of families'. The expected number of children was estimated at around 4,230. A breakdown of professions and occupations showed the majority to be shop-keepers, store-keepers, carpenters and clerks. The report added:

> In view of the suffering and deprivation already experienced by these people
> concerned, it would, we believe, be disastrous if once having arrived in Leicester
> they were to be the subject of public discussion again and regarded as a problem.
> At the same time, we see that their unexpected arrival could cause difficulties,
> especially in the education field ... How difficult this would be would depend on
> the period during which they arrived, but in view of the fact that children are already
> having to wait for admittance to school we believe that this matter is serious enough
> to be drawn to the attention of the authorities in Leicester.

The accuracy of the report was confirmed by the events of 1972. It estimated that around 7,000 'as the upper limit' would eventually make Leicester their home, and that this would have particular consequences for the allocation of secondary school places. The range of occupations too was closely in line with those who reported to the reception centre set up by the British Asian Welfare Society for Ugandan refugees. In a further report (July 1971) the JCWI noted that in Uganda 'many people are living in an atmosphere of fear and unpredictability very uncertain of what will happen next.' But Mary Dines, the Secretary of the JCWI, then an organization with a mere handful of full-time workers operating from a small office at the back of Toynbee Hall, London, was unable to influence the politicians.

When news of the expulsion of the Ugandan Asians came in August 1972, the *Spectator* was not alone in pointing out that at least the government had received warning 'this time'.[50] During the first six months of 1968, when 60,000 British Asians had come from Kenya alone, there had been no warning. By 14 August 1972 the JCWI, had issued a blueprint of recommended emergency arrangements for 'The British from Uganda'. It stated that at least two-thirds of those leaving Uganda would have friends or relatives in Britain, and because of the distribution of the present community from East Africa they would be likely to head for three areas: London, the East Midlands and Manchester. 'Leicester is likely to be the main receiving area … It is estimated that as many as 20,000 (including women and children) could have friends or relatives in the City.' The document ended with a note addressed 'to final points of destinations':

> Inevitably people will wish to live in areas where there are others of their own community in the first place … There will be a need for a solid group of people who will not only assist but will be able to stand up to any backlash from right wing organisations that may develop.

But despite these forecasts, when the 'inevitable' was made irreversible by Amin's expulsion in August 1972 of all Asians from Uganda, the immediate reaction in Leicester – and not least by its City Council – was that of astonishment and anxiety. Forgetting its affluence and its moderation in politics, Leicester retaliated to the news by advising the Asians to keep away.

PART ONE

Arrival and Resettlement

Chapter 1 The expulsion from Uganda: background and causes

Explanations of why General Idi Amin decided to expel the Asians from Uganda in 1972 range from those which regard events as merely stemming from his erratic and irrational personality, to those which search for much deeper causes, located in the role played by the Asians in the social and economic structure of Uganda.[1]

In the period before the Second World War there was very little interest among scholars in the small but economically significant settlement by Asians in East Africa. Neither did the Asians themselves (with a few exceptions) record their own achievements, perhaps because businessmen generally do not bother much with things around them so long as their own businesses are unaffected. One commentator warns that there is a danger of 'creating reasons' to explain certain behaviour and this is easily done when trying to account for relations between Africans and Asians in Uganda. Apart from these speculations, there have been debates over the legality of the expulsion. The only systematic evaluation made by the Ugandan Asians themselves about their fate was documented by Adams in 1975.[2]

1. AMIN: VENDETTA OR OPPORTUNISM?

The tabloids at the time of the expulsion explained events as being caused by Amin's growing paranoia. Typical of this was the *Sunday Mirror*'s headlines 'He's Nuts – Chequers Crisis Talks on General Amin – Heath is Warned'.[3] These reports seriously underestimate Amin's capabilities[4] and popularity as distinct from his brutality.[5] Much more serious for the Asians were the direct repercussions this kind of journalism had on events in Uganda where the papers were distributed. This portrayal of Amin as just a 'big, stupid black tyrant' was seen by some analysts of the mass media as part of the consistently negative attention by the Western media which manipulates and selects information on black leaders.[6]

Amin indeed provided lucrative media material for all the years that he was in power, well illustrated by a film made in 1980 by Sharad Patel, a Kenyan Asian, which has been described as being in the worst Fleet Street tradition of treating Amin as a joke.[7] Though the Leicester refugees had first-hand evidence of or knew at second hand about Amin's enjoyment of sadistic scenes such as public executions, nevertheless they frequently spoke of his guile and the skills by which he remained in power for almost a decade. One of them described him as 'an evil primitive genius. He was a corporal but never a clown.' The film, like another made in 1974 and purporting to be a documentary about Amin,[8] proved unpopular with Leicester Asian cinema goers. Although the 'documentary' drew huge crowds in Paris and was popular in London, when it was screened in Leicester it played to half-empty houses – this at a time when local Indian cinemas were drawing large audiences. The general reaction to these portrayals of Amin was summed up by one young student who said, 'Why should we pay what money we have to see a film about Amin whose life is no way a source of laughter to us?'

Amin's apologists reserve their support for his actions rather than for his character. Some assert that Amin would have been content to be a professional soldier, but because of the incompetence and corruption of civilian politicians he took over leadership. He was the exception to the general lack of faith that Africans have in the ability of fellow Africans.[9] He might have been a pragmatist, approaching problems with an 'empty mind', but he had an instinctive popularist appeal. Although the Western press might laugh at Amin's account of God appearing to him in a dream and telling him to expel the Asians, this was 'Africa's genuine dream'.[10]

Amin had a penchant for bold policy pronouncements without forethought.[11] The background to his first announcement on 4 August 1972 that all Asians would have to leave Uganda was not, it has been said, a reasoned policy of using the Asians as a means of diverting attention from Uganda's deteriorating economy. For this to be so Amin would have had to be informed about the state of the economy, and he neither listened to his ministers nor did they dare tell him. The fact was that he wanted money. His expenditure on weapons (estimated to have risen to over $90 million compared with $20 million before he seized power) and his recruitment of tribesmen from the West Nile and Madi districts were features of his free spending on a restless army which he hoped to contain, for it was the army which had backed him when he overthrew President Obote on 25 January 1971.[12] His financial problems were made worse by Britain taking a disturbingly long time actually to deliver the £10 million loan promised in 1971. There was nothing unusual about Amin's speech on 4 August being delivered away from Kampala: indeed it was a feature of East African political life for highly placed government officials to do this. Speeches about Asians not being wanted had been made before. What was different about Amin's August 4th speech is that he may have thought of a ready solution to his financial predicament while he was actually speaking. The decision to expel the Asians could have been a hurried one, but it was the British media which turned it into headline news.[13] The local media did not make much of it. Amin was an ardent listener to the BBC Overseas Broadcasts and there what had been 'asides' about Asians in a speech dealing with other matters assumed unpremeditated importance. His methods were grotesque and dramatic, and may have caused a wave of sympathy for the Asians outside

Uganda, but they struck a chord in the heart of the masses of almost every African country.

2. THE ECONOMIC BACKGROUND

Most commentators, particularly African, believed that the expulsion of the Asians was not just a spontaneous event, and that any ruler of Uganda would have sought to destroy the Asian economic block and thus Africanize the economy. Amin's first attack on the Asians had come within a year of his seizing power. In December 1971 a conference was called. It marked a break in tradition in that Asian representatives were called *by district*. (Previously consultations had taken place on the basis of the various ethnic and religious groups within the Asian community.)[14] Both British Asians and Ugandan Asian citizens were invited, without any distinction being made. Once they had assembled, what had been previously thought of by the Asians as an exercise for the amelioration of race relations turned out to be a verbal assault on their 'malpractices' as 'saboteurs'. Amin charged them on two scores. First, he referred to their manner of conducting their businesses, which included charges of hoarding, creating false shortages, overcharging and violating the income tax laws by keeping two sets of books, and writing their accounts in Gujarati. Secondly, he complained of the undervaluing of exports and overvaluing of imports, the difference being paid into overseas accounts.

That there was validity in some of these charges is stressed by at least one Asian commentator. Patel[15] cited what he classed as deliberate acts of sabotage: the inflated rents to which African businessmen were subjected by Asians, and price discrimination in favour of fellow Asian traders, which helped to undercut African traders. The admission of Africans into businesses was a mere token, real power being retained by the Asians.

As well as commercial malpractice, Amin's memorandum to the assembled Asians attributed poor Indo-African relations to their disloyalty in not returning to Uganda after studying overseas. If they did return they went into 'private practice', forgetting the fact that the Ugandan government had paid for their tuition, whereas they should have shown their gratitude by serving the public sector. After blaming the Asians for their non-integration into Ugandan society and their maintenance of a rigid endogamy, Amin dealt with their citizenship status. Although he promised to honour those issued by Obote, he warned that the outstanding claims for citizenship would not be processed and were cancelled. Fresh application would have to be made. Amin's message to the Asians was: 'It is yourselves, through your refusal to integrate with the Africans in this Country, who have created this feeling towards you by the Africans.'

Amin (and the other Africans) failed to give any credence to a document published by the Asians the day before the conference began. This gave the Asians' version of many of the features which caused offence. They complained about their treatment in the local media, their exclusion from official functions, and that they were not given the opportunity to serve on governmental and parastatal bodies. They emphasized that their conservatism, especially over marriage, was to be found in any society in any country in the world. They claimed that the fact that 12,000 applications for citizenship had not been finalized could hardly be blamed on them, and they pointed to general bureaucratic delays. Perhaps most important of all, they asked for a clear statement by the government which would define the areas of economic activity where they could be allowed to concentrate. The Asians pointed to their past record in developing the primary produce processing industries (for example, cotton ginning, oil seed crushing, flour milling), their part in manufacturing (cotton, glass, timber) and their expertise in the distribution system and service industries. They also showed that government policy after Independence had advanced African interests through the Co-operative Movement, which had given black Ugandans control of cotton, coffee and tea processing. The Uganda Development Corporation and the National Trading Corporation had helped Africans in the spheres of trade and commerce.

Though Amin's 8 December speech contained some conciliatory phrases, its emphasis on intermarriage certainly reminded the Asians of the nightmare of forced marriages imposed on other Asians during the time of Shaikh Karume in Zanzibar in 1963. By January 1972 the different Asian communities (including the Ismailis and Goans) were united as never before, and in a mood of indignation they again presented a lively defence of their position. They reiterated much of what was in their first memorandum, and this time added a reference to 'the resentment and revulsion felt by Ugandan Asians' at having to carry Asian Census receipts to prove that they had been counted in the Indian Census of October 1971. This they compared to 'the system of passes now in force in the Apartheid regime in South Africa'.

There was a period of surface calm for eight months between the December conference and the expulsion order, during which the Aga Khan visited Uganda and was given a reassurance by Amin that he himself did not condemn all Asians and would not bring about forced interracial marriage. However, no real action was taken to follow up constructive recommendations as to how integration could best be facilitated. The Asians stood aside when all Israelis were ordered to quit the country in March 1972. The state of affairs months after the December conference remained without any positive moves on either side, a situation to be expected after such a conference, when the General and the Indians talked *at* each other and when the possibility of progress seemed slight.

African resentment against Asian traders, and the Asians' role as middlemen in the bureaucracy, commerce and the professions, rather than their social exclusiveness, were the reasons for their expulsion most frequently mentioned by contemporary commentators in 1972. Belonging to what has been called 'industrious minorities', the Asians in Uganda shared with others of these groups – the Chinese in South-East Asia, the Parsees in India and Jews throughout the diaspora – the accusation that they were adept not only at making money but at keeping it within their group.[16] The essential contribution made by these groups to the economies of the countries where they have settled brings rewards to many of their members, but not to all. Their material prosperity is a visible attribute. Their very industriousness and their apparent monopoly in trade and commerce make them unpopular. Their cohesion and organizing ability seem directed to mere self-advancement and so even after generations they are still classed as outsiders. But the middleman minority is often numerically small, and depends for its power on the elite of the country where they have settled. In many instances, this middleman minority actually mediates interaction between the elite and the subordinate group, yet is all too often used as a scapegoat in times of stress. Bonacich[17] reviewed the whole field of literature on 'middlemen minority', describing them as being perpetual strangers, often brought into conflict with their surrounding societies: 'the recent Indian expulsion from Uganda has meant great personal loss ... other middleman groups have suffered worse fates.' Amin was often described as 'an African Adolf Hitler', and the Asians were seen as being like the Jews of Nazi Germany. But there were great differences, one of which was that the Jews were fully integrated into the social and cultural life of their country.

Another perspective on the Asians' economic role is provided by the theory that it can only be understood through a grasp of how colonialism worked in East Africa.[18] Instead of concentrating on the middleman 'neo-Protestant Ethic' characteristics of the Ugandan Asians, an explanation for their expulsion can be found in the way they were used by the British. The Asians were agents for Britain's 'colonial penetration process'.[19] Up to the immediate Independence period, the Asians were seen as aspiring to partnership with the Europeans, requesting that they be Justices of the Peace, and be admitted to high-ranking positions. They lost sight of their real subject status, and their political loyalty remained focused on Britain. Given this background it was not surprising that when the Africans actively entered politics in the period following the Second World War they aimed at the overthrow of the Asians. The speed at which they were able to implement this was, however, entirely unexpected. The Asians' loyalty to the colonial government was not reciprocated: from the beginning they had been disliked by the white settlers. The colonial government itself wanted to drive them out of the country, referring to them contemptuously as 'those dukawallahs', 'those bent Asian lawyers'.[20] The African middle classes, educated in the British-run school system, had their own prejudice strengthened by their teachers. Mukherjee[21] traced the restriction placed by Britain on Indian immigration to Uganda (for example, by the Immigration (Control) Bill 1948), and described the 'Colonial masters' as becoming 'cruel to the Indians' because they were no longer needed in Britain's post-war development schemes. He placed the blame on the Indian community for not playing a progressive part in African politics. Over a decade before the expulsion, Mukherjee wrote: 'The Indians are awaiting the hour to evacuate this country, and in the meantime, enriching themselves as best they can under the servile conditions, without regard for anybody else.'

The generally accepted enmity towards the Asians has also been described as the same resentment felt by the lower classes towards shopkeepers throughout history.[22] There was, too, the feeling that the Asians filled the jobs that Africans could take over. However, the particular resentment against shopkeepers may well be too sweeping and a blatant transference of Western political clichés to an African context, where it may well be meaningless. Resentment, it has been suggested, was not so much against shopkeepers as such as against what was seen as the general exploitation of ordinary people. But it was not confined to the ordinary African. Thus, Jorgensen[23] emphasized that pressure to expel the Asians came to Amin not suddenly in his famous dream but from experiences in his waking life: from the constant demands from the aspiring Bagandan traders, from Joseph Mubiru, Governor of the Bank of Uganda, and from the *Ugandan Argus* with its constant plea for state aid for African traders.

The 'historic indispensability' of the Asians in the building of East Africa's economic structure[24] may well have been exaggerated because of the Asian traders' visibility.[25] This visibility of the Asian dukawallahs or small traders led to the replacement of one myth (that the Asians first came to Uganda to build the Uganda railway at the end of the nineteenth century) by another, that they were a race of shopkeepers.[26] From the start Asians served as clerks in the colonial bureaucracy. But the anti-Asian feeling of the Africans was easier to manipulate against shopkeepers. In 1962 40 per cent of Asians in Uganda were classed as wage and salary earners but this was smaller than in Tanganyika and considerably less than in Kenya. The overall fact of the surprisingly small percentage of Asians in Uganda compared with the rest of East Africa was forgotten in the blaze of publicity about their expulsion.[27] Nevertheless, the importation of Asians by the colonial government to fill gaps in both the administration and economic sectors resulted in what Mazrui [28] called 'Indiophobia' on the part of Africans. Asian clerks commanded higher salaries than Africans, and that, coupled with their entitlement to periodic leave in India, made the colonial government move towards their replacement – hence the establishment in 1922 of Makerere College for the training of their African substitutes. Amin was far from being the initiator of Indiophobia. Its origin can be traced back to the early days of colonialism in the concept that East Africa was intended to be the 'America of the Hindus', a concept not introduced by the Indians themselves but by Sir Harry Johnson, who was Special Commissioner to Uganda at the turn of the century (1899–1909). Johnson saw them, too, as an important agent of colonial change, for he hoped that they would bring with them, though at second hand, the benefits that Britain had brought to India.[29]

Before Uganda gained Independence increasing attacks on the Asian monopoly culminated in 1959 in an attempted boycott on Asian goods.[30] Measures for squeezing out non-citizen Asians were devised by President Milton Obote in 1969. In March 1970 the Trade Licensing Bill restricted non-Ugandan traders to special areas and also controlled the goods they could sell. The Immigration Bill controlled the entry of non-Ugandans and established a system of work permits for particular posts. Verification of the fact that these new laws were designed to give Ugandans most of the jobs and enable them to carry out most of the country's trading activities is contained in contemporary newspaper comments. Under the Immigration Act, which came into effect on 1 May 1970, Asians (and other non-Ugandans) who were born in Uganda, or who had lived there for many years, were no longer allowed to take up jobs without specific permission; permits were only granted if a job could not be done by a Ugandan. By the Trade Licensing Act, which came into force in January 1970, non-Ugandan Asians were only allowed to trade in specific areas in the larger towns, and could not trade in a list of key commodities. The real aim was to force Britain to acknowledge responsibility for British subjects, for many Asians who held British citizenship decided to apply for entry to the UK rather than face further restrictions on their lives.

The restriction of Asian traders in rural areas resulted in their ceasing to trade, perhaps becoming destitute or leaving the country, or alternatively opening shops in the towns. African and Asian were, in fact, in non-competing categories; African trade was in traditional products (butchery, fish, fresh produce). Rural Africans increased their visits to the towns to avail themselves of services (such as repair of tools) that the 'new' African traders could not perform. Thus Amin's expulsion order can be seen in the light of the fact that he and others realized that as long as the Asian traders in the towns controlled the supply of consumer goods, no real success could accrue to any attempts at Africanization.[31] In the process of post-Independence nation building, all East African governments adopted policies of 'economic proselytism' in order to create an African commercial class.[32] But appeals made to Asian businessmen to take Africans into their enterprises were bound to be ineffective because of the Asians' essentially family business structure, with its strongly personal element. In contrast to Kenya, Africans in Uganda had a longer history of economic activity and moreover there were fewer Asians. This, combined with Amin's impatience, helps to account for the fact that it was Uganda which expelled Asians, although they were equally unpopular in Kenya.[33]

The institution of the 'duka' (the abbreviation for 'dukawallah') was in fact an effective agency linking the rural areas to urban centres. This class was active where small investment was the requirement. The small profit margins of the up-country duka, with labour-intensive demands involving the whole family, and its austere life style were nearer the truth than the popularized stereotype of an exploiting unscrupulous wealthy Asian class. The universal affluence of the Asians was a myth believed even by other Indians in the subcontinent. Certainly Africans regarded Asians primarily as 'banjani' (traders), given to displaying superior airs. Africans were more prepared to accept exploitation and particularly 'superiority' from the European ruling stock.[34] The abject poverty of some Indian families in the slum areas of Kampala and the small profit margins of many Asian shopkeepers were ignored. Mamdani[35] argues that Amin's expulsion of the Asians was naïve. They were only a dependent *compradore* class ('the petty bourgeoisie of Capitalist underdevelopment'). The only effective measure towards Africanization was when Amin challenged the

British banks in December 1972. But the more general view is that the colonial pattern of development, with its pyramid three-tiered systems of stratification of British, Asian and African, had produced a built-in friction between Asian and African that ran through the entire economic and social fabric.[36]

3. SOCIAL EXCLUSIVENESS

The Asian's social role cannot be easily separated from the economic:

> Vis-a-vis business, an Asian primarily sees himself as a member of the joint family and later at the centre of a number of overlapping circles (such as caste, language group, religious group, network of kinship) which comprise the total Asian society. Within the Asian society business activity is part of the total social activity. The same individuals and groups which interact socially do so economically as well. By comparison, social participation (particularly institutionalised social activities) outside the Asian society is inter-personal and minimal.[37]

Various ethnographic studies conducted in the era of decolonization in East Africa describe some of these 'circles' of caste (such as Patidar and Lohana) and religion (such as Khoja Ismaili).[38] What emerged from these is the essential communalism and 'circles' of autonomous subcultures, the result of which was that they formed a barrier to the Asians' ability or willingness to participate in political life in Uganda. In addition, the Asians in East Africa, more than any other Indian overseas groups, maintained strong ties with their kin and caste in India. At the same time they did not initiate among themselves the social reform movements and modernization taking place in urban India. Although, then, the Asians appeared to be an exclusive group, concerned with their own social life, there were social and religious divisions among them. Outsiders might have labelled them a 'community', but the exclusiveness of the communal-centred leaders and elders prevented younger members from taking an active political part in supporting African independence. Those individuals who did were seldom popular with their own community. But more importantly, this exclusiveness and concern with perpetuating communal traditions were interpreted as racial arrogance and superiority.

Tandon[39] argues that the Ugandan Asian communities were certainly not blameless in the crisis which led to the expulsion, for their cultural arrogance and sense of racial superiority vis-à-vis Africans were at times as bad as those of the Europeans. Moreover, each of these distinct Asian groups had its own internal system of social status. When these features are combined with the fact that the Asians' social organization was closed to *all* outsiders, it is not surprising that they were accused of being clannish and exclusive. In contrast to their dealings with Asians, the Africans, particularly in the towns, had some idea of what was entailed in European life styles and culture through their contact with schools and missionaries. It is easy to see why the Asians appeared to be contributing nothing to the society in which they lived. Their hesitation about taking local citizenship confirmed this idea.

In the post-Independence era, there were many utterances by heads of states about the necessity for Asians to integrate with the Africans, but the exact meaning and the implications of this process were not spelt out. The only form of minority–majority relationship that Asians could possibly have contemplated was that of 'pluralism', with its permitted diversity in personal and family life. When Amin talked of inter-racial marriage as *the* answer, he was not only threatening the most sensitive of primary relations, but also showing a lack of understanding about racial contacts. 'A crash programme of racial marriage cannot be the solution to the racial problems.'[40]

What is important, though, is the amazing resilience of the communal structure of the Ugandan Asians, which has survived the trauma of expulsion and resettlement in the UK. When Parsons[41] speaks of the direct effect of Amin's action as resulting in the destruction of the Asian community, with its social networks irrevocably broken, he ignores the reconstruction which has taken place, involving substantial regrouping such as in Leicester. There is plenty of evidence of the endurance of endogamy rules and even sub-caste (*gnati*) occupational roles, particularly among Lohanas and Patidars.[42] The communities have their own social centres, and indeed much of the voluntary self-help of resettlement was on a communal basis.

4. THE ASIAN VIEWPOINT

For the 68 families of Ugandan Asians who settled in Leicester and provide the basis for this book, the main reason for the expulsion was often seen in terms of Amin's personality. The perceived irreconciliation between the two processes of 'integration' and 'Africanization' was also frequently mentioned, particularly by those who regarded the expulsion as totally unjust and even criminal. One ex-government clerk pointed out that there was no equality of opportunity in the Ugandan government service, with Africans being promoted 'even when there were far better Asian clerks who had been there longer'. There were references as well to 'Asians being pushed aside' in entry to the university (only Ugandan citizens were admitted) and to the secondary schools, yet blame was attached to those who sought education overseas. A motor mechanic working in Leicester summed up his view of the position: 'We Asians were never political. But I don't think it would have made much difference. In Kenya, there is today only one Asian MP.[43] We did not seek power, we only wanted to stay on and carry on working.' He went on to say that he and his brothers had decided to stay in Uganda, even after Obote had announced that transport businesses would be nationalized. He added that 'if any blame is to be laid', then it was because his family like so many others were taken in and tricked by promises that Uganda needed them and could not manage without them.

The Asians' bewilderment about their misplaced optimism over what the 1971 coup against Obote had hoped to achieve, featured frequently. A typical response was: 'We thought that Dr Obote was threatening us with all his ambition about wanting to nationalize everything. Amin's Africanization turned out to be much worse.' This theme of self-blame for not having sensed the warning signs was repeated over and over again by the younger members of the group. Blame was also transferred on to those individual Asians in Uganda who did give real cause for being disliked, and whose actions were thereby used to justify African dislike of the whole community. Those who were particularly singled out were the affluent who transferred large sums of money out of the country. A teenage daughter of a shopkeeper said:

> It's in the past now. No use looking back ... but they are living in luxury here
> in the UK. They gave us a bad name. What mattered to the Africans was the things
> they could understand like some shopkeepers overcharging. So the poor man behind
> the counter was an easy target, while the big boys got away with it.

Another aspect of this self-blame was the fact that the cornerstone of every Asian success story in Uganda had been an outward show of affluence in the form of television sets, refrigerators and above all cars. All these, especially the cars, were also the symbols of success amongst Africans, but they were possessed by a much smaller number. A few years before the expulsion it was estimated that for every two Asian households there was one private car and one commercial vehicle. The public service vehicles, too, were largely in Asian hands. These symbols were the features that 'pinched the African mind most'.[44] African ownership of cars came earlier in Uganda than in Kenya, and it was a very important feature, signifying affluence in its modern form. A Sikh auto-engineer said that 'the Africans either had Mercedes or cycles. We had cars like Peugeots or Mercedes trucks ... we needed these for our businesses.' He pointed out that Africans accepted the Europeans having cars ('partly because they had always had them, and they were the ruling class'); however, not only were cars essential for Asian business purposes, but it was a fact that 'we paid for them out of our own profits'; as an auto-engineer and salesman he knew that most of the Europeans had overseas grants for their cars.

Jealousy of Asian economic success was seen by the Asians as the main reason for their expulsion. This is hardly surprising since 49 of the 68 heads of households studied in Leicester were themselves in some form of business in Uganda. It was noticeable, though, that not one of them described himself as a 'dukawallah'. In fact when this term was used, it was dismissed as an all too familiar but derogatory term ('that's what the Africans called us ... it's really an insult, a putting you down'). Much more favoured was 'merchant', though the goldsmiths always described themselves specifically as such. In any attempt to describe the general economic status of Asians in Uganda, individuals used the caste term 'Banyant' (trading castes). As far as the Leicester group was concerned, they ascribed to themselves the accepted stereotype of 'traders'. When asked whether, since this was the label applied by commentators who were not themselves part of the Ugandan Asian society in Uganda, it was accurate, the typical rejoinder was that of course among their numbers there were 'professionals (even priests) and civil servants', but essentially they saw themselves as a business and trading community. This was illustrated by descriptions of the vertical organization of most Asian business concerns: for example, in Uganda, and now in Leicester, the Asian clothing manufacturers are linked with Asian retail outlets. One ex-hardware merchant said: 'Asians in Uganda were all related by blood and trade.' References were also made to the way in which members of the family, though they had other occupations, still kept in touch by investments or giving occasional professional help to the family business. Jaymini, who was by 1977 a secretary in a city centre office, maintained that: 'All right, we were not all shopkeepers or in business in Uganda. But my uncle had a shop. I did his typing in the evenings. My cousin who is an accountant did the books. My father was in transport. He never charged, but had his share of the profits.' She said that a lawyer uncle gave free advice. Her mother also served in the shop. A sister who was a schoolteacher had helped during the school holidays in ordering stock: 'you don't have to look far for a business in most of our families'. Another former retailer explained: 'My generation was in trade by and large. After Independence we encouraged our children to go in for other occupations, but they still had the family business at their backs and in their minds. That's why the African government turned on us.'

None of the group, young or old, expressed any deep dislike of the Africans. The older members tended to spell out at some length how they had always extended credit to their African retail customers (for example, 'When we shut our shop, they said, "Who is going to let us have goods in advance of cash payment now?"'). There were frequent references to the fact that the relationship was normally that of 'good master–good servant'. The way in which the Asians gave all their household possessions to African servants in September–October 1972 was constantly reiterated. One of the group emphasized that 'regardless of what was thought, I never heard one Asian insult an African by saying such things as "Mali ya nyoko!" ("Take yourself off!").'

What then of the reported universal African dislike of Asians? When the Leicester group spoke about this, they spoke in terms of specific and personal interactions between individuals from the two races, some of which were good, some bad. However, they were all agreed on one point: that there was a rapid acceleration and articulation of pent-up resentment on the part of Africans after the expulsion order. An older man (who had spent months trying to get work in Leicester and had failed to do so) asked his daughter Hamita to explain to me: 'My Dad says Amin made them avaricious. They became like "Kondos" [robbers] and we were glad to leave Mubende.' The Africans' dislike of Asians because of their experiences of exploitive business practices was continually challenged, especially by the older members. An ex-director of a wholesale firm said: 'Business is business. But our record was better than the Africans[45] and we were more honest than those African co-operative societies. They were set up by the government but they were full of bad management and embezzlement. It was the country that was corrupt, not the Asian businesses.'

What then of the contention that Asians had no emotional attachment or loyalty to Uganda? It was especially the younger members who disputed this; after all they had been born there, they knew no other country. They emphasized that though Asian money had been sent out of Uganda or had been used to endow purely Asian institutions (such as schools, hospitals and communal halls), things were changing. This change came not only through an imposed policy of Africanization but on a genuine personal and attitudinal level. One young man, Amritlal, and his younger sister explained this. Amritlal said:

> We no longer called the Africans 'Kalia' ... we had been to school with them,
> they were our class mates. When the Asians were there in the early days, they rode
> around on bikes, spoke Swahili, mixed with the Africans. We were going back to
> those times – the Africans needed our hard work and capital.

His sister added that the younger Asians were learning Swahili in school and 'within a generation we might have been eating their motoke [mashed green bananas] as well as curry.' Many others expressed their sense of loss not only over their share of the abandoned Asian property but also in terms of human investment and experience.

Coupled with this sense of loss, there was resentment over Amin's vacillations and changes in policy. A Sikh, father of two small children and a self-employed motor mechanic from Jinja, complained:

> Amin had no plans. He played games with us. He took away Asians from owning
> coffee factories. He took away cotton businesses ... He forced us out of country
> areas ... in the end, those Asians left in Uganda after the expulsion were forced
> back to work on the land. You see now ... he had no plan ...

In any of the discussions about how overcoming mutual distrust and peaceful coexistence might have been achieved in Uganda, a potential 'melting-pot' of the races by intermarriage was never regarded as having any validity. Two young men agreed at one point in one conversation that 'It wasn't impossible, just a few of us were thinking about it ... but probably would not have done so, when the family got to know.' A far more typical response came from Bharat who said:

> Our position has nothing to do with feeling superior. It's just culture and tradition.
> How many Asians in Leicester have married West Indians? They are our equals
> here. Besides there were so few of us Asians in Uganda we had to marry each
> other or become completely absorbed. So I am not being patronizing about racial
> marriage, just practical.

Although never categorized as a prime reason for their expulsion, the women amongst the refugees frequently mentioned Amin's own intentions to have an Asian wife.[46] A young factory worker was adamant: 'We knew it as a fact. He was going to marry an Aga Khan girl. She was to be his fourth wife. Her people sent her to India and he blamed and hated the lot of us ...'

Some of the Asian family members emphasized another aspect, that the older

Asian leaders lacked the foresight to encourage their communities and move towards integration. Sandra, a Polytechnic student, spoke of 'even a British Prime Minister talking about the winds of change ... but our leaders looked away'. Another viewpoint (mentioned often by Hindu and Jains) was surprise at the fact that Amin, a Muslim, expelled other Muslims and even those who had taken out local citizenship. When the topic was mentioned by one Muslim family (though the head of the family had entertained Amin in his own house) they said that Amin was not a conventional follower of Islam, but rather a 'Black Muslim'. The father of the family added that he had heard from his cousin who still travelled frequently to Kampala from Nairobi that many of the best ex-Asian businesses now had Muslim names.[47] The reason was that when the Ugandans applied for these they assumed Muslim names, and because they were black and Muslim they were favoured by the government. He also spoke about other features: 'There are many Libyans there flashing more wealth than we ever did. So what matters is that if you are Asian and Muslim you are not accepted.' He stated too that 'Amin tried to be a Black Muslim, but he made false promises to Stokeley Carmichael and other black Americans about offers of jobs in the Civil Service vacated by the Asians. So it's just the same thing, being American makes them not accepted, though they say they are Muslim.'

Many regretted that Amin worsened a situation which, given a few years, might have solved itself. The Asians were already leaving Uganda at the rate of 200 a month. At that rate the Asians could have left Uganda within seven years. A former goldsmith said: 'We are a cautious people. Amin's personality and the British government's rationing of vouchers caused a flood not a flow.' Another view was summarized by an Asian girl who was just entering secondary school when the expulsion took place: 'No one alone can be blamed ... the trouble with us Asians was, we were too smart in business, too few and too different.'

5. IMMIGRATION CONTROLS AND THEIR REPERCUSSIONS, 1968–1972

The expulsion of the Asians from Uganda can be viewed as forming part of a more general movement of Asians from East Africa. Notwithstanding this, President Amin's ultimatum on 4 August 1972, that Britain should take over responsibility for all Asians holding British passports and that this should take place within three months, posed the Conservative government with the most dangerous political issue since it had come to power. Control of immigration had been one of its major planks during the General Election in 1970; another election promise had been that there would be an attempt to control *where* those admitted would be allowed to settle. Speaking at Walsall in January 1969, Edward Heath, the party leader, had said: 'Our proposals would enable the authorities here in Britain to make sure that before anyone is allowed in, the social condition and community resources in the area in which he works are adequate.'

The events in Uganda occurred when the government was hurriedly steering its new Immigration Act and Rules through Parliament.[48] The Act fulfilled yet another electoral promise: it replaced the former dual codes, one for aliens and another for Commonwealth citizens, by a single comprehensive code.[49] In so doing it widened even further the gap between those Commonwealth citizens with direct personal or ancestral connections with the UK, that is, those with a UK-born parent or grandparent (patrials) who had the 'right of unrestricted entry and of abode', and those non-patrials who had no such connections. The UK passport-holders in Uganda were not slow to recognize that the Act's general criterion for admission was based on country of origin. This became very apparent when in June 1971 there was an increase in the immigration quotas for East Africa but at the same time there was a decrease in immigration quotas for the rest of the Commonwealth (that is, for other non-patrials).

These new quota allocations introduced by the Conservatives increased the number of entry vouchers available to the UK passport-holders in East Africa from 1,500 to 3,000. Kramer[50] claimed:

> At the same time the Conservative Government negotiated a yearly grant of eleven and a half million pounds to Kenya ... but [it] was also apparently contingent on a pledge from Jomo Kenyatta, Kenya's President, that as long as the money kept coming, the Asians in Kenya would be allowed to stay.

A similar deal was being negotiated with President Obote just before he was deposed. He and Prime Minister Edward Heath were in the process of negotiating an agreement which aimed at clarifying the confusion surrounding those Asians who had applied for Ugandan citizenship in return for an increase of vouchers for those who wished to leave. The agreement was one of the subjects to be discussed at Singapore during the 1971 Commonwealth Conference, when at home in Uganda Amin successfully ousted Obote. So 'a golden opportunity of solving the problem of stateless Asians in Uganda was lost',[51] for Obote might well have initiated a more efficient and fair system of granting local citizenship to those Asians who wished to take it. The so-called 'Maudling quota' included a special allocation on a once-only basis of 1,500 vouchers for the most desperate of cases caught in the backlog, and 500 for those who had gone to India to join the 2,200 people on the waiting list there. The Conservative government hoped to avoid a repetition of the 'shuttlecocking' spectacle of Asians trying to get admission to the UK which rose to a peak in the final months of the Labour government in 1970. At that time, keeping down the numbers of East African Asians had become 'an obsession for Mr Callaghan', then Home Secretary in the Labour government.[52] After the General Election in June 1970, the British Asians had appealed to the European Commission of Human Rights in Strasbourg, using the provisions of the European Convention on Human Rights. The Commission found against the British government, so the Conservatives reacted by bringing in the 'Maudling quota'. However, it was pointed out by the Joint Council for the Welfare of Immigrants in July

1972 that frustration was building up among British subjects, particularly in Uganda.[53]

Even after Amin's ultimatum, the government stressed that there was no other way of dealing with 'the problem in a humane way: it should be by an orderly quota arrangement.'[54] Interviewed on the BBC programme 'The World This Weekend', David Lane (Under-Secretary of State, Home Office), stated: 'We are an overcrowded island and immigration must and will be strictly controlled ... successive British Governments have said, "Yes but we can only absorb you at a limited rate ... You must wait your turn in the queue."'[55]

In Uganda itself the 'crisis' for the Asians had been developing since 1966, when President Obote changed the constitution. At the time of Independence (1962) it had been declared that anyone born in Uganda could become a citizen by right. The alteration of this promise was a deliberate move on the part of Obote to disqualify Asians from automatic birthright citizenship. It is possible to view this from an African perspective: the colonial power, Britain, was responsible for introducing the Asian population to East Africa but did not nationalize it. Had there been a 'different kind of definition, the Asians would never have been regarded as aliens'.[56] In 1966 Obote had rejected the principle of acquisition of nationality by *jus soli* (law of the soil). This was at a time when large numbers of Asians had received no reply after having applied for Ugandan citizenship.[57] Citizenship had originally been offered on condition that the Asians should legally renounce British citizenship within three months, which involved the British High Commission in having to refer many cases to London, for renunciation of British citizenship depended on the establishment of entitlement to it in the first place. As a result substantial numbers of Asians did not obtain renunciation certificates within the three months allowed.

These complicated processes were also connected with the right of the Asians to trade. In 1969 the Ugandan Licensing Act (which came into force in 1970) not only required non-citizens to apply for special permission to continue business, but also asked for a bank deposit of 80,000/- (£4,470). In addition the Ugandan Immigrant Act, passed at the same time, required all non-citizens in Uganda to obtain an entry permit. Those who could not obtain a permit could be expelled, fined or imprisoned. It was Obote's intention that by 1977 all resident aliens should have been replaced by Africans.

Between 1968 and 1972 various surveys,[58] conducted by very different organizations such as the Conservative Bow Group and the Joint Council for the Welfare of Immigrants, found that there were growing numbers – variously estimated from 2,000 to 9,000 families – of British Asians who were unable to work or carry on business. There was a new and frightening development in Uganda: the creation, particularly in the smaller towns like Lira, of virtually refugee communities consisting of Asians who were homeless and without work or money. The situation was described as being far worse than it was in Kenya, and the future for Asians in Uganda as bleak indeed. There were accusations that various practices introduced by the British High Commission were making life even more difficult for those Asians wishing to leave, along with suggestions that the situation was of the Asians' own making because they had not applied for Ugandan citizenship; but the considerable numbers who had done so had often had their applications rejected, or received no reply. All these reports urged a higher level of voucher allocations than had been granted in 1971 by the Conservative government. However, the government largely ignored campaigns such as 'Admit the British' (whose Chairman, Himat Lakhani, was later to become prominent in the resettlement process of the Ugandan refugees). But in addition the Joint Council for the Welfare of Immigrants and the all-party Committee on United Kingdom Citizenship warned of the inadequacy of the current quota system. The government chose to disregard reports that appeared in Kenyan newspapers in January 1971, which claimed that several hundreds of Asians were planning to fly out of Uganda as a result of Amin's announcement that citizenship applications from 12,000 Asians were cancelled. Even against the background of Amin's instructions to his military police to 'crush' senior civil servants and Asians who held political meetings, the British High Commission stated: 'As far as we are concerned there are no signs of exodus. The rhythm of consular work has remained absolutely constant throughout the three months since the new quota allocations were introduced.'[59] By contrast, Luff[60] wrote that 'a hundred thousand Asians with British passports are stranded in a no-man's land of statelessness ... they have been declared aliens and are deprived of their jobs ... Labour and Conservative legislation has successfully staunched the flow to the UK, and caused a queue of poverty in East Africa.'

6. MIGRATION PATTERNS BEFORE THE EXPULSION ORDER

Of the 68 families which are the focus of this book, just under a half had intended to come to the UK and their plans to do so were under way before the expulsion order. For the remainder, their view was that 'Uganda was the only country we had ever known ... it was our home.' So they had intended to go on living there. But even these families had contacts with the UK – frequently because one of their daughters had married and settled either in Leicester or London.

Those families who had already decided that there was no future for them in Uganda had a typical pattern of phased migration. An adult member (most frequently the oldest son) would be the first to leave and get employment in the UK. He then acted as a 'pioneer' preparing for the time when the others would eventually join him. He would find accommodation, buying a terraced house in Leicester's Highfields. He would make arrangements with local schools and Further Education Colleges for places for younger brothers and sisters, who would also come to Leicester to live with him. Meanwhile, back in Uganda the parents still waited for their entry permits. Since the full implications of the Ugandan government's Africanization policies still remained unclear, often one member of a family (usually a younger son) hoped to stay on there. This was especially so if there was the hope of continuing profits from a well-established business enterprise.

For those who had lost their jobs or were unable to go on trading and knew there was no future for them in Uganda, the waiting period for entry visas to the UK was a difficult time. They described how their life savings were gradually used up. They blamed the bureaucratic delays and *de facto* rules imposed by both the Ugandan authorities and the British High Commission. Some admitted to having been tempted to use up what money they had left in order to pay the fees of 'agents', who were able to obtain a quota or visitor's pass for the UK within a fortnight or so of being approached. One of the group claimed that for around 1,000/- everything could be 'arranged: even accommodation in Leicester'. Others of this group had made plans to go to India. The British and Indian governments had an agreement by which Asians who intended to 'settle' in India were permitted to enter that country if their passports bore a certificate of entitlement to enter the UK. They also had to sign an undertaking not to work. But they could apply to come to Britain as part of the special voucher allocation.

Only two of the 68 families had absolutely no one, whether relative or friend, with whom they were in contact in the UK. Among the rest, even among those who had not planned to leave Uganda entirely, a small number had actually visited Leicester before the expulsion. Through personal experience or widespread correspondence with relatives already in Leicester, most had an accurate picture of both the difficulties and opportunities to be expected in such an English city. Their vision was certainly 'not a rosy one'.[61]

The Asians in Uganda were caught up in an incredibly complex system, so that in one family at the time of the expulsion decree there might be four classes of citizens. Grandparents might have retained Indian nationality. Parents and children could have kept British nationality, or could have been recognized as Ugandan citizens, or could be British protected persons with British passports, though their possession of British passports (which, stamped 'D', were known as 'D valued passports') did not give them automatic entry to the UK. There was yet another group who might in fact be technically stateless, because of the delay in the processing of the required renunciation of British citizenship when they applied for Ugandan citizenship.

Among the Leicester refugees there were examples of numbers of families who were involuntarily split up for a considerable period before 1972. In one such case, the wife had applied for a passport for herself and her four children. Her passport was stamped with an entry permit for the UK. Her husband remained behind with two teenage daughters. He was without a job and had been waiting for 18 months for a voucher. The wife worked for a while after coming to Leicester but then became ill. She was living on Supplementary Benefit until, as she related, 'Amin reunited us after nearly two years ... people say Ugandan Asians can settle in any place ... but people forget that we do so, because we are made to do this thing.'

Chapter 2 The ninety days: 5 August - 7 November 1972

1. REACTIONS TO AMIN'S THREATS

News of Idi Amin's speech in which he made it clear that non-citizen Asians were no longer needed in Uganda reached most of the Asians on 5 August 1972, the day after it was delivered. Ninety days later, on 7 November, only a handful of Asians remained in the country. In the time between these two dates the contradictions and shifts in Amin's policy statements confused everyone, both inside and outside Uganda. They also served to distract attention from what was his real intent from the first: the 'Africanization' of Uganda. Certainly for the first few weeks, most of the Asians found it difficult to realize the finality of this and its implications for them.

There had been threats to their position before, the most recent in December 1971. Then Amin had accused a conference of all the different Asian groups of arrogance towards Africans and of caring only for their own interests. But in the first half of 1972 there had been little public reaction to this. One positive step had been taken by the Madhvani enterprises, which had sought to recruit 'suitable applicants for the sugar works at Kakira as part of the firm's "Ugandizing" policies'.[1] In May 1972 Amin had started on his own Ugandanization. He expelled several hundred Israeli technical and military advisers, accusing them of poisoning the Nile. Colonel Gaddafi of Libya was Amin's chief backer for this expulsion.

When Asians featured in the news, they were those who had already left Uganda and were looking for a way to gain admission to the UK. There were accounts of the Indian government putting pressure on Whitehall to increase the number of entry vouchers to the UK for some of the 10,000 East African Asians who had gone to India. They had done so in the hope of settling in Britain more quickly than if they remained in Africa.[2] Towards the end of July stories were printed of small groups of Asians from both India and East Africa arriving at Heathrow Airport without the necessary documents. They had not been allowed to enter the UK and had become shuttlecocks or 'migronauts' looking for asylum elsewhere.[3] It can be speculated that Whitehall's policy towards these people triggered off Amin's resolve to force the issue of Britain's responsibility for British Asian citizens. When he addressed the staff and students at the Uganda College of Commerce, in Kampala, Amin spoke of foreigners having too much power.[4] Asians were not mentioned as such, but Amin might already have sent a secret memorandum to his civil servants about an impending major move against them.[5] Nevertheless, very few were prepared for the implications for their future contained in Amin's speech to the Airborne Regiment at Tororo on 4 August. These were summed up by the next day's headline in the *Ugandan Argus*: 'It Will Be Britain's Responsibility. The Future of Asians in Uganda'.[6] The soldiers were told that 80,000 Asians holding British passports 'were sabotaging Uganda's economy and encouraging corruption'. The troops were also told to arrest any Israelis who tried to return to Uganda. Amin was more specific about Asian sabotage when he spoke on International Co-operative Alliance Day. He told the farmers that 'the Asians milked the cow, they did not feed it.' He went on to praise the moves to Africanize cotton ginneries (where machines separated seeds from raw cotton) and coffee factories: 'no Asian gave loans to small farmers ... the marketing of cash crops used to be in the hands of Asians, who never bent down to dig.'[7]

The official edict which put the expulsion into effect was the Final Order issued by Amin from his command post at Kampala on Wednesday, 9 August.[8] Three months later, in his message 'congratulating Muslims on completing the Holy Month of Ramadhan', Amin remarked that the Feast of Id-el-Fitr also 'happened to be the day on which the people of Uganda are witnessing the end of one chapter in the history of this country and the beginning of another one'.[9] The Asians had been thrown out.

2. HOW THE ASIANS FARED

Accounts by people who were resident in Uganda at the time give contrasting views on what happened there. For one Asian university lecturer, Mamdani,[10] the expulsion came as a complete surprise. When its inevitability became apparent, he blamed delays at the British High Commission in processing entry visas to the UK for causing further apprehension. This coincided with the increased physical attacks on, and even murders of, Asians. These took place not only up country but in Kampala. Others, too, witnessed beatings, killings and abductions, particularly by the military on the road to Entebbe Airport.[11] The US ambassador, Thomas Melady, who had just arrived in Uganda, noted that the Africans seemed as surprised as the Asians about the expulsion. What struck him was the degree of non-resistance that the Asians displayed. Their acceptance of the situation partly explained the fact that they attempted no physical resistance.[12] The Ugandan Foreign Minister, Wahume Kibedi, was 'surprised that anyone should be surprised at Amin's edict'. The Asians were so unpopular that Kibedi had expected Amin to have moved against them earlier.[13]

Assaults on Asians increased in September when Tanzania invaded Uganda. The Asians were also caught in the crossfire of Africans seeking out fellow Africans disloyal to Amin.[14] As always in a time of uncertainty the rumour factor resulted in exaggeration of events. In the main Asians suffered loss of property, robbery and extortion.[15] The East African Correspondent of the *New Statesman* (8 September) wrote that 'the real crisis seems to be in London – here [in Kampala] there are no anti-Asian marches.' There was evidence of ugly events in western and southern Uganda, but most of the Asians lived in the eastern region or in Kampala itself. Those Asians queuing outside the British High Commission were more worried about difficulties facing them in the UK: 'none have complained of physical violence here.'

Anyone who asks a group of refugees about their recollections of the immediate weeks before their forced evacuation from a country that had been their home for generations can justly be accused of insensitive intrusion. Yet none of Leicester's Ugandan Asians showed reluctance to talk about what they went through during those last days. It was as if memories of the good days in Uganda were strong enough to sustain them in their recollections of the unexpectedly sudden and certainly very unpleasant termination of their lives there. Only four of the refugees claimed that they had foreseen the events as they had happened. They had been convinced all along that Amin was mad and getting progressively worse, so as one of these said: 'A madman like Amin hits out ... he took over from Obote with blood on his hands. He had had his share of African blood, and then it was to be Asian.' The majority, though, said that the Tororo speech came like a thunderbolt. If Asians appeared to take things calmly, it was because they thought it was a false alarm or they did not think that it applied to them individually. Some said that they just could not explain their feelings. One of the women refugees explained: 'When you've lived through a time like August to November 1972 in Uganda, you can't remember what you really believed about your position there previously, or how events come out in your memories now.'

3. THE FIRST DAYS

During the first few days most of the Asians comforted themselves that the worst would not happen. After all, they reasoned, they had lived through a whole series of government restrictions on their trading activities, their employment in the public services sector and their school system. Since Uganda had become independent from Britain in 1962 Asians had survived, even though bribes and other devices might have often been necessary. The Asians were in a different category from the Israeli 'foreigners'. Besides, if the worst came to the worst, only non-citizen Asians had been referred to in Amin's speech. However, a few of the younger refugees recollected that they had been less complacent: 'the older generation stuck their heads in the sand ... they were reading only the small print.'

Various items in the *Ugandan Argus* and particularly in the *East African Standard*, showing that governments *outside* Uganda were taking the situation seriously, however, brought the situation home to the Asians. Britain was to cut its aid to Uganda. India announced that the Asians were 'Britain's problem'. Then Foreign Minister Kibedi threatened 'if they remain in Uganda they will soon see what happens to them', and suggested that Australia and Canada should be alternatives to Britain as new places of settlement. Finally, with all the channels on the radio service repeating the headlines of Britain's newspapers, Asian families started to face up to what was in store for them. Daniel Arap Moi of Kenya told reporters that his country had no intention of providing a refuge for 80,000 Asians and the frontier was to be closed. Zambia blamed the Asians for not identifying with the Africans of Uganda, and Tanzania 'was making no comment'.

Few of the Asians, however, were as resigned as the two 'Indians' who agreed to be interviewed by the *Ugandan Argus* on 8 August and who said: 'We have given our service with a clean heart and we think that Ugandans will accept this. We have no quarrel with anybody and if it is the wish of the Government and the people of Uganda to see us leave, we are prepared to do so.' The 'wish of the Government' was contained in the 'Final Order' signed by Amin on 9 August 1972 and which was to come into force from the day of signing. Asians holding British passports and also now the nationals of India, Pakistan and Bangladesh, except those in essential occupations, would have to leave Uganda within three months. The *Ugandan Argus* (9 August) was jubilant:

Are there any critics this morning of President Amin's statement on the Asians? No! At least not in the minds of all fair minded people in Africa, Asia and Britain ... The hands that went up in horror now hang limp ... The only Asian who is being told to leave the country is ... the person who milked the big fat cow but let someone else feed it.

By contrast, the other English medium newspaper, the *East African Standard* (10 August), was more compassionate:

Consider this morning the plight of 50,000 or more Asians holders of British passports living in Uganda ... you who read this comfortably seated at your breakfast tables ... consider the fear, the knock at the door ... President Amin could be right. He could kick out the luckless, trembling Asians who hold British passports ... and ultimately every non-Ugandan citizen. What happens in the U.K.? Can they be assimilated? Only in high tented Camps on Salisbury Plain.

Certainly 9 August was remembered as a very significant date by most of Leicester's Ugandan Asians. One described it as 'the day when the die was cast ... there was no going back, no not facing up to what Amin meant.' Now there was legal standing to what had previously been regarded as merely rhetoric.[16] But there was still uncertainty as to just who was to be expelled, though nationals of India, Pakistan and Bangladesh were now included. Other aspects of Amin's final order were far from clear. First, the list of those exempted from the Order because of their occupations included so many categories that even the *Ugandan Argus* admitted to their 'fuzziness'. So the paper pleaded for the ministers, who were to tour the country to 'educate the people' about the expulsion, to be given accurate information of the circumstances under which some Asians were to be allowed to stay.[17] The exemptions included not only persons in government service but also those in co-operative movements; professionals like teachers, auditors, lawyers, medical practitioners, but also managers of banks and insurance companies, and finally 'professionals and technicians' engaged in agriculture and marketing.

The vagueness of all this was summed up by one of the refugees who, three years later, remembered going to a meeting of the Jinja Hindu Sabha and speculating along with others there that this order could be interpreted to cover nearly every male adult Asian in Uganda: what, for example, did they mean by 'auditors'? 'All businessmen were auditors either by having a degree, a diploma or experience.' More important was the hint that those Asians who claimed Ugandan citizenship might not in fact obtain verification of this status. Amin had quoted the results from the government's mini 1971 census. This showed 23,242 Asians claiming Ugandan citizenship (8,791 by registration, 14,451 by birth). But newspaper reports stated that the government had reason to believe that the actual number might be smaller. All claims had to be verified by the Ministry of Internal Affairs. Then on Thursday, 17 August not only was the Exemption Clause for non-Ugandan Asian professionals cancelled, but also all those who had Ugandan citizenship were required to produce documents of proof at the Immigration Office. They were warned that if they had not done so by 10 September their citizenship would be void. Next Amin announced a new phase in his 'Economic War'. He accused the Asians of sabotage and arson. On 20 August he told a mass rally at Rukungiri, Kigeszi, that all industries, buildings and businesses owned by Asians would be sold. This would be done through a government agency. The private sale of everything except clothing, furniture and radios was to be prohibited. But most alarmingly of all, he also announced that *all* Asians whether citizens or not were to be expelled from Uganda.[18]

It was this pronouncement, made against even those who had chosen to remain citizens of Uganda, that was rated by the Leicester refugees as the most unfair and illegal of all of Amin's actions. Those Asians who had thought they were safe to carry on living in Uganda, who could produce their appropriate and original copies of documentation and had queued endlessly outside the Immigration Department in Jinja Road, Kampala to obtain them, now found their efforts wasted. It was about this pronouncement that the most real resentment and bitterness was expressed by the Leicester group. A student related his reactions. He and his grandfather had been born in Uganda and knew no other country, and both wished to remain there. They had waited three days to receive verification of their citizenship status at the Ugandan Government Immigration Office in Kampala. Citizens had been told to report there according to the region in which they lived. He emphasized that the delays and insults he encountered at the British High Commission were closely matched by the bureaucratic brusquesness and incompetence at the Government Immigration Office whose staff were totally unprepared for the rush of business. For his own family there was success in gaining verification of their citizenship status and 'we would have been loyal to Uganda. But we saw a motorcade of African traders in Kampala's City Square. They had posters saying "Asians we wish you a good journey".' Other Asians had not even had their citizenship validated. They were those who had queued for days to get to the counter at the Immigration Office, only to be told that their citizenship had been incorrectly processed. The main reason given by the Ugandan civil servants was that their applications had been received after the deadline set. Thousands who had thought they were safe now found that they were technically 'stateless'. They could not stay in Uganda and they had no right of settlement elsewhere.

Just two days after he had announced that all Asians should leave, Amin again changed tack. He told the visiting Sudanese Foreign Minister that those Asians who had managed to verify their citizenship documents at the Immigration Department could stay. By this time, however, the majority of the Asians who eventually came to Leicester had lost all confidence in Amin's promises. They felt that this about-turn might yet in its turn be reversed and that it was a temporary move by Amin to placate those who accused him of racialism. Besides, they thought something could be salvaged, for on the same day as the decision was announced (22 August) Amin sent a long telegram to President Nyerere of Tanzania. Among his complaints about Nyerere's misunderstanding of Uganda's policies was the clear statement that 'unlike Tanzania's nationalisation policy which had been carried through without compensation', Amin's policy was that 'everyone who will leave will receive the proceeds of his property.'[19] This promise, together with a statement by Prince Sadruddin, UN Commissioner for Refugees, that if Asians were made stateless the United Nations would assist them, and the fact that on 26 August Canada (where many of the citizens had relatives) announced that it would be setting up an Immigration Office in Kampala, persuaded those who possessed or thought they had possessed Ugandan citizenship that they should begin to make preparations to leave Uganda. The *Ugandan Argus* (24 August) gave its version rather differently: 'it is all happiness in the Ugandan Asian citizen's camp ... one Asian who has been in Uganda since 1900 said, "Let those who call themselves British citizens go, these Asians are very very bad."'

The British passport-holders as well as citizen Asians delayed their actual departure. Their main reason was the need to stay on as long as possible to receive instructions about how assets were to be registered. Also, they wished to clear the stocks in their shops. They hoped to take as many material possessions out of the country as possible. The real blow fell when at the end of August it was announced that the expellees were allowed to take only £50 per head of family. This was because under the previous exchange control regulations an estimated £100 million could have been exported. With Uganda's gross foreign reserves standing at £15 million it was no wonder that the regulations were changed.[20] The result of this was that many Asians were virtually destitute when they entered the UK.

It was not until 30 August that the Ugandan government required departing Asians to list their assets. Once again the Leicester group remembered still more queues and further confusion. A retired goldsmith recounted the fights which he saw among those Africans who were scrambling to get into the Ministry of Commerce and Industry where they were trying to obtain the necessary application forms for the sequestered Asian assets. Another incident frequently mentioned was the 'meeting of the queues'. Asians standing in line to register their assets waited so long that their line met up with that of other Asians who were getting their passports at the temporary offices at the Industrial Promotion Services (IPS) building.

This endless filling in of forms, the listing of their businesses in the newspapers and on the radio and television, together with the definite promise of compensation, resulted in the Asians believing that the longer they delayed departure the better their chance of seeing that their assets were properly registered. Thus, Deena (who by 1974 was working at the Imperial Typewriters factory in Leicester) gave reasons why she and her family delayed leaving: 'We Asians are property people and we wanted to save as much as we could. Yes, there were the attacks by soldiers. Most people in Kampala made room for relatives from outside to come and stay with them.' She also remembered that they 'stuck together for safety'. When they knew they could take only £50 and personal effects,[21] naturally they tried to bring as much as possible of the latter. Asians went out and bought jewellery, clothes and watches. Moreover, they were told they could take only 30 kilos of luggage on the plane, so they gave away their heavy possessions to their African servants. Others bought new electrical appliances which could be resold in Britain. Not all Asians went on these shopping sprees. One of the poorer Asians, who had lost his job in 1970, was described as being happy that he was no longer living on charity: 'Kicking the Asians out is terrible for those with money. For me it is the opening to paradise.'[22] Another way of getting money out of the country was by buying airline tickets. Internationally standardized air fares are quoted in American dollars, and agreements for the transfer of tickets from route to route made them in effect a form of world credit. The tickets were bought by black market dealers in London and elsewhere and resold to small airlines operating mainly in the Middle East. After the 'racket' had been featured in the *Daily Telegraph* (26 August 1972), Pan-American and Trans-World, two of the airlines being used in 'the racket', imposed restrictions on their tickets issued in Uganda.

Other reasons for not leaving during this period included the difficulty experienced by those who had Indian passports of getting to the coast. The worst 'stop and search' tactics of the military and the police were near the Kenyan border. Eventually passengers were transported to Mombasa in closed trains. Some 4,500 Indian citizens went on this route. Many were the older members of the families who had been born in the subcontinent. But this operation did not start until mid-September. The offices of the Indian High Commission did not begin to process registrations until 28 August.

Even those Asians who were prepared to leave as soon as possible, or to send just one member ahead to prepare for the arrival of others of the family in the UK, were delayed by the sheer mechanics of departure. The first Asians who left before 29 August did so on scheduled flights. They had already planned to leave before the expulsion order, they had the money for the tickets and were in fact helped by Amin's decision. The clearance of this group of 3,000 families (who had applied for vouchers before 9 August) took three weeks. A report in the *Ugandan Argus* (29 August) gave a breakdown of their destinations: two-thirds were going to the London area, 70 to Leicester. Their occupations included 23 motor mechanics, 34 clerks, 35 merchants, 22 teachers and 7 labourers. At the end of August details were announced about the airlift of the evacuees. Thirty flights a week were to start from 1 September. The airlines asked the British government to guarantee flight expenses. Once these arrangements had been made, there were yet other queues, this time for tickets from East African Airways at yet another emergency office opened in the Bank of Uganda in Kampala Road. These queues, according to the recollections of the Leicester group, were the worst of all, with only a hundred tickets being issued a day, and an average wait of four days to obtain these.

Another factor which helped cause the delay and which accounted for the extra flights being cancelled in mid-September, was the insistence on the part of the British government that five days' notice be given for the special flights to enable them to give necessary landing rights. The *Ugandan Argus* (23 September) claimed that this caused as much delay to the exodus as did delays at the British High Commission.

Critics of the delay in the exodus have largely ignored the practical difficulties at Entebbe Airport. First, given that six or seven air flights every evening were calculated as necessary, there was the limited capacity of the fuel tanks. Secondly, the ground staff included a large number of Asians, many of whom were candidates for the flights. Thirdly, there was the lack of a 'movements office', that is, an administrative office, staffed by officials authorized to cut through the red tape and able to deal with large numbers of passengers. Fourthly, there was the problem that the flight timetable was in the evening, when a high altitude airport is under maximum usage. Most commercial flights on the long-distance run to Europe passed through Entebbe at night. Thus there were problems over the maintenance of safety standards. Lastly, some of the congestion might have been avoided had there been a shuttle service to Embakasi Airport, Nairobi. But Kenya did not co-operate in this.[23]

The charge for air tickets was 2,000/– (equivalent to £100 sterling) a head, with children charged at 10 per cent, which was actually above that charged for the scheduled flights, but 30 kilos of luggage was allowed instead of the normal 20 kilos. These air fares were difficult for some of the families to find, particularly if the family was a large one, and those families had been left without ready cash, even after selling off as much as they could of their assets. Several families in Leicester spoke of people in their community not being able to raise this amount and how 'for the very first time people from every community helped each other out.' One of the refugees, who within a decade of the expulsion was successfully re-established in a flourishing car sales enterprise in a town in Leicestershire, was firm in his conviction that 'the British Government should have provided free air passages ... we would then have been relieved of some of the immediate worries over paying for air tickets. This was especially so for large families...'

Most of the passengers on the first special flight were those who had been waiting for over two years for vouchers, and were now at last going. The others, crowded together in houses in Kampala, waited to hear what was to happen in the UK if relatives could not help them. The Ugandan press and radio spared them nothing in their reports of the hostile reception they might expect. Several of the Leicester group reported that they had heard news of the anti-Asian march of the Smithfield meat porters and demonstrations at Heathrow. They balanced this against their faith in the traditions of the essential fairness of the majority of the British. Several of the Leicester group referred to 'speeches of leaders like Sir Alec Douglas-Home', who spoke in their favour. They also weighed reports that Leicester was compiling a list of those who had accommodation for them[24] against the frequent warnings that they should not go to 'saturation' areas and should go instead to settle 'in newer housing estates in towns with few immigrants'. They were urged by the one Asian member of the British government's newly established Ugandan Resettlement Board to show the same pioneering spirit 'which had characterised the early days in the Asian settlement in Uganda'.[25]

Then on 15 September the first insertion by Leicester City Council appeared in the *Ugandan Argus* advising people not to come to Leicester. What then was the collective reaction of the Asians to this? The majority of them, as events proved, were not deterred, especially if they had already made up their minds to come to Leicester. This was not, as was frequently said, because the Asians concluded that there was something well worth coming for if a city went to the trouble of warning them off. Instead the first reaction, and the one most frequently mentioned, was expressed by an ex-teacher: 'When you are being expelled from a country you think of the refuge with your relatives ... you think of their house, not the city where it is ... we thought of a roof over our heads.' The second reaction was that refugees still clung to their respect for the ultimate tolerance and fairmindedness of 'the Leicester people'. Thus Fatima (like many others) was adamant: 'We had made our arrangements to go to Leicester. We were expected there. We felt that if we stood on our own feet and asked for little we would win approval ... the British are like that.' The third reaction, which did contain a proviso, was summarized by Devan: 'You ask me about the Leicester notice. It made some of us think we would wait for a bit, perhaps go to the camps. But it's not true it made us want to go there more than ever before, or made people know that there was a place called Leicester.' Several of the group pointed out that though Leicester was the only local authority to actually insert a notice in the local papers, other areas had been mentioned both on the radio and in the press as having made moves to discourage Ugandan Asians, and indeed had done so before Leicester. Brent and Wembley, as well as Ealing, were known to be discouraging. All the attempts, then, to persuade the Asians to go to 'non-

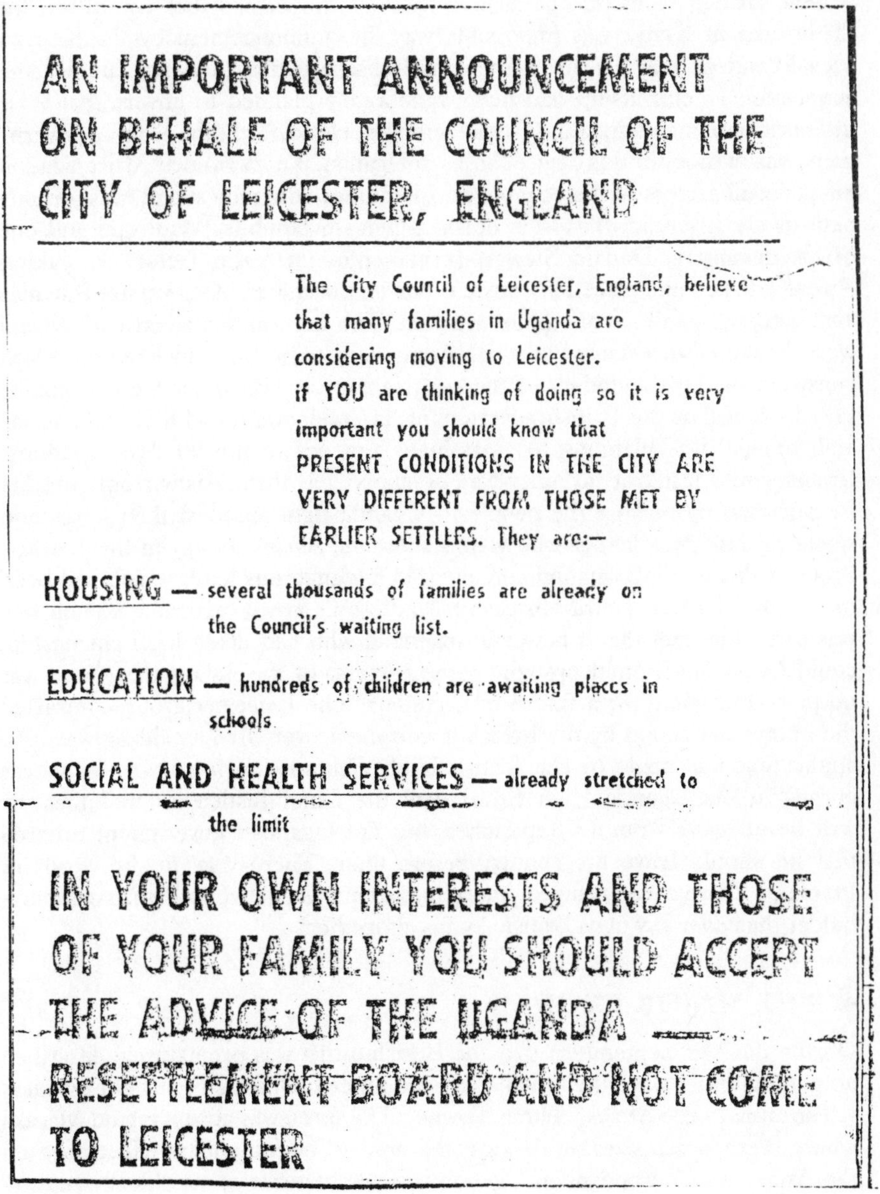

AN IMPORTANT ANNOUNCEMENT
ON BEHALF OF THE COUNCIL OF THE
CITY OF LEICESTER, ENGLAND

The City Council of Leicester, England, believe
that many families in Uganda are
considering moving to Leicester.
if YOU are thinking of doing so it is very
important you should know that
PRESENT CONDITIONS IN THE CITY ARE
VERY DIFFERENT FROM THOSE MET BY
EARLIER SETTLERS. They are:—

HOUSING — several thousands of families are already on
the Council's waiting list.

EDUCATION — hundreds of children are awaiting places in
schools

SOCIAL AND HEALTH SERVICES — already stretched to
the limit

IN YOUR OWN INTERESTS AND THOSE
OF YOUR FAMILY YOU SHOULD ACCEPT
THE ADVICE OF THE UGANDA
RESETTLEMENT BOARD AND NOT COME
TO LEICESTER

Figure 1   Advertisement in the *Ugandan Argus*, 15 September 1972

saturation' points in the UK were futile. Summing it up, one representative said: 'If we had relatives in a place, that decided the matter.'

One further event that persuaded most of the Asians that any future for them even in Kenya was impossible was the announcement by the Kenyan Vice-President that his government had observed that in Asian families the acquisition of citizenship had been deliberately planned to ensure that their interests were maintained in several countries. Henceforth, the Kenyan government was to monitor this device for, as in Uganda, it undermined Africanization plans for all sectors of the economy.[26] In addition, the richest and most prominent of the Ugandan Asian big businessmen – Manubhai Madhvani and one of his managers, Donald Stewart (manager of the sugar factory at Kakira) – were arrested and placed in army custody on the charge of subversive activities and sabotage of the economy of Uganda. The accusations against Madhvani were contained in a statement which Amin made to his Security Council, which consisted of representatives of the army, air force, prison service and police. He claimed that the British government 'in collaboration with British Asians and Israelis' was planning to assassinate him before the 90 days' deadline. Britain could think of no other way of stopping British Asians from entering Britain than by making the people of Uganda fight amongst themselves and replacing him by a leader who would allow the Asians to stay in the country. Proof of this was information contained in a 'dangerous letter which had been intercepted by the security forces'.[27] Madhvani's arrest signalled that no one was safe. The fact that a powerful magnate, who had taken local citizenship, could be so imprisoned brought home to most of the Asians that there was no point in hoping for a future in Uganda.[28] The Leicester group contrasted the immediate action by the British government over Mr Donald Stewart. An application was made by the British High Commission for a writ of habeas corpus in the Uganda High Court, and the Chief Justice ordered that the writ be effective from 13 September, but the Ugandan government ordered that he should leave the country before then. There was, in the words of Pranlal, a 20-year-old refugee, 'more fuss over this one white British passport-holder than over any of us British Asians altogether'.

4. THE MAJOR EXODUS

On the day (18 September) that the British airlift was prematurely described as 'getting under way', the local papers announced 'Uganda Fights Off Invaders – Tanzania Force Attacks Three Towns'. The force was advancing on Masaka where there was a sizeable Asian community. The immediate effect for both the Asians and Europeans in Uganda was the increase in roadblocks and the 'stop and search' tactics of the police, for the purpose of identity checks. As the editorial of the *East African Standard* (18 September) put it: 'General Amin has two acute obsessions – the Israelis and the Asians, with Britain as a close third ... there is the idea that the invasion is linked with insurrections.' This attempted invasion has been described by Meisler[29] as President Nyerere's

'Bay of Pigs', for he was mistaken in his belief that the Ugandan army, weakened by tribal conflict, would crumble with the invasion from Tanzania by Ugandan exiles. Writing at the time of the invasion Meisler stated: 'Nyerere was mistaken, for anti-Asian hatred has inflated the popularity of Amin ... the soldiers are drunk with power. Diplomatic sources report that since the invasion an average of five Asians a day have been shot by the invaders ... without the army intervening.' In the pervading uncertainty, it was to be expected that rumours would fly around, despite the fact that two days after the attempted invasion official sources were announcing victory and that life was normal in Kampala, 'with its South Street car park as busy as ever'. Yet reports from Kenya spoke of Asians arriving at Mombasa trembling after robberies in broad daylight, clinging to their parcelled possessions and explaining that 'in Uganda we already mistrust people there so much, that only when we see will we be convinced of our continuing ownership.'[30]

The other effect for the Asians of the abortive Tanzanian attack was the government warning that though Nyerere and Obote might have planned to disrupt their expulsion, and there was evidence that 'the Israelis and the U.K.' were hoping to send in troops, the Ugandan authorities, and particularly the military, would not tolerate any further the delaying tactics of the non-citizen Asians. Only 4,000 had come forward to begin the exit processes and they were warned that 'they should never in any way attribute this to the Tanzanian invasion ... if they want peace with the Ugandan army and the entire Ugandan public they should come out quickly to have their documents processed.'[31]

The Ugandans blamed the delay on the British High Commission; the Foreign Office in its turn blamed the Ugandan administration. The airlifts were cancelled on two days because of lack of passengers. The *East African Standard*'s editorial on 25 September stated that 'part of the reason why the airlift has been delayed is fear – fear of being manhandled on the roads by ill-disciplined and licentious soldiers ... will the merchants dealing with the Ugandan authorities ever get their money? ... £50 per head is a cheap price for safety.' Yet whatever examples they gave of assaults either personally experienced or reported, the Leicester refugees were emphatic that these fell into insignificance both in scale and intensity compared with those inflicted by Africans on Africans, particularly by those soldiers recruited by Amin from the West Nile and the South Sudan. An ex-insurance broker related that 'Makindye Military Prison was the worst. But we lived near the police station at Mbarara, and even before the Obote invasion we had heard the cries in the night.'

On 22 September members of the Ugandan Security Forces were directed by the government to 'ensure that all British Asians who have been cleared by the Bank of Uganda must not remain in the country for more than 48 hours'. And once again the British High Commission was blamed for delays. The Ugandan government published comparative figures proving the superior clearing capacity of both the Bank of Uganda and the East African Income Tax Department. The authorities now planned 16 extra flights per week, together with scheduled flights making special calls at Entebbe. Thus it would be certain that 'all Asians have returned to their homeland by November 8th'. The cancellation of two flights and the non-take-up of seats on scheduled flights on 19 and 20 September showed that the Asians were deliberately not coming forward, and again the *Ugandan Argus* (23 September) said: 'this is at the expense of the same taxpayer that has been milked by British Asians for almost a century.' In what were described as 'the first representations made in Whitehall by actual Ugandan refugees', two Asian businessmen compared the 'round the clock' service, including weekends, mounted by the Ugandan authorities with the strict office hours of the British High Commission. They suggested that passports should be automatically stamped to enable prompt clearance.[32]

The Leicester group mentioned that by the end of September there were positive incentives to hasten their departure. The fact that Malawi offered to take some 1,000 expellees meant that some could join relatives there (the Asian community numbered around 6,000). Again, India announced that those with UK passports would be given an initial two-year entry permit and that the UK government had promised to help India 'with several millions' in the resettlement there.[33] Eleven thousand refugees had applied for settlement in Canada on the grounds that they had relatives there. Arrangements for flying 6,000 to Canada were now organized by the Canadian High Commission in Kampala. When the British High Commission ceased to publish press announcements of the passport numbers of those who should report there was a last-minute rush. Shops were closed for their owners to start queuing at 6 a.m. and there were several scuffles caused by late comers who wanted to be served first.

Reassurances were given that Asians going to areas in the UK where services were reputedly overstretched (termed 'red areas' by journalists) would not be denied help if they were determined to settle there, and also to those who had been unable to make their own arrangements for resettlement. The *East African Standard* (26 September) reported that half of those who had already arrived at Stansted Airport had 'no place to go to', and a second resettlement camp to supplement Stradishall was announced. Two events featured in the memories of the Asians still in Uganda in the last few days of September. Kampala was deserted on 22 September, following what official sources called 'an unexplained hoax'. The police held many Asians for questioning for several hours. The second event was the seizure by the security forces of cash from the Aga Khan Mosque in Namirembe Road, Kampala. One million shillings in cash was hidden in biscuit tins, ready to be smuggled out. Naturally the Asians were trying to take with them as many possessions as they could. Sharda related how she had posted a parcel to her sister in Kenya under the eyes of Customs Officers: 'We were walking jewellery shops. We Indians have always trusted gold, but we were now weighted down with it. No wonder we were attacked. Now in Leicester our homes are robbed for the same things – jewellery and gold.' However, most refugees arriving at Heathrow were now stating that things were becoming better and there were no longer attacks on Asians, especially on those on the road to the airport.

Those Asians who had hoped for an extension of the 90 days were disappointed. Uganda's permanent representative at the United Nations accused the UK of trying to bully Uganda. He maintained that under Article 2(7) of the United Nations Charter the expulsion was an internal dispute. Amin told the Sudanese ambassador that 'any leader who tries to suggest that the Asians should stay longer does not understand the feelings of the people of Uganda'.[34] The Readers' Letters to the *Ugandan Argus* continually demanded instant expulsion and the speeding up of processing the applications of intending buyers of the businesses owned by the Asians.

On 4 October Amin repeated that the deadline still stood and that he had never hinted he would change his mind, despite the threat of an alleged invasion plan by Britain, India, Tanzania and other countries. To show his determination he authorized thorough checking of every building in Kampala and other places to find out which Asians had not yet left. The time had come to actually place their properties in the hands of Ugandans 'because everything in the country belongs to them'. One deadline was extended – the time by which the outgoing British Asians could declare their businesses and properties for publication by the Ministry of Commerce. Importantly, Amin issued a statement to the United Nations stating that this was not confiscation, for there would be compensation. He told the students at Makerere University that 'we are not nationalising any of the Asians' business.'[35]

One opinion put forward by some of the Leicester Ugandan Asians was that Amin was determined to show progress in his expulsion plans by 9 October, as this was the date of the tenth anniversary of Ugandan Independence. They related how the search along the Kampala Road, as part of the thorough check of every building in Kampala, revealed Asians were still trading though they possessed exit clearance papers which automatically cancelled their work permits and trading licences. Rough handling, with their explanations shouted down and detention at an army station, inevitably followed these searches.

On 6 October (the day when the 'Don't Come to Leicester' notice appeared in the newspaper for the third time), 300 Asians with identity cards showing their Ugandan citizenship took part in the rehearsal of the Independence Day march in Kololo Park. This was the first time that Asians had participated and Amin reassured them that if they continued to come out and identify themselves with Ugandan Africans they had nothing 'to worry about'. He went on to warn them not to keep themselves aloof and promised to attend their weddings when they married Africans. On 13 October he promised that the small numbers of Asians who were permitted to stay would be 'happy ... they would be appointed into the public service, country gombololas [councils] and even as district commissioners.'

In his broadcast on the Independence Anniversary Day Amin once again repeated that non-Ugandan Asians should leave within the 90 days, adding that Ugandans now had opportunities to enter commerce and industry brought to their doorsteps. Reinforcing this were the frequently repeated announcements on Radio Uganda reminding the Asians of how few days there were left. Half-page advertisements in the *Ugandan Argus* by the British High Commission, 'Please come quickly if you need an entry certificate', and 'Visa Ready' notices of the United States Embassy appeared daily. The efficiency of the Canadian High Commission, which arranged its first free chartered flight to leave on 27 September, was the subject of comment by some of the Leicester group, who also claimed that preferential treatment was given to the Ismailis (including those who had no real family members in Canada, a prime consideration by the Canadian authorities). Notice also appeared urging all Indian citizens leaving Uganda 'to complete immediately all departure formalities'. Then the Intergovernmental Committee for European Migration announced that 'certain countries in South America' would accept some of the refugees.[36] In early October Sir Charles Cunningham paid a short visit to Kampala, but this was accorded very little publicity either on the local radio or in the press. He stated that the fate of 'stateless' people was no concern of his Resettlement Board and that the issue should be conveyed to the British government. A few days later news came from Geneva that stateless Asians might be admitted into refugee camps in Europe. This would be the first stage before they were provided with documents needed to move to other countries. Mr Joseph Godber, the British Minister of State in the Foreign Office, was at Geneva to have talks with the UN High Commissioner for Refugees and the President of the Red Cross.

By the first week of October 10,000 to 11,000 Asians had entered the UK. It was estimated that there were 10,000 or less stateless Asians left in Uganda ('about half the number originally estimated'). The High Commissioner for Refugees had accepted that stateless people would become his responsibility, 'if they ceased to live in the country which was their "natural habitat"'.[37] This report like others emphasized that the original total of British Asians which had been put at 57,000 did not take into account the fact that 15,000 of them had already entered Britain before the expulsion order. An editorial in the *Ugandan Argus* (6 October) argued that these smaller numbers were an additional reason for not extending the 90 days.

At this time the International Red Cross agreed to act as the agents for the United Nations High Commission for Refugees and to open an office in Kampala during the last week in October in order to organize the documentation and welfare of the 4,000 '*genuine* refugees'. The United Nations High Commission would only agree to take the 'genuine stateless' Asians, leaving the UK with no alternative but to accommodate the Asians whose Ugandan citizenship was revoked on technical grounds and who under British law remained British subjects. The *Ugandan Argus* (17 October) pointed out that a planned High Court case to test the validity of this principle had been 'quietly dropped', because 'for domestic consumption' Whitehall had had to soften the impact that another 6,000 Asians were to be admitted.

The Industrial Promotion Services (IPS) building in Kampala was to host yet another temporary office. This was the United Nations Centre 'to assist those members of the Asian Community who [were] of undetermined nationality and who [were] required to leave Uganda by 8th November'.[38] On the day that this office was opened, the first special flight left to take stateless Asians to the United States, and the news came that the American Council of Churches had offered to take 2,000 Asians in addition to the 1,000 that the US authorities had already agreed to accept. This offer was welcomed by the Asians: the fact that the ACC offered to provide the full range of welfare services, jobs and houses in an affluent country, and moreover an English-speaking country, made it a far more attractive haven than camps in Europe. Although Australia and New Zealand offered admission for only 600 people, Australia did offer £25,000 to the International Committee for European Migration, which had been set up after the Second World War to help resettle refugees into countries where they had been accepted.

All this detail needs to be translated into human terms. Ten years later a refugee woman took part in a phone-in on local commercial radio in Leicester. She was emphatic that what had happened was to be put behind her. But she said: 'Our family in Northampton and Leicester is together ... but our real family, the family we were in Uganda has scattered throughout the world. Some in Canada, some in Sweden, some in India ... We are safe but separated.'

To the very end the Asians were still trying to smuggle out those assets that remained. The cache from the Aga Khan mosque was destined for Kenya. Some of the Asians hoped to sell their businesses to fellow Asians from surrounding East African states who were temporarily resident in places like Fort Portal and Kampala. Amin spoke of this 'syndicate with Asians ... these dirty tricks ... this sabotage of the economy' to President Kenyatta,[39] and he made it clear that the 'blood suckers' who were manipulating the take-over of property would not be permitted to do so.[40] On 25 October Amin signed a new Immigration Decree from his room at Mulago Hospital (where he was 'resting'), which invalidated every entry permit or certificate of residence issued or granted under the Immigration Act 1969 to any non-Ugandan Asian. This meant that Asians from Kenya, Tanzania, Zaïre, Zambia or any other country were to leave with the Ugandan Asians on or before 8 November. A second decree signed was the Declaration of Assets (Non-citizen Asians) (Amendment). This established a Board of Custodians of six Cabinet ministers to administer properties and businesses abandoned by their Asian owners. The Board of Custodians was to consist of the same ministers as those who composed the Cabinet Committee on Asians.

A week before this decree the government had emphasized in its 'Decree 27' that every departing non-Ugandan Asian was obliged to declare all property, business and fixed assets. The Minister of Commerce also prohibited the transfer of any business for which there was no documentation lodged with him. People who had taken over vacated Asian businesses were warned that they did so at their own risk; they might be asked to quit when the government began official allocation. The Ugandan delegate to the United Nations, Mr Peter Ikia, explained to the General Assembly's Social, Humanitarian and Cultural Committee (during a debate on the elimination of racial discrimination) that Asians being expelled from Uganda were allowed to take £50 only, 'because they have already put their money in British banks'.[41] First, creditors of departing Asian businessmen were advised by a government spokesman to take their complaints to the courts even if the Asians had left the country. Asians who attempted to sell their businesses privately faced the threat of up to two years' imprisonment and a fine of 50,000/–. Moreover, Decree 27 stated that the agents appointed by the Ministry of Commerce should ensure that the property was properly looked after until it was sold. If any business was not properly registered with the ministry before the Asian owner left it would be vested in the government and no compensation would be paid. Amin himself warned British and Asian banks that took care of businesses and houses of Asians who had left, and had put up notices claiming that they had taken over the property, that they were wasting their time. These banks were not deterred. Three British banks (Barclays Bank DCO, the National and Grindlays Bank, and the Standard Bank) controlled 80 per cent of Uganda's commercial assets, compared with the 10 per cent held by other foreign banks (including such Asian enterprises as the Bank of Baroda). The remaining 10 per cent was controlled by the two Ugandan banks. Despite the dominant position of such Asian capitalists as Madhvani and Mehta, finance capital was still largely controlled by British capital. The majority of the expelled Asians were small-time businessmen heavily indebted to the banks.[42]

This was emphasized by an expellee, now an accountant practising in Leicester. Discussing the question of compensation he said: 'How can a small businessman, like my father, be compensated for what he owed the bank? Our assets were the goodwill of our enterprises...' Ritha, who was an office worker in Kampala, and on arrival in Leicester worked in a hosiery factory, left on 27 October. She described in graphic terms what it was like in the last days in Uganda: 'It was like being an item on a cash register. People in my family were "rung up" one by one. Grandparents in India, an uncle in Canada, we came to Leicester...'

The British High Commissioner left the country, and the very last official announcement that he made was to warn the Asians that 'there are only twelve days left'. Those Asians still awaiting a flight remembered the chaos of those last days. The military threatened to take over Fort Portal. There was a growing shortage of food. Abandoned cars were immediately seized by soldiers and driven away. The news now in the *Ugandan Argus* was that refugees were being persuaded to leave the 'comfortable' resettlement camps 'and face up to life in Britain'.[43]

In Tororo there was only one Asian trader left by 2 November. Although Kampala was described as taking on the appearance of the capital of an independent country, there was an undercurrent of discontent by Africans over the time the transfer of businesses was taking. Finally on 8 November, with last-minute sales in the big stores such as Deacons and Anilyaliamanyam, and with Africans strolling round hopefully inspecting business premises which they hoped to acquire, and pedestrians able to walk in the middle of the main roads because there were so few Asian cars around, Amin issued his statement on the completion of the Holy Month of Ramadan celebrating the end of one phase of the economic war.[44]

The Canadian High Commission closed its office having issued 6,000 entry permits. The *Ugandan Argus* stated that by 7 November there were no longer any Asians waiting outside the British High Commission. It was conceded that with the help of extra staff and volunteers documentation had been speeded up and the Commission had issued entry certificates to 28,000 people. On 6 November just 28 heads of family and 11 wives collected documents. The United Nations Office had issued documents to between 3,900 and 4,000 Asians of 'undetermined nationality'. A third of the total was under 16 years of age and the staff were planning to seek out Asians who had not yet obeyed the order to leave. Amin also directed that there should be a physical count of all Asians left in Uganda, to start on 9 November. The purpose was to determine who were Ugandan citizens and who were not. The count began in Kampala where the Asians assembled at Kololo Airstrip. Although they had voluntarily stayed on, and among them was a former Member of Parliament (Mrs Visram Namubiru), they were accused of continuing all the practices for which their fellow Asians had been expelled. Amin produced letters containing over 3,500/– included in Diwali greetings posted for overseas destinations. But in the presence of a United Nations official the Asians were assured that they would not be molested by any black Ugandan. On 12 November Amin announced in a speech at the Mutolere Secondary School, Kigezi, that the 'Ugandan citizens of Asian origin' were to be transported 'physically' to various districts to work in the fields and asked that they be taught to dig hard and seriously.[45] The number of Asians in this group has never been given with any degree of accuracy. The *East African Standard* (9 November) gave an inflated estimate of 8,000, of whom half were the professional group allowed to stay on because of their specific skills, with the rest business people who were those ordered to sell their assets and work the land. Later the *Standard* (11 November) gave the number as 'less than 2,000 of whom only 500 were Ugandan citizens'. The abandoned assets were estimated at £100,000,000.[46]

One of the non-citizens to leave after the official deadline was Mahendra Mehta, the multi-millionaire whose group of companies rivalled in wealth those of Madhvani enterprises. He was ordered to leave on 8 November. By the end of November the Madhvani and Mehta properties had been vested in the Abandoned Property Custodians Board, as well as other companies such as Kassam Motors and Camera Centre Limited.

On 30 November the second phase of the 'economic war' was initiated when Kampala, Entebbe, Masaka and other locations were allocated to four sub-committees for the checking and redistribution of abandoned businesses to Ugandans.[47] As part of this phase by December 1972 all British firms in Uganda were acquired, and the British families airlifted out. They were allowed only £50 in foreign currency, but in addition £500 in personal effects. On 25 November a 'Live Letter' from Mityana was published in the *Ugandan Argus*, which captures the general tenor of all those others printed during the 90 days. It is also indicative of increasing resentment over what was to happen to their abandoned property:

> A lot has been said about the Asian exodus. And the common talk today in the country is 'taking over the property left behind by the Asians'. I personally call it rehabilitation of our lost property which was exclusively monopolised by the ravenous Asians ... The Asians have gone physically but the current problem is that there is a lot of deep-rooted Asian mentality left behind. The tea industry is a very good source of national income ... the big estates previously owned by the Asians should be taken over by the Government ... signs are showing that people are likely to be favoured for high positions on religious considerations ... and family connections.

The Asians did not attempt to sabotage their property before leaving Uganda, and the Africans whom they once employed continued to protect Asian shops and offices against the threat of looting by the 'kondos' (violent robbers). Asian houses soon had self-appointed African owners. Altogether the Asians left property 'amounting to between £100 and £150m'.[48] To date no British Asian has received any compensation. One of Leicester's Ugandan Asians gave her view on the end of the Asians in Uganda thus:

> Perhaps Mr Thorpe was right. He called Amin a Black Hitler. But it was the Africans who were his victims. They say that 400,000 were murdered. Very few of us Asians suffered like that, though people are calling us Leicester's New Jews. Even now though I can't believe that it was God who directed Amin to do these things to us Asians.[49]

5. THE *UGANDAN ARGUS* AND THE ASIANS

The reports and readers' letters published in the *Ugandan Argus* during the 90 days were consistently vitriolic and abusive about the Asians of Uganda. By comparison, articles in the other local paper, the *East African Standard*, were objective and balanced.

Immediately after the first announcement that the Asians would have to leave the *Argus* reflected the understandable jubilation felt by the Africans that 'at last we are going to get our share of the economy of our country.' ('Ugandans Hail Move on Asians', 9 August 1972). But soon groups such as the Bukedi Traders were stating that 'the deadline of three months is too long and can afford them time to play dirty tricks on our economy like the Israelis.' Then various local councils had letters published stating their grievances. Kampala City Council complained that 'at Mbale Secondary School Asians never wanted Africans to sit at the same desk ... no more imperialism or Zionism.' Gulu Town Council thanked President Amin 'for the performance he has shown to rescue the economy of our country'.

Other letters expressed the pent-up resentment of Africans against the Asians and urged that the Asians should be expelled within a week: 'We Ugandans are fed up with their tactics of causing the sugar shortages.' 'Why should

Britain reject her own passport holders? It reminds me of the great chieftain who married 100 wives and refused to take responsibility.' Among the 'Live Letters' on 17 August was one from 'An African Christian': 'Our Asian friends have been in a deep sleep since they were coolies for the railway line ... may I wish the British Asians a long and very cold winter. Let all Asians and non-Ugandans quit our country.'

The cartoons drawn by 'Mzee' also depicted the 'humour' of the situation for the Africans (although the characters are drawn not as African or Asian but European). One cartoon (14 August) shows eager customers reading advertisements for Asian shops and asking, 'How about these adverts? "A hair dressing business at Cut Price..." "Gold Mine for sale at rock bottom price".'

Despite all its support and even sycophancy for Amin, the *Argus* was warned by him on 30 November that he would close all newspapers 'if they published unchecked facts'. Here he was referring to a report in the *Argus* that there continued to be a serious sugar shortage in Jinja. By December 1972 Amin ordered the *Argus* to change all its staff and its name to the *Voice of Uganda*.

6. INTERNATIONAL REACTIONS

The initial 'sad silence' of politicians inside the UK[50] about Amin and the Asian expulsion was matched by that of African leaders, who apart from President Nyerere of Tanzania and President Kaunda of Zambia preferred to remain quiet throughout the 90 days. At the United Nations, the position of Secretary General Dr Kurt Waldheim was one of extreme reluctance to intervene or even criticize what he defined as the internal policies of a UN member state. The Pakistani daily, *Dawn* (2 September), and the West German *Frankfurter Allgemeine Zeitung* (19 August), however, both considered that the task of resettlement should be shared by the ten EEC countries, South Africa, India and Pakistan. The German paper asked, 'Should all be left to Great Britain, that one unfortunate heir of European colonialism?'

The International Commission of Jurists attacked the expulsions, stating that the Ugandan constitution protected Asians with Ugandan citizenship. The suggestion that the expulsion could be justified on the grounds of alleged treason by some Asians could not be upheld, since 'those guilty should be brought to trial and others should not be held guilty by association'.[51] Other legal experts[52] argued that the expulsion was in breach of the law of the United Nations concerning racial discrimination. The expulsion was also described as a 'genoport', and a contravention of the Universal Declaration of Human Rights ('overtly racist ... a gross violation of human rights').

Despite being urged that the time had come for 'confrontation not appeasement' and that it should prove itself to be not just 'an exercise in futility', the United Nations only offered to the Asians 'the comfortable news that they would be held to be refugees'.[53] It was not until September that Britain took the case before the General Assembly and then requested an early discussion. The Foreign Secretary, Sir Alec Douglas-Home, adopted the strategy of an appeal about the humanitarian aspects of the expulsion and did not ask the UN to deplore the expulsion as such. By this means he hoped that some African and Arab nations would at least admit the question to the UN agenda. But there was no possibility of gaining a two-thirds majority necessary for an emergency debate. Besides, the UN debate could only have been timetabled for mid-October, which was hardly effective, bearing in mind the 7 November deadline.

The move by the Foreign Secretary was interpreted by observers as doing only two things: reassuring opinion in the UK that he was doing all he could, and giving opportunity for further initiatives if Amin carried out his threat to round up the Asians and put them in camps.[54] But following a speech by Uganda's ambassador Mr Grace Ibingira, in which he gave explicit assurances about the treatment of Asians, the British delegation did not insist on the question being debated further. In addition, the UN Sub-Committee on Human Rights (after two attempts which were defeated on majority voting) gave up the proposal to send a telegram to Amin expressing serious concern at his proposed action. The *Sunday Telegraph* (17 September) described this as yet one more example of the United Nations' failure as an international forum, in that it failed to condemn racialist acts because the perpetrators had black skins.

An Indian commentator[55] argued that once Britain had made it clear that it would not shrink from its responsibility to its passport-holders, it won abundant support from the world community, and in particular India. Since the activists of the Organization of African Unity had shown no willingness to interfere in Uganda, and there were members of the Commonwealth amongst them, by not pursuing the issue the UK avoided splitting the Commonwealth. Instead it gave it a new lease of life, and internationally the UK did not lose face by its lack of open confrontation of Amin.[56] The situation at home, however, was not so clear-cut.

Chapter 3 The press and the politicians: national and local reactions

In August 1972, when crisis reporting and xenophobic fears reacted on each other, neither the Conservative government nor the other political parties made any great effort at public education to prevent deep antagonism towards the coming of the Asians to Britain. They did not tackle what Richard Bourne in the *Guardian* of 5 September 1972 aptly called 'statistical terrorism' (that is, 'information' by the media about the expected numbers from Uganda, or suggestions that their admission would be a precedent for other UK passport-holders). Because it was the time of the Summer Recess and Parliament was not sitting, the media had the monopoly of public debate over what was described as 'Britain's duty' in a 'grim crisis'.

Some press correspondents themselves criticized contemporary reporting. Hugo Young of the *Sunday Times*[1] examined the choice of words ('invasion', 'flood', 'influx', 'a refugee problem') and their importance in not challenging but rather confirming people's fears. He concluded that in the first four weeks after the expulsion order, the *Daily Express* had set 'an unrelenting pace in crisis building and fear mongering'. The journals *Race Today*, *New Statesman* and *New Society*,[2] monitoring the part played by the press, radio and television in advertising the activities of extreme right racist groups such as the National Front, Colin Jordan's British Movement and the Immigration Control Association, found that these received much more attention in the media than did demonstrations of goodwill to the refugees. In its editorial, the *Sunday Times* (27 August) once again singled out the *Daily Express* with its 'orchestrated attempts' to prove that there was no legal duty to admit the Asians. Criticism was also made of the quality of some 'I.T.N. news bulletins ... with instant projections into national prominence of the National Front'; and the wide-spread general publicity given to a few protesting Smithfield meat porters demonstrating against 'the invasion of Britain'. After the Ugandan Asians had arrived, the specious arguments and the bias were analysed by academics and media studies specialists.[3] Among their findings was that four separate opinion polls which took place between August 1972 and September 1973 actually revealed a much more tolerant set of attitudes to the Asian refugees than was reported by such national newspapers as the *Daily Express* and the *Daily Telegraph*.

Some observers argued that, in spite of its decision to honour Britain's commitment to the Ugandan Asians, the government 'never intended to allow the bulk of them into the country and was prepared to resort to any means ...

to keep them out'.[4] The more general view was that the Conservative policy initially aimed to persuade Uganda to delay the expulsion, by using an accelerated version of Kenya's 'pole/pole' or 'gradual' plan. Then efforts turned to persuading other countries to receive the expellees. The *Indian Weekly* (10 August) at this point said, 'the whole situation is being complicated by bringing India into it.' But the *Indian Weekly* (24 August) also remarked that 'a shade of surprise is permissible, that in this matter of coloured immigration the Tories are showing up better than Labourites.' Mr Geoffrey Rippon, Minister Without Portfolio, who had been sent by the government to negotiate with Amin failed to gain more time for the Asians, or a reduction in the numbers to be expelled, or any agreement over compensation. He stated on 16 August that the Asians would be admitted: 'The British public accepts that when people have been given United Kingdom passports . . . and have been given assurances by successive British Governments, that they will honour them if they are expelled, those assurances must be fulfilled.'

Although the Conservatives' decision to admit the Asians sometimes earned praise for its 'strong and determined leadership requiring a considerable amount of political courage',[5] there was growing criticism of its lack of zeal in doing anything to counteract the acceleration of fears and anxieties in places like Leicester. These fears were at their height before the Asians actually arrived. When Robert Carr, the Home Secretary, was given the sole charge for receiving and settling the refugees, this was hailed as 'at last providing a leadership that had been so sadly lacking'.[6]

The decision to admit the Asians also presented the first issue on which the right wing of the Tory Party hoped to attract a following from the more moderate sections of the party. Mr Enoch Powell, MP, argued that Britain had no moral or legal need to admit the Asians. No special obligation had been given to them in the past. They were the 'thin end of a very thick wedge', and one-and-a-half millions of other Asians had by this precedent a right of entry.[7] The Conservative Monday Club faced a move from some of its members to expel Mr Rippon for committing 'heresy' against its policies, because of his statements about the right of Ugandan Asians to be admitted. Another member of the Monday Club, Mr John Biggs-Davison MP, accused the government of keeping the British people 'muzzled and angry . . . the Ugandan Asians should be a charge on overseas aid funds.'[8]

Meanwhile Labour politicians remained silent: 'not a squeak is heard from the Socialist hierarchy.'[9] At the Standing Conference of Asian Organizations, Praful Patel stated that 'the Labour Party which had championed the cause of the Third World, should come out with a clear call to the working class to welcome the Asians.'[10] Transport House press office issued no statement. There was no public reference to the recommendation made earlier in 1972 by the Labour Party Study Group on Immigration that there should be free entry for all UK citizens of overseas origin who had no alternative citizenship. Breaking this silence on 2 September the Labour Shadow Home Secretary,

Shirley Williams, stated that Britain had a clear obligation to
to the refugees, but the government should adopt a more acti
dispersal of those who had no family connections 'to less cro
the country' was to be encouraged. When he ended his holid
Labour leader' Harold Wilson said that he had supported the
action; had he disagreed then he would have spoken earlier.[11]

Whether Labour's silence was indeed 'contemptible', the party which claimed
to be 'the party of the inner city' did little to remove fears of the people in
these areas, particularly when they were sensitive to what was described as
'appalling unemployment', nearing one million.[12] Victor Feather, the Trades
Union Congress General Secretary, was outspoken about these fears. Applaud-
ing the government's decision to admit the Ugandan Asians, he went on to
urge the government to make its intentions clear on what was to follow their
entry: 'If there is indignation in Britain over Amin's actions that is fully justified,
if there is apprehension then we should not be surprised.'[13] But as the *Observer*
(3 September 1972) pointed out, it was much easier to sit back and deplore
proletarian prejudices than to do much to help.

1. POLITICAL REACTIONS IN LEICESTER

From August 1972 Leicester was to gain the reputation as the city above all
others in the United Kingdom that was the most unwelcoming to the Ugandan
Asian refugees. It was characterized in the national media as the authority
which conducted the most vigorous of all the current public campaigns against
the refugees coming to its city, especially if they intended to settle permanently.
But was the policy adopted by the Leicester City Council really so out of
line with responses elsewhere? If so, how can this be explained? Was it the
case that the city's leaders genuinely believed that it was better even for the
refugees themselves if they were dispersed and settled elsewhere? Was its
decision to advertise in papers like the *Ugandan Argus* merely a disastrous example of 'going public' whereas other authorities confined their debates within
their local Town Halls?

The one action that singled Leicester out as the place where 'though it
was enjoying the good life ... prejudice came before pride' was its insertion
on 15 September (and for three subsequent weeks) of a half-page advertisement
in the *Ugandan Argus* declaring that there was no room for any more Asians
in the city. This signalled the abrupt and public abandonment of the *laissez-faire*
policy adopted since 1968 towards immigrants by Leicester's elected Council
and chief officers. Even some of the city's Asian leaders themselves advised
that Leicester should not be 'a dumping ground', and that the Ugandan Asians
should choose somewhere other than Leicester for permanent settlement. The
Leicester Mercury's 'daily diet of thundering Editorials' and its letter columns
'which often contained racialist nonsense of the worst kind',[14] and the petitions
that were circulating in some of the city's local engineering works and in Leicester's suburbs, coincided with the local Labour Party leaders' determination

ιot to take any action until Central Government provided accurate details
of the numbers to be expected and the financial aid that Local Authorities
might expect from government. The City Council's controlling Labour group
clung to this policy until the end of August 1972. In contrast, the Conservatives
on the Council cried out for 'action', and two of the Conservative councillors
presented a 'giant petition' against the Asians' arrival in the city. But on 31
August Labour gave way and an all-party delegation went to the Home Office
to tell Whitehall that Leicester was 'full up'.[15]

The Council's Emergency Meeting on 31 August with its references to 'the
fabric of our City at risk' was followed by Leicester getting what it wanted:
a visit from the Uganda Resettlement Board and a promise that the refugees
would be steered away by persuasion. The decision to insert the advertisement
in the Ugandan press was taken on 6 September. The Labour leader Edward
Marston stated he was certain that it would be effective: 'this will show the
people of Leicester that we are doing everything we can do to put their view
across.'[16] The action won the approval of Prime Minister Edward Heath when
he visited the city at the end of September. By then the actual numbers coming
from Uganda had fallen from an estimated 80,000 to between 20,000 and 30,000,
which Heath described as 'considerably less than scaremongers have tried to
make us believe'. He went on to say: 'My final message to you in Leicester
is this. You have been quite right to express your concern about the possible
extra burden on your resources.'[17]

But if a Conservative Prime Minister had praise for a Labour-controlled
authority, the latter was faced with a much publicized revolt from within its
own ranks. On 16 September, the day that national newspapers carried headlines
about the 'Stay Away City'[18] and Leicester gained the reputation as an avowedly
racist city almost overnight, nine of its Labour councillors defied the Council's
ruling group's policy. They saw this policy as 'a massive negative act of public
relations' and stated that it failed to present the true picture. The actual decision
to advertise advising the Ugandan Asians not to come to Leicester had been
taken in a meeting of the General Purposes Committee of the City Council.
It had been followed by the Presidents of the British Asian Welfare Society
sending a telegram to the British High Commission in Kampala advising the
refugees 'to avoid such areas as Leicester'. What the reaction of the Ugandan
Resettlement Board was can only be guessed at. Probably it fell short of outright
approval of a Local Authority 'going it alone'. Leicester's City Council had
effectively gone against the Board's policy for the deployment of the Asians
so that they could be persuaded to settle and 'would cause the least possible
disruption to the race relations and social services'.[19]

The revolt within the Labour group had already started at a Special Emergency
Meeting of the Council on 30 August, when there had been a call for the
city to take a lead in positive reception plans. Some of the Labour members
had pleaded: 'There may be no room at the inn but some help was supplied
and I hope that we here will supply some help as far as we are able.' 'God
forbid that they leave an inhuman situation in Uganda and find an inhuman

situation here.' The revolt culminated in nine Labour councillors breaking away from the rest of the controlling group's policy about the Ugandan Asians. The *Leicester Mercury* labelled them as just local party rebels, and concentrated on questioning them whether individually they would be prepared to house Ugandan Asians in their own homes (four said they would do so). To the *Mercury* the whole incident was simply an internal Labour Party dispute, continuing a previous 'unrest' which had taken place over the chairmanship of the committees after Labour gained control in May. The 'new Socialist members ... challenge the old guard personified by Alderman Edward Marston and Alderman Sidney Bridges ... they lack patience and foolishly believe it is possible to change the City overnight.'[20]

Outside Leicester the revolt assumed a much greater significance. To the *Guardian* the nine were 'crusaders' who symbolized that a prosperous city like Leicester could indeed be geared to cope with the refugees. The nine councillors had challenged the current picture of Leicester as a heartless, even racist community which fell short of what had been its high standards of tolerance, efficiency and common sense in 'absorbing peacefully tens of thousands of Commonwealth immigrants' in the past. For the Labour MP Paul Rose the nine Labour members represented something more than just a group of crass newcomers. Their dissent had saved not only Leicester but the Labour Party itself from complete ignominy. The silence of all but a few in the party, the lack of leadership ('the Labour Party is a crusade or it is nothing') and the xenophobia of the party as a whole had resulted in 'Powellism ... no longer being, if it ever was, the sole prerogative of the Conservative Party'.[21]

The Ugandan Asian refugee 'crisis' occurred at a crucial time for Leicester Labour councillors. They had gained control of the city, by winning 11 seats, in the recent May elections. Previously the Conservatives had controlled the City Council for five years. In 1969 Labour had only ten elected members on the Council. The main issue facing the Council was the administrative reorganization necessary before the County Council took over many of its functions under the reorganization of local government scheduled for 1974. Labour councillors were aware that many of their supporters opposed any whittling away of the city's powers and a take-over by a Conservative shire authority. Now, a few months after gaining control, faced with an estimated cost of £500 for each refugee in the first year of resettlement, Labour leaders joined with Conservatives to reassure 'Leicester citizens' (that is, the voters) that the 'burden of the rates' should be kept as low as possible.[22] If Leicester had to accommodate the Asians, then measures would be taken willingly to receive and shelter the refugees but these would be 'temporary'. But whether anyone took this short-stay strategy seriously is to be doubted. It was a Conservative alderman, Terence Harris, who gave it as his opinion that 'of course, we are going to get many of these Asian immigrants in Leicester. To describe the situation as Leicester's worst emergency seems to suggest that we have lived a very sheltered life.'[23] But the *Leicester Mercury* in its editorials constantly reminded the politicians: 'what the people of Leicester are saying ... that they don't want the Ugandan

Asians here ... this does not mean there is a lack of sympathy for these unfortunate people.'[24] The *Leicester Mercury*, too, presented a picture of an electorate thoroughly let down by its elected representatives. This message, repeated in many forms, could not have failed to impress the Labour leaders. Even before the Ugandan Asian expulsion, one of the main points stressed by the National Front in the May 1972 elections was that 'Labour is no longer interested in the British working man.'[25]

If the Labour leaders needed any more reminding of what 'the people of Leicester' thought about the Ugandan Asians coming to the city, it came in the shape of what purported to be 'an independent and non-political survey' advertised anonymously in the *Leicester Mercury* (5 September). This claimed that it had received '304 replies of which 303 opposed any further Asian immigration'. The *Mercury* gave space for a former Leicester City footballer, Mr Tony Mathers, to publish the replies that he had received when he wrote to five local MPs about the 'Ugandan Asian question'. Tom Bradley, Labour MP for Leicester North East, had replied:

> I believe that we in Leicester can do no more ... I am sure if the Government
> had stood up to Amin in the first place, much of this mess would have been avoided.
> I fully support Leicester City Council's policy of alerting the Government of the
> dangers of this critical situation.

Even so this did not satisfy the ex-footballer; he told the *Leicester Mercury*'s reporter: 'You get the feeling that nobody is talking as ordinary people are talking.'[26]

Stepping into this alleged vacuum came the coterie of the national right-wing splinter groups. They agreed to unite 'to end alien occupation of Britain', and significantly chose as their meeting place the district of Blaby on Leicester's outskirts. Colin Jordan, of the British Movement, said that 'this Leicester decision will set a shining example to the rest of the country.'[27] The National Front, the National Democratic Party and the Immigrant Control Assocation, helped by a contingent of the Bradford-based British Campaign to Stop Immigration (with the British Movement following in the rear), marched through Leicester on Saturday, 9 September. The National Front claimed that with 600 people on the march it was the 'biggest ever anti-immigration demonstration in Leicester'. In an interview a member of this alliance said: 'The Leicester City Council constantly claimed that everything in the garden was lovely. Now they suddenly admit that without a single extra Asian they are at breaking point ... the Ugandan Asians ... have made the public aware.'[28] In October a pro-Enoch Powell Group was formed in Leicester (although his secretary said that Enoch Powell had not heard of it). The Group proclaimed the same theme, that local politicians had not listened to the protests of the ordinary citizen: 'We are an anti-immigration party ... we are not connected with the National Front ... we have had no support from Leicester politicians.'[29] When Enoch Powell suffered an official defeat at the Conservative Party Conference, the *Leicester Mercury* stated 'Don't write off Enoch Powell ... The Conservative

Party has accepted Government action over the Ugandan Asians, but is aware that the fabric of life is threatened.'[30] 'Respectable' right-wing activists also capitalized on local tensions. The Leicester branch of the Monday Club was not formed until 1973, but its national chairman, Jonathan Guinness, who lived in neighbouring Bosworth, was politically active locally in 1972. To coincide with the Prime Minister's September visit to the city, Guinness issued a statement that there was no obligation for Leicester or any other place in the UK to admit Ugandan Asians.[31]

Leicester's decision to advertise its difficulties was, however, condemned by the Liberal Party at its National Conference. In the latter's view, Leicester Council had panicked and sullied the city's reputation for good race relations: 'A Labour and Conservative alliance had openly flaunted the inadequate services of the City, although they had previously boasted about having cut the rates.'[32]

The only organized public action in favour of the admission of the Uganda Asians took place when a local left-wing voluntary group, the Inter-Racial Solidarity Campaign, organized a march on 23 October. Five thousand people took part as a protest against the right-wing activity. Other contemporary observers pointed to the fact that in Leicester both Labour and Conservative elected members had stood 'white shoulder to white shoulder', and by thus combining against the Ugandan Asians coming to the city, both hoped to retain their share of the white working-class loyalty and votes.[33]

For the first week after the news of the expulsion broke, the local Labour leaders received no strong lead from the National Home Policy Committee, although the Committee did eventually extend a belated welcome to the refugees.[34]

In Leicester the Labour controlling group were led in 1972 by long-serving party veterans. Alderman S. Bridges, the deputy leader, was in his seventies, and saw inequalities in society as 'general concerns' and favoured 'the same policy for *all* the working class coloured or otherwise'.[35] He and the Labour leader Alderman Edward Marston can be, and indeed were at the time, accused of reflecting what has been labelled the insularity and xenophobia of the people they represented. In their defence, they were well aware that although Leicester was still a city where unemployment stood at only 2½ per cent in 1972, and economic decline was not yet apparent, nevertheless its knitwear firms were working below capacity. Slight though it was, the city was described as experiencing serious unemployment for the first time in its history. The Labour MP for Leicester North West, Mr Greville Janner, expressed his concern in the House of Commons when he stated that 'the unemployment rate in the Leicester area had doubled during the period [since June 1970]. Is not the Hon. Gentleman aware of the tremendous hardship caused by unemployment in a previously very prosperous City?'[36]

The *Sunday Telegraph* pointed to the plus side.[37] Leicester was still a 'rich City'. Its unemployment was set at well below the national average of 2 per cent. There were plenty of job vacancies on the postcards in the windows

of the Department of Employment office and private employment agencies had
many too, especially for women. Moreover, although there were 9,500 families
on the council house waiting list, Leicester was building 1,000 new homes
a year. When pressed, Sidney Bridges ('a bluff North countryman') gave it
as his opinion that with the full co-operation of all its citizens ('never likely
to be forthcoming') Leicester could accommodate 20,000 refugees: 'No good
protesting, we have a job to do. Like spitting into the wind.' Almost a decade
later, in a study of Labour voters in Willesden, Miles and Phizacklea[38] noted
fears about 'immigrants' contributing to unemployment and inner city decline:
a message which the voters had received through ideas mediated by both newspaper and television programmes.

The provincial press is particularly influential in shaping public opinion
in the sphere of race relations.[39] In a detailed study of levels of racial antipathy
in Leicester and Manchester, Troyna[40] argued that the *Leicester Mercury* helped
to 'highlight and reinforce the conception of "race as a problem" in the City'.
He cites its treatment of the Ugandan Asian refugees in 1972 as particularly
important. In its own defence, the *Leicester Mercury* claimed that it indeed printed
on its Page Four a representative sample of letters about the Ugandan Asians.
It also ran a feature in September 1972 in which its columnist attempted to
redress the balance of its general reporting.[41] 'It is generally agreed that the
silent majority is solidly behind right wing extremists ... but this silent majority
has been misrepresented ... it is not of one body and no one should presume
to speak for it.' Also one editorial on 28 August urged:[42]

> The anti-immigration march through the streets of Leicester should be ignored.
> The Leicester Mercury would like to see an all-party committee from the Commons
> ... come to Leicester. A walk around the shops, factories, streets and clubs and
> pubs would enable them to judge for themselves the widespread concern that exists,
> concern caused by reasons that are far from racialist.

The cumulative influence of this local newspaper with its power of 'agenda
setting',[43] together with its publication of so many Readers' Letters and its
use of cartoons[44] all of which purported to show how 'the people of Leicester'
viewed the coming of the Ugandan Asians to the city on the thinking and
policies of Leicester's political leaders, can only be speculated. But with the
paper's estimated readership of 169,094 in 1972/3 they could scarcely remain
unaffected by the message it so frequently transmitted.

2. LOCAL POLITICS: THE AFTERMATH

As well as trying to gauge the climate of opinion among its supporters, the
Labour group was mindful that in a few months it would have to test out
its popularity at two sets of local elections: in the city seats for the new county
authority in April 1973, and for the new Leicester District Council in mid-June.
The National Front and other extreme right-wing groups decided to make
Leicester their showplace for these elections. In May 1972 the National Front

gained 399 votes per candidate in the city elections. In 1973, although another 'race relations' topic had become prominent (the strike of the largely Asian workforce at the Mansfield Hosiery mill in Loughborough), the main plank of the National Front's campaign was that one in five of all Ugandan Asians who came to Britain had settled in Leicester. It claimed that a growing number of people had joined the National Front mainly, as stated by Mr Graham Eustace, the National Front's chief local organizer, because 'they believe that the Tory, Labour and Liberal politicians just don't care about anyone but themselves any more.' He went on to claim that in other parts of the country, branches of the National Front were made up largely of people to the right of the Conservative Party, but that was not true of Leicester. 'Most of the people who have come in used to support the Labour Party.'[45]

The Leicester Enoch Powell Support Group in their turn challenged Labour's statement that because they had pressed the government so hard, Leicester's ratepayers did not have to bear 'the burden of resettlement' costs,[46] by issuing an estimate that each Ugandan Asian had cost the British taxpayer a matter of £124 'so far'. 'One asks what some of our own British unfortunate people, the sick, infirm and disadvantaged could do with £124 each.'[47] In the April 1973 elections the National Front and the Enoch Powell Support Group's total of 19 candidates polled 13,500 votes, the *Leicester Mercury* commented that this was 'not a lot, but probably enough, with three candidates reaching four figures and beating Tories in one ward'.[48] Although in the June 1973 elections the National Front scored 683 votes per candidate, Labour increased its majority, winning 37 seats out of 48, and electing its first Asian councillor (who was prominent in the Gujarati Welfare Society). The extreme right wing increased their percentage vote but won no seat.

In the end, then, the policies of the 'old guard' of the Labour Party towards the Ugandan Asians seems to have had little direct effect, despite what the National Front and its other right-wing opponents claimed, and the 1973 elections showed an increase in Labour's popularity. The party had closed ranks after the initial rebellion by its nine members, and one of the latter (Councillor Jim Marshall) became the new party leader in 1973. After 1973 too there was a shift in attitude, and one of the 'new guard' Labour councillors elected in 1973 stated that, 'ashamed of its "don't come here advertisement", the Labour Party "fell over backwards" to make racial harmony work.'[49]

The Inter-Racial Solidarity Campaign, however, claimed that the significant change by Leicester's Labour Party in its attitude came later and was caused mainly by fright over the National Front's success in the 1976 city elections. The National Front polled nearly 18.5 per cent of the total votes and in the Abbey Ward came within 61 votes of victory. But in 1977, this time in the county elections, their total share slumped to 13.5 per cent. If 1977 was a year of bitter disappointment, then their performance in 1978 was 'a very bad nightmare'. Inter-Racial Solidarity emphasized that this was due to effective campaigns conducted by itself and the successful rise of the broad-based Unity against Racism Movement. 'More recently the Labour Party has [also] launched a strong and long overdue stand against the Nazis.'[50] In 1976, however, as part of the massive country-wide swing to the Conservatives, Labour lost control of the City Council. Among those who lost their seat was the former Labour group leader, Edward Marston. Although there were other factors, both nationally and locally, that were responsible for Labour's defeat (locally the issue about the purchase of the New Walk Centre to house all the Council's departments was seen as an extravagance 'on the rates'), it was immigration that the National Front made the central theme of their election campaign. In an editorial 'Swing with a Sting', on the day after the polls (7 May 1976), the *Leicester Mercury* commented:

> All the major parties in Leicester must be a little thoughful about the votes collected
> by the National Front ... Clearly they are never going to be a real influence in
> the Town Hall but the message of the measure of their support is that there is
> a sizeable minority not satisfied with the way immigrant problems are being tackled.

3. REACTIONS OUTSIDE LEICESTER

In one of the first policy statements of the Uganda Resettlement Board, made on 24 August, its Chairman promised that 'all the persuasion that is available' would be used to guide the refugees from areas where immigration had already laid 'great stress on the social services'. In the media coverage of these 'magnet towns', it was Leicester that was given the most attention. However, the *Financial Times*[51] pointed out that among the local authorities most concerned about the practical effects of the influx, protests in plenty had come from other Labour-controlled councils too. Ealing, with its 33,000 immigrants, had a ruling Labour group which said that 'it is a physical impossibility to accept more.' Brent, again Labour controlled, stated: 'We can't build a fence to keep them out.' The deputy Labour leader of Birmingham, Councillor Stanley Yapp, reported that there was no question of his authority putting extensive contingency plans in hand: 'the influx was a national matter.' A similar statement was made by Bradford's Labour group: 'We should not go out of our way to show that they would be welcome here.' The explanation of these Labour-controlled Councils' reactions was seen by *Race Today*[52] as a logical line of development of Labour's position since 1962, when the party had abandoned its principled opposition to immigration control. So the questioning by these various towns as to whether they should reject or accept the Asians was inevitable and predictable, once the principle of control had been accepted.

Another viewpoint was expressed in the *Municipal Journal*.[53] It emphasized that the most disturbing aspect was not that Labour Councils like Leicester and Ealing had said they had no room to spare, but that no other sizeable authorities, whether Labour or Conservative, offered positive hospitality. Only a handful of smaller authorities offered to take a few families. So it was left to individuals, such as the Archbishop of York, who wrote to *The Times* on 1 September urging that places like York, Norwich and Lincoln should welcome the expelled Asians. He was promptly criticized for not offering a place in his palace. In York, too, the leader of the Labour-controlled Council declared that the archbishop's idea was not practical: 'The social services in York are woefully underdeveloped ... the housing situation is no better than it was ten years ago.'

The Foreign Secretary also urged similar obligations 'both moral and legal'. But for every town like Pontardawe and Lincoln which did offer homes, there were others, such as Cheltenham, where a prospective Conservative parliamentary candidate responded to the Archbishop of York's plea by stating 'We are not racialist ... we couldn't absorb any number into our community.' (Cheltenham in 1972 had a population of 78,000 with about 100 immigrants.) The Secretary of the Cheltenham Croquet Club said she had no objection to Ugandan Asians living next door 'just as long as they keep our standard'. The Secretary of the Gloucestershire Royal British Legion summed up what his friends thought: 'We are not in favour of affording help to cast-off foreigners who are prepared to accept the hospitality of the country and knife us in the back ... I don't think they will be popular here.'[54] Norwich said it had no room – it had 3,000 on its housing list. The town which won approval as the most hospitable was Peterborough, where the Labour Council was the first of the few who did offer to accommodate some (50) families.[55] It brought out a special edition of its ratepayer's newsletter, *Focus*, to answer the letters which poured in abusing the leader of the Council and the Town Clerk. The houses offered were in fact empty and waiting for demolition, not those which were newly built by the Peterborough Development Council.

In the New Towns there was a good case that accommodation, which after all had been built at the government's expense, should be made available to the refugees, but the New Towns Commission's first reaction was that it was unlikely that this would be so. In September it decided that its homes could be offered in four of its new towns: Crawley, Hatfield, Hemel Hempstead and Welwyn Garden City. But at Crawley the chairman of the Labour-controlled Council said, 'We already have a housing problem of our own second generation ... the Government's decision is in fact an imposition on Crawley.' The Labour MP Mr Robert Maxwell was reported as stating that it would be unfair to offer houses there to the Ugandan Asians, because Londoners would be deprived.[56] Although Corby said it could offer accommodation to only five or ten families, an observer noted that on one estate alone there were 40 empty houses 'to lure employees to the town'. Runcorn had been advertising for the previous 12 months that it had empty houses and employment opportunities, yet in September its General Manager claimed that the waiting list for houses was growing. Skelmersdale New Town, which had been advertising its 500 empty properties on television, suddenly ceased to do so. In Basildon New Town the local press and politicians created a crisis about the allocation of just five houses, and caused a split in the Labour-controlled Council.[57]

Of the large urban authorities, Birmingham was if anything more negative in its initial reactions to receiving the refugees than Leicester.[58] Shortly after the news of the expulsion and before any Leicester MP or local politician made any public announcements about the Ugandan Asians, Mrs Jill Knight, Conservative MP for Edgbaston, stated that Birmingham's schools were 'at saturation point' with an average of 30–40 children arriving each week. Mr J. Kinsey, Conservative MP for Selly Oak, said that 'any further influx would be unwelcome and unwise ... we do not want anything to interfere with the integration now going on.' Both Mrs Knight and Mr Arthur Bottomley (Labour MP for Middlesbrough) used the phrase 'we are at saturation point' when they made a joint broadcast as fellow members of the Select Committee on Race Relations (BBC News, 8 August). Birmingham's Conservative Alderman Charles Collette said that social services would collapse if there was an uncontrolled 'peaceful invasion' by Ugandan Asians. He forecast serious racial trouble in the city within the next decade if the Asians were allowed to come. Birmingham's Conservative leader, Alderman Neville Bosworth, like his Leicester counterpart, called for an 'emergency meeting' of the Birmingham City Council which took place on 24 August. However, when Birmingham sent its four-man delegation to the Home Office they criticized the futility of Leicester's policy of advertising: 'We do not have passport control points on Birmingham's boundaries. It is quite useless passing resolutions of the Leicester type and imagining that the problem will go away.' But Leicester's Conservative leader Alderman Kenneth Bowder on an ATV programme on 15 August gave as a reason: 'Leicester does not sprawl, we are a community ... in the short term I doubt whether we have room to take the Asians.'

Leicester was not the first Council to approach the Home Office over the need for the refugees to be 'dispersed'. Ealing decided to do so on 14 August, its Labour leader stating on the BBC News that 'an extra 4,000 will have a devastating effect, both political parties are united on this ...' When its Council representatives appeared on the ITV programme 'This Week' on 31 August, they emphasized that 'the Home Office can't give us a packet of land.' This theme was also taken up by representatives of the Southall Tenants Association who appeared on ITV on 30 August: 'We have been asking for dispersal before this ... you can't squeeze an extra sock into a full suitcase.' Ealing Council too held an emergency meeting. There the public protest outside was bigger and more vociferous than the one in Leicester's Town Hall when a mere handful of housewives from Blaby gathered. And when Colin Jordan attempted to make his 'Keep Britain White' speech during the Leicester Council's debate, he met with little public support outside in Town Hall Square.[59]

The Community Relations Commission hastily compiled a report from 11 areas that already had concentrations of East African Asians (Brent, Birmingham and Leicester were among them). Leicester was singled out, but only along with other authorities, as expressing doubts about capacity to provide adequate employment opportunities. Yet in a previous press leak of the same report, Leicester's unemployment rate was emphasized as being below the national average. It was stated that Leicester had clerical and commercial opportunities for the large number of clerks expected to arrive.[60]

Finally, Leicester went on record as being heartless in comparison to its near neighbour Nottingham. The Runnymede Trust published a survey of the dispersal policy of the Resettlement Board. This demonstrated that the division of the country into 'red places' (from which the refugees were to be steered) and 'green places' (where they would be encouraged to settle) was determined less by actual difficulties of absorption than by the shrillness of political protests of the local councils.[61] The authors of the survey (Robert Briant and Dipak Nandy) knew Leicester personally. They pointed to the fact that Nottingham had been classified as 'green', yet it had 7,468 unemployed compared with Leicester's 4,495, and had almost as many people on its council housing list (8,151 compared with Leicester's 9,500). Nottingham won approval for its lack of protest over the Ugandan Asian settlement there. But the report ignored the fact that Nottingham's coloured population was not in the main from East Africa, and also that its Housing Committee chairman had stated that no Ugandan Asian would be given any preferential treatment in council housing (BBC News, 19 August). It has been argued that attitudes to immigrants vary from one community to another and the most positive places are those which are most stable.[62] If this is true then Leicester's political leadership certainly did not reflect much civic confidence in 1972.

The chorus of responses by other Local Authorities has been detailed in order to show that they were in essence the same as, or even at times harsher than, Leicester's, and that the reluctance to accept the Ugandan Asian expellees was almost universal. Although singled out as the most unwelcoming of all places in the UK, Leicester gained this reputation only because of its decision to advertise its advice that they should settle elsewhere, an action which proved largely ineffective.

As a footnote to Leicester's reactions to the Ugandan Asian refugees, it is interesting to look back to the events of 1956, and the refugees from Hungary. When that country was invaded by the USSR Britain was then said to have accepted more than its share of moral obligation for these mostly non-English-speaking non-citizen refugees. Their numbers (30,000) were slightly larger than the total of Ugandan Asians who came in 1972. On the day in 1956 when, because of another crisis (the Egyptian nationalization of the Suez Canal), petrol rationing was introduced, the *Leicester Mercury* announced that the Lord Mayor had launched a 'Help the Hungarian Refugees Fund', with the words:

> There should be no delay in making an appeal to the City and to all men of goodwill who live, work or transact their business here … we should demonstrate our practical concern for the suffering of those overtaken by the tide of adversity which has so suddenly overwhelmed them.[63]

Within a few weeks, Leicester had raised over £10,000 by voluntary subscription for the Hungarian refugees. Leicester of the 1950s showed a great deal more goodwill and practical concern towards a European group who had decided to leave their own country rather than live under Soviet communism, than was extended 20 years later towards Asians who were British citizens and had been given no chance of staying on in Amin's Uganda.

Chapter 4 Reception, not resettlement: strategies for settling the refugees

1. INTRODUCTION

The reception of the Ugandan Asians as exemplified in the government's 'resettlement programme' was seen by a number of observers as second rate and less than enthusiastic. Attitudes filtering down from the 'bureaucratic top', that is, the government-sponsored Uganda Resettlement Board set up in August 1972, certainly caused some misunderstandings among Local Authorities (such as Leicester), on whom the Board relied for the reception of the refugees into their areas. Lord Wade, the Liberal peer, described the first three months of the operation as 'one long story of improvisation'[1] and said it compared unfavourably with that of the planned reception of refugees from Indonesia by the Dutch in the 1950s.[2] Other commentators such as Dipak Nandy and Brian Jackson[3] saw the whole of the government's proposals as primarily designed for reception and dispersal to ensure that the refugees placed no burden on the taxpayer, and in effect left them to their own devices. But the *Observer* (11 November 1972) described the initial reception as being 'exceptionally well handled on the whole' and David Lane, MP, Under-Secretary of State at the Home Office, stated that 'some journalists have been looking for petty things to carp at and criticise, and have failed to give a due measure of praise to what had been achieved during what was essentially a crash operation.'[4]

Nowhere were these contrasting evaluations better illustrated than in two BBC programmes made in 1973. A radio documentary, 'From Riches to Rags' (30 August), found that every area and official appeared to have dealt with the special problems of the Asian refugees in their own way. Once they had left the Reception Camps set up by the Resettlement Board, there was no monitoring of their progress or difficulties. A variety of pressure groups were shocked at the deficiencies in the Welfare State that the coming of the refugees had highlighted. Yet it seemed that the Asians were not complaining; indeed a typical comment in this broadcast was: 'We are born optimists. We have struggled from nothing before. Before the last war our capital in Uganda was low. Then came success. We have lived through the Wild West of Kenya and Uganda. No one opens the door for you, you have to push it.'

The other documentary, 'The Promised Land', was televised on 7 September. This traced the fortunes of two families. As fast as they were out of the camps the members of the successful family moved from the refurnished derelict house in Peterborough and then to their own home (with a 100 per cent mortgage). The other family featured were itinerant musicians who had already spent a year in the camps and had no prospect of employment outside. The difference in the fortunes of these two families illustrated that much of the resettlement was to depend on the resources of the individuals rather than on help from any outside agency.[5] Some of the refugees put their own social memories into writing.[6] Among these were the recollections of a number of refugee schoolchildren who had a naïve optimism about their future life chances in a new country. But most of the other accounts reveal how families had to come to terms with the loss of all their possessions, and found adjusting to life in such towns as Cambridge, Tunbridge Wells and Huddersfield a daunting task, even though they were helped by some of the local people. By contrast, the series of insensitive and racially inspired insults began at the airports and continued both in their temporary hostel accommodation and when they were 'settled into the community'.[7]

Most reports and surveys were disturbing and pessimistic about both the reception and resettlement schemes. A team of academics from the University of Wisconsin interviewed refugees in Wandsworth and Slough during late 1972 and early 1973, and were almost optimistic about the Asians in terms of their acceptance, acculturation and absorption ('the group is well advanced into the first phase of the cycle'). But a far more depressing picture emerged when they surveyed families in the same locations in 1975. They noted a growing degree of disillusionment because of underemployment and unemployment. Some had no permanent homes, one in four was jobless and most had no contact with English people. The research was severely criticized by Praful Patel who said it gave a totally false picture.[8] Others, however, continued to assert that the Uganda Resettlement Board had been largely ineffective, especially in its efforts to disperse the Asians throughout the UK. This, it was claimed, was a public relations effort to appease general opinion rather than a seriously constituted practicality. The Resettlement Camps, it was admitted, offered in theory a potential base for a really worthwhile programming to launch the refugees into British society. But the Board viewed them as temporary expedients from which people were to be dispatched as soon as possible. Many of the Asian refugees were destined to swell the ranks of the Welfare State. The problems that the refugees encountered were the same as anyone in a similar situation might encounter, but made worse by the refugees' desperate need to accept *any* job or shelter.[9] What is significant is that the particular difficulties of the refugees were only revealed in those few areas where there were specially appointed Welfare Officers who took on an activist role and devoted themselves to acting as full-time mediators between the Ugandan Asian claimants and the statutory services. There was no such officer in Leicester. But the Uganda Resettlement Unit at Wandsworth Council for Community Relations warned: 'The success or failure to resettle Uganda Asians will be seen by immigrant communities as an indication of Britain's attitudes.

Their present insecurity is a constant reminder to immigrant communities of apathy, prejudice and alienation and constitutes a threat to integration.'[10]

The Co-ordinating Committee for the Welfare of Evacuees from Uganda, an umbrella organization for the various voluntary groups that had not been nominated by the Resettlement Board as having the most appropriate skills 'for dealing with emergencies', had been set up in August 1972 on the initiative of the British Council of Churches and the United Kingdom Immigrants Advisory Service. The CCWEU was among those who claimed that the resettlement programme had been a failure:

> Of course, race relations and immigration are political issues. Of course, special treatment or positive discrimination is seen as explosive. The fact remains that the Government's view of its responsibility to the Ugandan refugees has been, not to help them re-establish their lives with dignity, but to regard that responsibility as terminated when the Asian families take their rightful place on the poverty line.

This report made it clear that it was not monitoring success but examining evidence of failure. But to blame the Resettlement Board would be naïve. Criticism was directed at particular aspects of its operations, but the main criticism 'must be directed at the Government for the terms and policies within which the Board had to function and our society for the overall context in which the resettlement took place'.[11]

Other accounts also detracted from any complacency about the resettlement process and concentrated on the inflexibility of the Supplementary Benefits Commission (or rather its local offices) in applying rules to the refugees. Not only were these rules not geared to the refugee situation, but the refugees, through lack of knowledge of the workings of the system and language problems, were particularly vulnerable in dealing with a complicated bureaucracy where the onus is laid on the claimant to prove entitlement.[12] It can be argued that the families quoted in these reports were those in greatest difficulties, and that most of the information came from areas like Wandsworth where the general housing situation alone was a disturbing symptom of community stress. Indeed this was acknowledged by Lewis Donnelly, the Director of London Council of Social Services, in a foreword to a report on elderly refugees: 'This is not a report about a typical cross-section of the people expelled by General Amin. It is *not* about the young, the healthy and those who made the transition successfully.'[13]

Another group with acute problems were the 'divided families' – those whose head of family was officially stateless, having applied but not received official recognition of Ugandan citizen status before the expulsion order. These refugees were now living in refugee camps in various European countries and were under the protection of the United Nations Commissioner for Refugees. Others had found temporary asylum in India or Pakistan.[14] Everyone who came into contact with their families in the UK saw that there was an urgent need for the government to relax its immigration rules so that the families could be reunited.

The continuing needs of the refugees and the insufficient attention being paid by the normal agencies featured in a report, *One Year On* (1974), by the Community Relations Commission.[15] In a second report (1976) the Commission emphasized that a tenth of all the families who came from Uganda in 1972 still had no one in the household who could support them.[16] The Chairman of the Commission, Mr Mark Bonham-Carter, said that the publication should do something to modify the general picture of the Ugandan Asians arriving, settling in and 'promptly and profitably opening grocery stores which remain open until midnight up and down the land ... this conceals the 10 per cent of the refugees who have been forgotten and whom people want to forget.'[17]

All of these reports and the Resettlement Board itself recognized that the British government should ask the Ugandan government for compensation. The Leicester refugees were convinced that finance was the real key to resettlement. The Uganda Evacuees Association, set up in Harrow in 1972, recommended the arrangements made by the Uganda Resettlement Board with the clearing banks and the government for loans to enable people to set themselves up in business: 'It is evident that a large number of British citizens from Uganda were traders and are unsuitable for any other occupation. These people are likely to remain the most difficult to settle unless some kind of loan arrangement can be made.'[18] But the Home Secretary decided against any action on loans. Both the government and the Resettlement Board thought it 'more sensible' for the refugees to take up a job and get to know 'life in this country'. The Uganda Evacuees Association also took on other financial concerns. The Association worked with the Foreign and Commonwealth Office on claims for compensation for all the Asians' assets left behind in Uganda. Another aspect of their attempts to obtain financial compensation for the refugees was their co-operation with the Life Offices Association for insurance policies taken out in Uganda with British-based companies, to be encashed to the policy-holders in sterling rather than in Ugandan rates of exchange. With a few exceptions this plea was turned down by the insurance companies. But the Uganda Evacuees Association did publish details about these insurances and dealt with the large numbers of enquiries that it received, before directing insurance-holders on to the Life Offices Association headquarters.

In January 1973 the Community Relations Commission asked all local Community Relation Councils for their 'assessment of the Ugandan Asian situation'. By February Navnit Dholakia, the Senior Development Officer of the Commission, had compiled a comprehensive list of the replies from 38 areas. In almost all places the co-ordinating committees of volunteers had been initiated by, and continued to be based on, the local Community Relations Council, and the chief Community Relations Officers were servicing these committees. Ealing had a West Middlesex British Ugandan Relief Committee on which the Community Relations Officer and executive members were committee members. Wandsworth's reply was: 'The Community Relations Council is fully responsible for the 700 individuals from Uganda who have already arrived here.' Only Leicester replied that there were two committees: one was a 'committee

at officer level' – the Director of the Social Services, the Secretary of the
Council for Social Services and the Community Relations Officer; the second
'set up by the Asians was based at the British Asian reception centre and spon-
sored by the British Asian Welfare Society'. Both of these organizations were
helping 'the 3,218 refugees from Uganda who had come to the city'. The
Commission also asked its local officers to assess the 'effectiveness of the local
committees' in helping to resettle the Asians from Uganda. Twelve areas gave
a reply to this, and these were in the main areas such as Oxford and Woking
where only a few families had settled and the replies were optimistic. Ealing
alone out of the places that had considerable numbers of refugees rated its
reception committee 'effective'. Leicester did not answer this item in the
enquiry.[19]

2. THE UGANDA RESETTLEMENT BOARD AND THE VOLUNTARY ASSOCIATIONS

The Resettlement Board

On 18 August 1972 the Home Secretary announced that the government would
establish a Board to organize the resettlement of displaced Ugandan Asians.
He also stated that he envisaged the voluntary organizations playing 'an im-
mensely important part' in the process.

The nearest previous parallel to the Board was the Anglo-Egyptian Resettlement Board set up in 1957 to assist some 7,000 British citizens expelled from
Egypt. Sir Charles Cunningham had been its accounting officer ('a typical
product of the alpha plusses in our Civil Service')[20] and he was appointed
Chairman of the Uganda Resettlement Board. The one newcomer to the Board
in terms of Whitehall experience, and its only Asian, was Praful Patel. But
as the secretary of the all-party Committee on United Kingdom Citizenship,
and as a Ugandan Asian whose family's business at Jinja had been closed
through Africanization and as someone who had been closely associated with
Indian groups since coming to the UK in 1958, Patel saw his task as the
equivalent of an MP's constituency work. Contrary to every other prediction
made at the time he gave it as his belief that 'the Ugandan Asians ... tend
to go where there are no great numbers of Asians. They will integrate very
quickly. All they want is assurances about their house, job and education for
their children. They already have a good appreciation of all that is English ...'[21]

Although Patel praised the creation of the Board and said that it marked
the start of a new epoch of consultation with immigrant groups, this consultation
did not extend to discussing the vital question about which parts of the country
the Ugandan Asians should be encouraged to settle in. Even before the Board
had been formed and without consulting any immigrant groups, the government
had worked out the numbers to be allowed in the different areas. After the
Board had been set up, the task set for it by the Home Secretary, Robert
Carr, was difficult and indeed as it turned out virtually impossible – to disperse
the refugees away from those areas where they would be an extra strain on

housing and education. In fact this meant the very areas already favoured for settlement by the families and friends of the refugees. But there was the other factor previously described: these were the places whose political leaders protested most loudly that they could not cope with the extra numbers and made their opinions known both to the government and to the Board.

Other members of the Board were Mark Bonham-Carter (Chairman of the Community Relations Commission); Douglas Tilbe (Director of the Community and Race Relations Unit of the British Council of Churches); Mr Brian Wilson, the Town Clerk of Camden; and Mrs Charles Clode, Director of the Women's Royal Voluntary Service (and the only woman member). After the first official meeting, additional members were announced by the Home Office.[22] But there were still gaps in its expertise. The employment question was at that stage considered the most difficult problem, yet there was no trade union representative, nor was there anyone representing those local authorities (such as Leicester and Birmingham) that had been expressing their anxieties over the prospect of being magnet towns for the refugees. Missing too was any representation from the more patently activist agencies, particularly the U.K. Immigrants Advisory Service and the Joint Council for the Welfare of Immigrants, yet both of these had full-time officers who had built up a considerable amount of specialized knowledge about the difficulties of Asians in East Africa, especially since the restrictions on their entry to the UK imposed by the 1968 Immigration Act.

At its first meeting, on 30 August, the Board published its priorities: the immediate reception of families; finding temporary accommodation near arrival points for those who could not go straight to their destinations; and using persuasion to disperse refugees away from areas under social pressures on housing, education and social services. Other tasks were to find jobs and to open a register of offers of accommodation. There was also a vague promise (important for Leicester) that the Board was prepared 'to reimburse any reasonable expenditure incurred by local authorities in making immediate arrangements'. It also pledged to co-operate with voluntary organizations in setting up teams at points of entry into the country. This list, apart from the setting up of Resettlement Camps and the actual naming of areas from which refugees should be 'persuaded' away, embraced most of the work that the Board undertook before it was finally dissolved in January 1974.

After this first meeting, the Board was already being condemned for its lack of a bold strategy in a national crisis.[23] Officials in Leicester complained about the Board's lack of urgency (during the first weeks of its operation its office and switchboard closed down at weekends) and its failure to appoint a press officer. But the Board was working in the dark. It was in no position to give Leicester or any other place details about the numbers of refugees. When it was first able to give information this was misleading because it was based on the figure of 2,000 men, women and children who had already made arrangements to come to the UK before the expulsion order, or who had the means to make such arrangements very quickly. Most spoke English, and very few were destitute. So the scale of the problem was unknown initially, and as it turned out far more needed government accommodation than the Board had previously calculated. Some of the Leicester refugees were able to give a further reason for this situation. Before leaving Uganda they had told the British High Commission that they had accommodation waiting for them, assuming that their relatives or friends would help, but many of these could not accommodate whole families. Others did have the definite promise of accommodation in Leicester, but they were afraid to say so because they knew that the Board would try to persuade them away from the city. A further complication was that many of the arrivals were women and children, sent ahead whilst the breadwinners stayed on to close down their enterprises.[24]

Though the total number of refugees arriving in the end proved to be much smaller than forecast, the Board was faced with a far more complicated and long-drawn-out process than had been anticipated. The early intelligence about the Asians, revealed in newspapers, research findings and the pronouncements of various Asian representatives, built up a picture of skilled, semi-skilled or professional workers;[25] nothing was heard of the destitute who were living in poverty after having lost their businesses through Africanization, and too much was made of the example of how well the Kenyan Asians had settled in. Because of this over-optimism the Board was faced with numbers of refugees for which it was ill prepared, and during September and October 1972 Transit Camps had to be hastily prepared for some 21,800 destitute Ugandan Asians. The population in the camps was at its peak on 9 November, when over 13,000 were in the renamed 'Resettlement Centres'.

By October the Board was so heavily involved in coping with the numbers of refugees who wished to have temporary accommodation in the Reception Centres that it had virtually given up its attempts to steer people away from non-approved areas. The Board had no powers to acquire housing and property even on a temporary basis. All it could do was to request Local Authorities and private individuals to offer accommodation to house the refugees. The response by the Local Authorities was disappointing, and when Sir Charles Cunningham took part in the Radio 4 programme 'It's Your Line' on 21 November 1972 he commented:

> We have many offers of houses from Local Authorities and many offers from private individuals ... but these are not all in areas where the jobs are, and I think that what we want, much more than offers of jobs, is more offers of houses, because the experience is that where it is possible to house a family, it is not too difficult, given the range of skills which have come with the Asian families from Uganda, to find employment.

The Board counted the response to its appeal for accommodation by Local Authorities in Scotland as one of the success stories. Yet the hopelessness of the dispersal policy was illustrated by the 'de-resettlement', the numbers who by 1973 had taken 'the highroad back to kinship' and had drifted back from Scotland to Southall and Leicester.[26] By 1976 it was estimated that 80 per cent of the Ugandan Asians were living in areas where East African Asians generally had settled.[27] Even in countries like Israel and Canada where the absorption of immigrants is part of the national ethos, direction of newcomers away from overcrowded areas where they have relatives has been found difficult to impose. Moreover, kin groups are a mechanism for guaranteeing support to recent immigrants with little collateral (whether material or social) in unfamiliar surroundings.[28] In Canada the Ugandan Asians were determined to settle in Toronto and Vancouver. The refugees who went to the USA joined fellow East Indians in New York.[29] So the attempt to persuade the Ugandan Asians away from the so-called 'red' areas (a term much disliked by the Board) like Leicester was a policy doomed to failure from the first. The Director of the Runnymede Trust said that the Board should be called the 'Dispersal Board' and that it was close to harassing the refugees. The Board wanted to keep these 'red areas' secret but they were named (including Leicester) by the *Guardian* on 18 September.[30] But apart from issuing a memorandum to counsellors interviewing new arrivals at Stansted airport, advising that people wishing to travel to areas listed as 'difficult' should not be given free travel warrants,[31] the Board in fact did very little else to deter the refugees from going to these places.

Another limitation on the Board was that it was an agency with very restricted powers to reimburse those Local Authorities that needed assistance in their attempt to help the refugees who had arrived in their area. The government preferred to channel money through the rate support system, and in 1973–4 this was increased by £2 million. Local authorities also received help for the payment of the salaries for some of the extra staff employed to help the refugees settle in, for there was provision for reimbursement under the provisions of the 1966 Local Government Act. The direct reimbursement made to Local Authorities by the Resettlement Board was £610,000. This was used for 100 per cent grants for items such as grants to students, salaries for social workers, hiring rooms for the reception arrangements and school transport. These were for one year only. A 75 per cent grant was for 'capital projects such as temporary school classrooms'. In a series of editorials *The Times*[32] argued that the Board should have been given greater powers in distributing finance. But Sir Charles Cunningham in response stated that the Board did in fact have a great deal of operational freedom, but this was 'subject to strict financial control of the Home Secretary'.[33] However this dual role led to a great deal of confusion on the part of officials and Council members in places such as Leicester. In November 1972 Leicester sent a deputation to the Home Secretary to complain about the complications involved. It also led to councillors accusing the Board of reneging on earlier promises. When Mr Carr addressed the Association of Municipal Corporations at Eastbourne on 20 September he raised hopes by his statement that 'the Government would meet the full cost they would face in resettling Ugandan Asians.'[34] But in November the details of more restrictive financing, particularly over the money for houses for the refugees, was relayed to Leicester's officials.

In its final report, the Board gave details about the cost of its operation up to December 1973. It estimated this at £6.1 million. By far the largest expenditure (£4,904,100) had been incurred in setting up and running the Resettlement Centres. Apart from this and the grants to Local Authorities, the Board had spent £79,000 on the reception arrangements at four airports, £62,000 on transporting the refugees from their points of arrival and £59,700 on those who had wished to emigrate after a short stay in the UK. The rest of the expenditure had gone on the administrative expenses of the Board (£347,000), and only £62,200 had been given to the voluntary bodies to help with travel and subsistence costs. The Board made mention of its grants to the Co-ordinating Committee and the Shelter Housing Aid Centre for local advice on housing. The actual sum given is not revealed, but 'the generous grant of £5,000' from Oxfam for housing advice by Shelter is detailed. The report stated that 'it is of course impossible to estimate the value' of the voluntary sector's efforts. Among the Asian organizations, the Board singled out the Standing Conference of Indian Organizations, the Ismailia Cultural Centre and the Swaminarayan Hindu Mission for their part in the reception and their continued support of the Ugandan Asians. The Board estimated that a total number of 28,608 'passed through its hands' and on average £200 had been spent per head, but those 6,621 persons who made their own arrangements and did not go to the Resettlement Centres received the smallest official financial aid of all. To this £200 can be added the £5 per head which was donated by the Uganda Asian Relief Trust (set up in November 1972 under Lord Sainsbury and with a total of £120,000 raised from donations from the government and other sources). With this money the Trust hoped 'to supplement the work of the Board and make the entry of the Ugandan Asians into the community a little easier than it would otherwise have been'.

The voluntary sector

The officials of the Resettlement Board had to work alongside representatives from some 60 voluntary organizations. These were not accountable to the Board, they sometimes co-operated with it, but at other times acted as its most outspoken critics; this was particularly so in the Resettlement Camps.

The first meeting of these representatives from social, welfare, church and charitable organizations took place on 16 August 1972. This was two days before that of the Resettlement Board. The original name of the committee they formed was the Co-ordinating Committee for the Welfare of Evacuees from Uganda. The Committee agreed to set up advisory desks at ports of entry. They were optimistic, envisaging an efficient reception process. It was admitted that particularly Leicester would face problems, but since the participating organizations had been 'inundated with letters' offering accommodation, government Transit Camps would not be necessary: 'Whereas Transit Camps could be helpful to those who do not have a family to go to, anything in the way of refugee camps would be most regrettable. The establishment of refugee camps for U.K. citizens who happened to have brown skins could politically be dynamite.'[35]

After the establishment of its own Board had been announced, the Home Office met the volunteers 'in order to discuss how their joint efforts could be dovetailed', and it was agreed that reception teams should be drawn entirely from the voluntary agencies. The old RAF camp at Stradishall near Stansted Airport would be used as a debriefing centre, rather like facilities provided for returned prisoners of war.[36] Both the Board and the CCWEU thought that only a few of the refugees would need help with accommodation. Three weeks later Stradishall was overcrowded, and by October 16 camps (still called 'Reception Centres') were operating at the cost of £1 million a month.

By October, too, the CCWEU had an office in the Bayswater Student Centre. Its teams met every flight from Uganda, either at Heathrow, Gatwick or Stansted, and the Community Service Volunteers in particular (most of whom were in their early twenties) worked 16 hours a day. Schools in the camps had been started, there was a register of private accommodation and the Co-ordinating Committee was developing a regional network superior to that of the Board.[37] It also kept in close contact with the Co-ordinating Committee for the Welfare of Asians leaving Uganda which worked in Kampala as a counselling and advice service. However, the big 'uniformed organizations' – the Women's Royal Voluntary Service, the Red Cross and the St John Ambulance Brigade – decided to work outside the CCWEU, which caused problems. The WRVS, with its centre in almost every Local Authority area, was able to provide staging posts for the refugees en route from the airports to distant camps in Devon or Wales. Also, through its work in the Hungarian refugee camps and in accommodating elderly repatriates for the Anglo-Egyptian Resettlement Board it had developed considerable expertise,[38] and so it was asked by the Uganda Resettlement Board to vet offers of temporary accommodation. The CCWEU complained that this caused delays. The WRVS for their part disapproved of the unorthodox approach of some of the younger volunteers, who in turn criticized the 'tea and blankets' approach of the WRVS, complaining that this earned more than its fair share of public acknowledgment both in Parliament and from the Chairman of the Resettlement Board. This strained relationship was denied by the CCWEU's representative, Douglas Tilbe, but friction continued in 'a good dose of philanthropic muddle'.[39]

Although there were disagreements among its own members, much more serious was the CCWEU's impatience with civil servants sticking to well-defined rules, and with the camps' directors following the routines that they had exercised as officers in the forces or as colonial administrators. The CCWEU sent a telegram to the Home Office on 10 October complaining about the non-co-operation between the Board and volunteers, and recording regret that there were not more Asians working in the camps; they said that when they did produce an Asian worker for Stradishall 'he was looked on as a spy.' Although the Board agreed that the CCWEU should appoint a liaison officer in each camp to be responsible for the volunteers, the relationship between these officers and the camp's administration varied. Some of the CCWEU's members continued to accuse the Board of failing to fight hard enough, of being contented with a *laissez-faire* policy, 'of being painfully rudderless' and of 'acting in a fit of sulks ... making the situation worse for everyone',[40] and at the end of its existence merely handing over the Asians' difficulties to the Home Office.

The CCWEU continued to function until September 1973, and its progress reports reflected its concern about the pace of resettlement and the residual problems of migration. It appointed a Regional Adviser to visit different areas 'to discover what is happening and stimulate the creation of supportive groups where none exist'. Its Housing Section was transferred to the Shelter organization, but its education and employment work largely ended. It was closely involved in the attempts to get the stateless husbands of British passport-holding wives to this country. When in February 1973 it was announced that these could come to the UK, the CCWEU worked for those families still split by immigration rules. Despite the praise that the Board's Chairman gave to the Committee, the more vocal of its members continued to see it as a façade behind which the government could discharge minimal responsibilities, and an excuse for not giving sufficient funding to Leicester and elsewhere. But the voluntary sector was also described as being run on the cheap and ex-ploitive.[41] Nervous of the dangers of apparently favouring a particular group, the government relied on performing on a shoestring budget a task to which it ought to have accorded unsparing priority:[42]

> The British Government reacted tardily and chaotically to a crisis which the knowledgeable had been predicting for some time. What they should have done, instead of relying on nostalgic wartime faith in muddling through, is to have recruited professional staff, professional social workers and to have paid them professional salaries to do the job.

3. THE REFUGEES' VIEWS OF THE RECEPTION PROGRAMME

Most of the Ugandan Asians who came to Leicester went to the Resettlement Centres run by the Board. Some spent only a few nights there but others stayed for much longer: one elderly man was still living at the West Malling Camp in the spring of 1974. The Resettlement Centres, or as they were more generally called 'the camps', were set up in the autumn of 1972 in hastily refurbished ex-British or US military accommodation. They housed a total of 21,987 people for varying periods of time. Views of their role and usefulness naturally varied. Mamdani,[43] who was at the Kensington Centre, concluded that they were run as colonies by post-colonial bureaucrats whose main aim was to condition the Asians to be docile. Those of the refugees that were the most 'well behaved' were rewarded by being the first to be given information about jobs and accommodation outside. To the administrators of the camps the term 'resettlement' was just a euphemism for getting rid of the refugees. In its account of Mamdani's views the *Indian Weekly* (23 August 1973) pointed out that 'we now wait for the Uganda Resettlement Board's side of the story', but the Board itself gave no answer except to explain that the unpopular move of the refugees from the Kensington Centre was due to its being needed for the expected arrival of white British evacuees from Uganda. The Young Volunteer Force team who worked at Eccleshall Camp in Staffordshire emphasized that it was the Asian women who suffered most from camp life, and that competition for jobs and houses caused rivalries amongst the camp dwellers.[44] The psychological effects of having to live in the camps were variously described. There was little 'survivor guilt',[45] but there *were* degrees of 'refugee neurosis' made worse by the camps, which were so soul-destroying and caused the trauma of despondency, depression, dependence and lack of decision. Observers said that there were two groups in the camps: those who were waiting for the first opportunity to leave, and those who clung to even this cold security rather than attempting to cope with life outside. It was the latter who were the long-term casualties of the expulsion.[46]

The Leicester group of refugees challenged some of these descriptions. They spoke with gratitude about the volunteers who had helped in the initial reception, members of the WRVS in particular. Whilst journalists were preoccupied with the WRVS stereotypes – 'the hearty ladies', 'shiny buttoned ladies', 'middle aged women bored with the monotony of meals on wheels ... for whom the arrival of the Asians was the best thing that happened'[47] – it was the efficiency of the WRVS, if not always their sensitivity (one of the Muslim refugees expressed her 'shame' at being handed a mini-skirt), that was remembered by those most concerned. This gratitude can be explained away as a familiar trait in those who have experienced a traumatic upset.[48] But a different slant was offered by one of the Leicester refugees, a former garage owner in Jinja, who commented: 'Of course we did not like wearing second-hand clothes. We did not like queueing like beggars for food; but we are used to knowing just when you have to conclude an agreement. In business you have to know when to say "thank you" as well as "I demand".'

Others expressed their distress, as members of a culture where age confers status, at seeing older Asian men being advised and even counselled by the younger volunteers ('My father had lost enough without having to suffer this ...'). There was general agreement that a feeling of fatalism that life would never 'take off again after Uganda was lost' gripped whole families after the initial euphoria of escape from Amin's threats. Shiva Naipaul described this fatalism as habitual: 'an inability to come to terms with the reality of the situation they happen to be in – whether in Uganda or in England ... an inadequacy bred by generations of colonial dependence which resulted in a sort of mental paralysis'.[49]

But among the refugees were some people who remained in the camps for a year or more, some of whom used the facilities that were provided for their own purposes. One Leicester woman, along with a few others, stayed on in the camps until late in 1973, purely in order to campaign for her stateless husband to be admitted to the UK. The woman had been married to an accountant, and the last glimpse she had had of her husband was outside her house in Kampala; she and the children were bundled into the bus taking refugees to Entebbe, and her husband made his way to Jugrat in Southern India. Whilst at Lingfield Camp she had written to *The Times*, the Home Office and MPs. When Hobbs Barracks in Surrey closed down, she was moved on to the West Malling Camp in Kent, where with help from the Camp Administrator and the Liaison Officer she continued to campaign. Her husband was eventually reunited with her in her two-roomed 'flat' in Leicester where she and her two children were living after she finally left the camps. She might appear to have been one of the resettlement failures, left stranded in the camps after most had left; but in fact she and others like her had used their long stay there in a purposeful way to obtain support and legal advice in their struggle against the heartbreak of separation.

Another similar example was an elderly man who had lost everything he had in Uganda, but later became an activist for other elderly Asians in Leicester. He was in the camps for a year-and-a-half. He had left £35,000 in business concerns in Uganda and was living on Social Security at £2.30 a week. But he was active on the 'Residents' Committee' (his own words), and far from just accepting the camp administration, he challenged it ('I was there on the office door step every day at 9 a.m.'), raising complaints about accommodation and food. 'I helped to run all aspects. The Camp Commander said I could run the camp. I dealt with those Asians who were complaining. I started finding the right partners for the young people. I made life go on for myself and my people.'

Although acknowledging that staying on in the camps could be seen as avoiding the realities of what lay outside, Leicester refugees were emphatic that they had never allowed themselves to become cut off from reality. They used the camps as bases from which they could look at prospective accommodation and employment. One or two thought, however, that they had lost out by staying on for over three months, since by that time the more acceptable accommodation in Leicester had been taken up by those refugees who had gone straight to the city.

Several families who had spent a few months in the camps were anxious to say that they thought the camps could be seen as an acceptable feature of any refugee reception and partial resettlement. For the Ugandan Asians they had provided a safety valve until the more extreme opposition to the initial acceptance of the refugees diminished. Some of those still in the camps in 1973 referred to reports of petrol bombs being hurled at Ugandan Asian shops by extremist groups. These refugees acknowledged that rumours exaggerated the extent of these racial attacks, but the camps were at least safe and secure. The camps had prevented the sudden intake into any one city, and especially Leicester, from being as precipitous as it would otherwise have been. Indeed none of the Leicester group disagreed with the actual policy of using camps for the first phase of reception. As Amrit, a student, explained: 'No one in their right senses likes camps. If everything had been generous and good, then we would have had instant houses, jobs and loans. But without that, well it was camps or nothing.' What was most disliked were the isolated locations of the camps; some commentators at the time even alleged that these sites were deliberately chosen as being distant from any city with immigrant settlement, and especially those which had made most protest about the possibility of accepting the Ugandan Asians. But since the camps were commissioned at such speed in the autumn of 1972 it is difficult to believe that this was part of a preconceived plan by the government, the Resettlement Board, the Ministry of Defence and the Department of the Environment, all of whom were concerned with the rapid refurbishing of the accommodation. It is noticeable, though, that the Leicester refugees who had spent the shortest time in the camps were those who had been at the West Country camps and at Tonfanau in North Wales. They could neither reach nor be reached by their Leicester kin. Moreover, they had encountered a measure of the general rural dislike of strangers, especially coloured strangers. Although it was impossible to gauge the effect that the refugees had on local communities, there was certainly reported resentment at Piddlehinton, in the heart of the Dorset countryside, an area of high unemployment: 'We know the Asians have to go somewhere – and we are sorry for them. But this is going to ruin village life. First there were the gypsies – and now this.'[50]

Refugee members remembered features of individual camps. Plasterdown, on the slopes of Dartmoor, was situated within the army compound and had a barrier at its entrance. One of the refugees agreed with what the Co-ordinating Committee reported: 'Of all the camps, this is the most likely to give the Asians fleeing from the excesses of militaryism [*sic*] the creeps.'[51] But another family praised the same camp for its school, its efficient administration and the speed with which the Employment Officer worked. (Naipaul described 'its festive, communal atmosphere'.) One Leicester-bound family was in Hemswell Camp, which for them had the advantage that it was within travelling distance of their son who was already settled in the city and was looking for a house to accommodate them all. In March 1973 an official complaint was sent to the Resettlement Board about the 'squalor and meanness of the medical facilities, lack of English lessons, and the Camp administration generally at Hemswell'. Whilst agreeing with this, residents still claimed that the actual accommodation was good. They joined in the protest, not because they thought the camp (or its smaller annexe at Faldingworth) should be closed, but because they were not getting 'value for money we were paying in rent'. It was resented that 'the British public all knew that the camps were costing £1m a month to run', yet very few realized that residents of the camps were asked to contribute on a scale of charges (£6 per week for a husband and a wife, dependent children £1.50 per week). The Resettlement Board refused to accept the criticisms made about Hemswell Camp, stating that during its operation it had received 2,500 Ugandan Asians, 1,900 of whom had been 'resettled into the community'.

One feature people disliked particularly was being moved from one camp to another before they could leave of their own free will. Hobbs Barracks

Camp, for instance, won a temporary reprieve so that the Christmas celebrations could continue. But a spokesman for the Resettlement Board said: 'Obviously, all the centres will be closed eventually. Hobbs Barracks has wooden buildings ... and is a fire risk ... but there is no need to worry about Christmas. *These people have celebrated their equivalent and anyway they are very understanding and obedient people.*'[52]

In the early months there was certainly an exception to this quiescence: at Greenham Camp there was a threatened hunger strike. The English caterers came in for much criticism and eventually two Asian women were appointed to advise them. (The only precedent for the threatened action in a refugee camp occurred in 1958 when some 400 people in the Anglo-Egyptian resettlement camp at Kidderminster went on a strike when asked to contribute to the cost of their board.) Food habits are amongst the most distinctive of Indian characteristics,[53] and indeed it was their loss of control over providing their families' meals in the camps that was most frequently mentioned by the women in the Leicester group. Two mothers who had been at Tonfanau spoke not of its isolation nor of their families living in former cloakrooms, nor the long distances from cities which might offer chances of employment, nor even the special temporary Bailey bridge built by the army to reduce their walk to the nearest Welsh town from eight miles to two. Instead, they remember that a shop was opened by two enterprising brothers in the camp, from which authentic Indian spices could be obtained. In other camps a great deal of illicit cookery went on[54] ('As long as I could cook one meal, I was still a mother looking after all my family').

Those in the camps resented the publicity (given both here and in Uganda) to the claim made by Praful Patel that people were clinging to the camps rather than face life outside because the camps were too pleasant.[55] The refugees denied the truth of this. Those living in the camps knew that the overcrowded conditions and the lack of privacy made life far from pleasant. But they had made a rational decision that it was better to tolerate these things than risk leaving and attempting a premature 'resettlement' for which they were not yet equipped. They resented certain features of camp life, but they were not going to organize riots since they wanted to stay on until it was convenient to leave. What many were staying on for was the half-promised government loan. They wished to do nothing that would delay this. If docility was expected, then they would display just that, for as in Uganda attitudes and politics 'began and ended in their pockets'.[56] Even with all the faults of the camps fully acknowledged (for example, the punitive meanness of stopping free telephone calls to relatives outside the camp; the warning notices about not wasting electricity; the falling off of enthusiasm and increasing irritability noticed in some of the volunteers), there was resentment among those 80 families left in Stradishall near Newmarket when it was announced that the last five camps were to be closed by autumn 1973. They argued that the old and lonely would still be old and lonely when living outside: perhaps more so. Amongst those who had stayed on were the most determined not to make a wrong start outside. They had found jobs in local factories but continued to live in the accommodation in the camps. So they objected to the closure of Stradishall, Hemswell, West Malling, Gaydon and Greenham Common, for it was easier to find a job than accommodation. One of the refugees explained that the camps were 'closed down over our heads; but it was because there was a general election coming and the government wanted everything cleared away.'

Despite the fact that any refugee camp is highly visible, and draws attention to problems of resettlement, for some amongst the Leicester group the idea of semi-permanent 'camp colonies' within easy reach of Leicester was seen as an acceptable compromise at least for the first few years. In August 1972 Leicester's Social Services Director suggested that there should be a Transit Camp near the city;[57] but this was not seriously considered by his fellow officers. Nor was the tentative idea that the refugees should land at Castle Donnington Airport and be accommodated in the grounds and house of Beaumanor Hall which belonged to the County Council. This was not without precedent, for as Lord Hawke urged in a House of Lords debate (6 December 1972):

> The Ugandan Asians are extremely capable ... given half a chance they will establish themselves in this Country ... but they cannot do so from remote camps ... we used to have a Polish resettlement camp near us where the Poles lived for many years; from that camp they established themselves, and are now prominent in business, and so on. Why on earth cannot something like this be done for the Ugandan Asians?

But whether the refugees went to the camps or not, what disappointed them most was that the government failed to initiate a financial loan scheme, and this despite the offer from some richer Asians to give them backing. Although the Uganda Asian Relief Trust administered by Lord Salisbury did provide individual Asians with small sums to overcome their immediate and more pressing problems, this was felt by a number of Leicester refugees to have come too late. It should have come at the height of the crisis and not as it did a few months later in November 1972.

> [The Trust] allocation ... was a paltry sum to handle, but its effect has often been out of all proportion to its value. It gave a fillip at a time of desperation and hinted that someone cared about their plight. Naturally with a sum like this none could be assisted in any major project they wished to undertake and great disappointment has been expressed that money has not been available by way of a loan to give initial help to people wishing to buy property or start a business venture.[58]

The Leicester group gave as their main reason for staying on in the camps the hope that the loans would come about. As one said: 'If I could have had a loan for house mortgage or to start up business I would have been out of West Malling within a week.'

There were reports of touts representing Asian and British firms taking advantage of the delay. The refugees were offered unsecured loans at what was in effect over 40 per cent interest. The Asian leader Dr Prem, having visited 12 of the camps, claimed that most of them could be emptied in two months if the government could have overcome the obvious objections to loans: that it would be subsidizing competitive businesses and cause resentment among other businessmen. Despite early promises by the CCWEU that a loan scheme was being worked out, and a ruling that this would not offend against the Race Relations legislation, the protracted talks between the Resettlement Board with Barclays and Grindlays banks came to nothing. Yet many of the Leicester refugees pointed out that these two banks had gained in the past from their Asian customers and knew their credit-worthiness; but despite frozen assets in Uganda which could have been used for collateral, it was their lack of business experience in the UK which counted.

The Board's lack of will to pursue loan facilities marked it off from its predecessor, the Anglo-Egyptian Resettlement Board. The Leicester group believed that the Board feared opposition from white small business interests. The Board also felt that such facilities prevented the geographical dispersal of the refugees, since Asian businesses tend to start within ethnic economic enclaves. It was also believed by everyone but the refugees themselves that business skills appropriate to Uganda were not easily transferable to the UK. Sir Charles Cunningham stated that it was a matter of speculation whether it was in the interests of the Asians themselves to provide them with money to set up immediately in business: 'retail trade in this Country is in a very transitional phase ... it would be well advised that a number of these people seek employment in the retail trade rather than set up in their own little shop or business.'[59] But this ignores the fact that 'after all, the Ugandan Asians had run Uganda.'[60] And just as they had virtually settled themselves in the UK, they were left to prove their business acumen by themselves.

4. EMPLOYMENT

Not all the Ugandan Asians were 'sensible', and whether they had been in the camps or not, a proportion of them did open up corner shops and small business (such as garages) in Leicester and elsewhere. This activity was noted in a series of newspaper reports: 'Service with a Smile is Back in Britain', 'Amin's Asian Refugees Back in Business'.[61]

In September 1973 the Community Relations Commission asked the Leicester Department of Employment 'how the refugees had fared in their job search'. The reply was that those who had taken Sir Charles Cunningham's advice and tried to get experience of the retail trade by becoming employees had failed in their efforts: 'despite having experience, they do not have the quality of English to cope.' The Department also said that 707 Ugandan Asians had obtained work through its office but 'only 102 were still out of work', and knew of no refugees who had obtained jobs directly through the Resettlement Board's advisers. In general the pattern had been for the refugees to bypass the labour exchanges; instead they had relied on the advice of relatives or friends.

In March 1974 the *Guardian* claimed that only a few of the Ugandan immigrants had failed to find employment. But since the official policy towards unemployment among the refugees was to play down the subject as much as possible, the true situation remained hidden. Instead, in 1975 the Manager of Leicester's Department of Employment said that the effect of the Ugandan Asians on Leicester's employment appeared to have been substantial. He outlined that in May 1970 under 9 per cent of all unemployed in the city were coloured. Two years later the figure was just over 14 per cent, but following the main influx of Asians from Uganda, 24 per cent of the unemployment in Leicester involved coloured people: 'By August 1975 this proportion had dropped to 23 per cent, thus becoming slightly less prominent in unemployment and reversing the national trend.'[62] There was a substantial number of Ugandan Asians among the workforce of the Imperial Typewriters factory who took part in the bitter strike against the bonus system and other discriminatory practices in 1974, including, as some claimed, those who had once been managers themselves and could not tolerate bad management practices at the plant. After 12 weeks the workers went back, but within 12 months Littons, the multinational firm that owned Imperial, had closed down its Leicester operation.

Several reports on the employment situation for Ugandan Asians made mention of 'the mercurial figure of Dr Seth'. In a volunteer capacity he took over from the local employment exchange the hunt for jobs. Seth estimated that there were over 600 still without employment in 1973. But he qualified this by stating that these were mostly older people, who had refused to take labouring jobs, and it was just this group who 'wanted to start businesses and were still hopeful of getting loans on the strength of assets they were forced to leave in Uganda'.[63] Among other accounts of how the Ugandan Asians had re-entered the retail trade was one by the journalist Tony Wilkins, who wrote that Leicester 'corner-shops owned and run by Ugandan Asians and Kenyans have mushroomed, small factories have sprung up ... only a handful of the latest Ugandan Asians have failed to get jobs' (*Guardian*, 26 March 1974). The *Listener* (20 May 1976) featured a report – 'In Britain Now' – by Khalid Aziz, a former BBC Leicester employee, for which Aziz interviewed a number of local Leicester people about the employment situation of Ugandan Asians. George Bromley, the District Secretary of the Transport and General Workers' Union, said that it was his opinion that the Ugandan Asians 'had travelled furthest of all Asians in trade-union work'. Raj Nayer, the Regional Development Officer for the Community Relations Commission in the East Midlands, told Aziz that the aspiration of the Ugandan Asians (of whom he was one) did not 'allow them to be content with mere survival in this country'. But Nayer did refer to the detrimental effect of the closure of Imperial Typewriters: 'whole families were employed at Imperial's two assembly plants in Leicester ... when Litton Industries Inc. decided to close its U.K. operations 1,800 lost their jobs, 1,000 of them Asians.' One of these was also interviewed: Kanti Lakhani had borrowed £800 and had built up a flourishing photography business in the Belgrave Road.

Leicester, as has already been stated, had no equivalent to Wandsworth's specially funded Ugandan refugee unit. The pressing social needs, often caused because of lack of employment, were dealt with by two young women who worked at the Community Relations Office. These two, along with an Asian clerk seconded from the Social Services Department to help with the immediate reception, and later on another young woman (funded by CCWEU) who worked with Dr Seth and the British Asian Welfare Society, bore the burden of all referrals from the Local Authority Departments. Unlike their London counter-parts, none of these workers published reports on their work and the level of poverty suffered by groups of the Leicester refugees. But there is some indication of how high this level was in the fact that for their first term, in summer 1973, almost all the pupils who were at the 'refugee secondary school' – Wakerley Secondary – qualified for free school meals.

Chapter 5 The role of the voluntary associations

1. THE BRITISH ASIAN WELFARE SOCIETY

> The Resettlement Board has consistently taken the view that the Ugandan Asian families should rely on local support which is often provided by the established statutory and voluntary agencies in their locality. There is an important need which seems more in the province of the voluntary organisations. There is need for advice and assistance with the minor but nevertheless important mechanics of living in our community.[1]

In Leicester it was the British Asian Welfare Society (BAWS), a voluntary organization of Asian community leaders, that provided this 'advice and assistance'. In the first few weeks after Amin's expulsion order it was the only group to do so. No other city in the UK was to have an organization which attracted so much publicity and functioned for so long. Although this publicity was out of proportion to the actual local impact in the time immediately following Amin's expulsion order, the media were only too ready to use the information that BAWS gave about the numbers of Asians who would have to leave Uganda and would make for Leicester and elsewhere. And this was when the British High Commission in Kampala was not prepared to do so. The character of its leaders, its claims about how it 'resettled' the refugees, its attempts to appease public resentment over the arrival of the refugees into the city, were known by all, and resented by a considerable number of Leicester's community.

BAWS developed from the British East African Subjects Association founded at the time of the Kenyan exodus which coincided with the Immigration Act of 1968. Within four days of Amin's expulsion announcement the original organization had re-formed with a new committee and an office (behind a cinema in Belgrave Gate owned by its President). This building had already been used as an advice centre for 'Commonwealth citizens'. Its antagonists invariably referred to it as 'the Punjabi Committee', although its Vice President was from Kenya and its members included a Pakistani general medical practitioner and its Treasurer was Secretary of the Leicester Hindu Union. But, importantly, its founders were not predominantly East African Asian.[2] Most people believed, however, that it was (in the words of one of the refugees) 'owned and run by two people'. The first of these was the President, Mr Harbans Ratoo. A pioneer Sikh businessman, who had been in the city for a decade-and-a-half, Ratoo was prominent on the local Community Relations Council, President of the Indian League, and was later adopted as a Labour candidate in the local elections. The second and the more active in running the Society was its Vice-President, Kundan Seth. Known as 'The Doctor', Seth was from East Africa, where he had assets and had been important in 'social and cultural activities in Kenya'.

BAWS held its inaugural open meeting on 14 August 1972. The meeting was attended by 150 Asians, and a programme was drawn up. It aimed to keep a list of Asians in Leicester who would house the refugees, and promised to raise funds by a programme of film shows and collections among the Asian community. The President compared Amin to Hitler, but the Society gave little support to the Secretary of the Hindu League who suggested that arms be given to Asians in Uganda to protect themselves and their property.[3] The meeting was reported nationally, and BAWS was featured in *The Times* (16 August) as the centre of a 'flurry of activity'. Its programme of fund raising ('for at least £10,000') and its 'complete programme for resettlement' were described as a potential example for cities other than Leicester. Its grandiose schemes for providing accommodation were praised. The President planned to rent buildings and to convert them into temporary accommodation with beds and bathrooms, and hoped to propose a special mortgage scheme to the City Council whereby mortgages for the refugees would be made available, with local Asian business and professional men standing as guarantors. Above all, matching what was conceived as the inbred indigenous respect for self-help and independence, BAWS publicly promised the British government that the public 'should not bear all the burden for reception and resettlement'. BAWS would 'take the responsibilities and make preparations to help the people'. The reality, however, proved rather different.

2. AUGUST TO SEPTEMBER 1972: BAWS AND THE LOCAL MEDIA

The first announcement and prediction of the 'crisis' situation in the *Leicester Mercury* was the headline on 7 August: 'Many of Expelled Asians May Make for Highfields'. This report, which appeared on the inside of the paper, was a speculation by the Rev E. N. Carlile, Vicar of St Peter's, Highfields, that Leicester, with its East African community 'higher than any other city in Britain', and with the Asians' tradition of being 'very family minded', would attract the greatest proportion of the 40–80,000 British Asians expelled by General Amin. Mr Carlile (who had personal experience of East Africa) foresaw, like other public figures, strain on the Education Department which would necessitate expediting the school building programme. On the other hand, these difficulties would be counterbalanced by the fact that the expellees were middle-class, resourceful and adaptable. The *Mercury* itself gave more coverage in its 7 August issue to the activities of a group of Hell's Angels who were currently threatening people in Laurel Road (Laurel Road, located in the heart of the immigrant settlement, was notorious as a prostitute area). Members of BAWS replied to Mr Carlile the next day, when it was reported that Kenya would not give the Asians refuge. Dr Seth said that St Peter's parish 'was not going to be inundated': probably only 20,000 out of the 50,000 would be expelled from Uganda, and only 12,000 would 'look to Britain for help, but they would spread out'. Uganda was 'like a volcano which might explode at any minute', but General Amin ('known personally') was not as bad as he seemed. The Ugandan Asians would come bringing their own funds; only a few, particularly the old, would make any demands on the British taxpayer. They had become British subjects 'not by choice, but in order to have travel documents', and British officials (not defined) had assured him that Asians would have fair treatment. On 8 August leaders of the immigrant organizations in Leicester met under the auspices of the National Standing Conference of Asian Organizations (there was an overlap of membership between it and BAWS). They planned to meet MPs (despite the summer recess), send a deputation to the Home Secretary and dispatch a telegram to General Amin ('a personal acquaintance of Dr Seth's') asking for restraint. In the *Leicester Mercury* of 9 August, Dr Seth emphasized that, far from Leicester being a 'dumping ground', the refugees would be an asset, not a liability, to the taxpayer. On 16 August Mr K. Pandit, Treasurer of BAWS (and Secretary of the Hindu Union), told the *Leicester Mercury* that BAWS had been 'flooded' with offers of homes and as a result up to 1,000 Ugandan Asians could be absorbed straight away.

In the weeks before the Ugandan Asians arrived, BAWS – whose members were predominantly prosperous businessmen and professionals – were anxious to publicize their view that the refugees would be like themselves: self-reliant and making very few long-term demands on Leicester's ratepayers or public services. They looked to the *Leicester Mercury* to promote this attitude, and Mr Ratoo and Dr Seth were always ready to give interviews to the press. True the *Leicester Mercury* (particularly in its editorials) had always praised decent citizenship, independence and continuity of tradition, but the *Mercury*'s reports gave a different impression from that intended by BAWS. For instance, on the question of housing, BAWS told the *Mercury* it had had a large number of people offering to shelter the refugees. The *Mercury* headlined this as: 'Asians Are Offered 2,000 Homes in Leicester' (16 August 1972). Headlines have a 'particularly potent way of transmitting meanings',[4] and this one gave a distorted impression. It led to a spate of letters to Page Four referring to the shortage of council houses for those on the official waiting list. Other letters, though acknowledging that the Ugandan Asians would be housed in the private sector, raised the spectre of overcrowding and the flouting of the Housing Act. The chairman of the city's Housing Committee made a public statement that there would be no council houses available, which appeared under the headline 'We Can't Give Houses to Ugandan Asians, says City Housing Chief' (*Leicester Mercury*, 15 August). (No immigrant organization, including BAWS, had said that it should do so.) The *Leicester Mercury* ran an editorial: 'Formula for Disaster' (17 August) on the topic, claiming that it spoke for the city 'which topped the popularity poll with Ugandan Asians': the BAWS statement on housing was 'commendable, impractical or downright stupid', depending on 'your point of view'. The points of view were respectively assigned to 'the unhappy 55,000' kicked out of Uganda, to the city's officials and volunteer organizations, and to immigrants who were already in Leicester 'from other lands'. This last group were described as striving to build a new life and doing so under such difficult circumstances that they would recognize the stupidity of attracting the refugees to the city. The Community Relations Council was praised for its advocacy of dispersal (which, in fact, it had never advocated), but it was also criticized for its lack of realism in ignoring 'the hard facts' of the coming influx, which was the 'formula for disaster', because of its stance of 'bending over backwards to present a humane multi-racial image'.

Other *Mercury* headlines were also misleading and did not carry the message of what the content of the reports really contained. One such was on 26 August, when 'Welcome to Leicester Booklet for Ugandan Asians' covered a variety of other topics, and there was only a brief mention at the very end about the distribution of the literature. Then after a long account of Leicester events came the claim (by Dr Seth) that the booklets were in Kampala rather than in Leicester itself. 'City Slams Resettlement Board', on 30 August, implied that the Vice-President of BAWS was being strident and demanding. But the actual reported interview with Dr Seth merely recorded his complaint that the Resettlement Board was not co-operating over advance notices about the numbers of refugees heading for Leicester, which was no different from the *Mercury*'s own view. 'Mr Carr, the Home Secretary, must speak up boldly. He has promised close consultation with Local Authorities. Leicester must leave the special Board he has set up in no doubt at all about what it can and cannot do ...' And the President of BAWS, Harbans Ratoo, said the same thing: 'It is all very well people in London receiving the families, but it is the provinces which will be carrying the can.'

But Ratoo also said he was well aware that uncontrolled numbers of the refugees entering Leicester could bring 'unfortunate consequences' even for a 'fully employed City'. He also stated that although 10,000 to 15,000 of the refugees had 'already made contacts' with people in Leicester, the majority would only use Leicester for the immediate transit period of a year before moving to other cities: 'these Asians are known to be hard workers', and Leicester could provide jobs for some 2,000 to 4,000 additional Asians. But the *Mercury* in its editorial (*'But* They *Are* Coming', August 22) pointed out: 'It is arrogant for Mr Pandit and now Mr Ratoo to claim to know how many thousands the City can absorb.'

The *Mercury* ran no really sympathetic report in which the refugees were featured as people undergoing threats to their lives and property. During the whole of August and for the first half of September, it featured the Ugandan Asians as inanimate 'numbers' threatening 'the City's fabric'. The two 'human' stories featured in August were hardly likely to reassure the 'threatened City' and neither of these showed BAWS as an effective organization for alleviating the threat). The first story was of one Babulan Thakerar, who was not an expellee, but had been coming for settlement under the Voucher Scheme. He first made his appearance on page 1 under the headline 'Asians Here Penniless:

Plea for Aid' (25 August). The *Mercury* reminded its readers that 'the full nature of the crisis which may face the City' was epitomized by this middle-class accountant. The next day the paper ran his story again under the heading '"I Won't Be a Burden", says the First Man to Arrive'. Nevertheless it was pointed out that he had spent the night at the homeless unit at Hillcrest Hospital, before 'disappearing into the community', without making any contact with BAWS.

At the end of August, when Leicester had been officially declared 'full up' by the leader of the City Council, the second penniless Asian was featured, this time under the headline: 'Asians, We Have Done All We Can, Says Council' (30 August). The refugee Mr Vadher was a microbiologist who had left several thousand pounds behind but 'would pick up a living at anything'. Again, he had no contact with BAWS despite its 'plans' for cooking and sleeping facilities to be available at East Park Road, Melton Road and the Commonwealth Community Centre (the Sangam) in Belgrave Gate. At the same time the *Guardian* (31 August)[5] ran a feature on Dr Seth, who had stayed in Britain because he felt 'the Asian community needed a leader'. He was described as sitting in 'the dark recesses of an Indian cinema', with his register of arrivals ('so far only three names') and actually finding accommodation for people by negotiating for houses on the books of Asian estate agents. But the *Mercury* reported BAWS as not helping even Mr Thakerar 'because this man said he paid £6 a month for his son's education, and he had come on an old voucher ... he is not an evacuee.' In fact the BAWS estimates of numbers – which they put at between 10,000 and 15,000 – were unofficial and wildly inaccurate, and produced a backlash in the columns of the *Mercury*. To take one example of a reader's letter: 'According to Mr H. S. Ratoo Leicester can expect to accommodate 10,000–15,000 ... I feel this opportunity to play host should be decided by Leicester rate payers who, if not in agreement with Mr Ratoo, should withhold their rates. This action might even alert the whole country.'[6] And the National Vice-President of the Indian Workers' Association, Surjit Mann, issued a statement on 15 August denouncing 'the scaremongering' caused by these estimates. However, another *Mercury* reader asked where were the jobs which Mr Ratoo said could be found for 2,000 to 4,000 Asians when unemployment had risen to such heights and even 'our own school leavers' with 'O' and 'A' levels could not find jobs.

On 26 August BAWS formed a sub-committee to raise money so that any Asian arriving in the city could be given immediate financial assistance. Dr Seth claimed that there were '24 houses already available, together with offers of accommodation in shared homes, which had come from both Asian and European individuals'. But other members of BAWS were becoming impatient with the way in which its message that the expellees would not be a 'burden' on the city or its services was being interpreted and doubted. A founder member, a Pakistani medical specialist, Dr M. Shakir, wrote to Page Four of the *Mercury* on 30 August: 'I find it difficult to understand the attitude of the City Council who say we cannot take one more British Asian. I feel once a man has been admitted here as a British Citizen he is free to go where he wishes.'

But in general, BAWS did not challenge the local media since its continued aim was not to confront but 'to co-operate with the host community'. It would in any case have needed to employ a full-time officer to answer all the criticism directed against itself or the refugees. From 16 August, when the first two letters appeared from 'patriots not racialists' who worried about 'the do-gooders welcoming 50,000 ... but not into their spacious houses', the *Mercury* defended its decision to publish these views; on 25 August it stated:

> 'throughout this week, letters have poured into Page Four, criticising often bitterly and in emotive terms, the prospective arrival in Leicester of a large proportion of Asian holders of British passports ... No usable letter which could help to redress the balance of opinion has knowingly been withheld, but has already been published in whole or part ...'

During August 1972 there were 42 headlines in the *Mercury* dealing specifically with the Ugandan issue. Of these only two referred to the Asians as anything other than a problem or a threat for Leicester. Despite this, BAWS left unchallenged even the syndicated article, 'The People Who Wanted the Best of Two Worlds', by an Indian journalist Sonny Rao, which referred to the refugees as 'gullible Gujaratis obsessed by their national craze for metal ... Uganda's small shopkeepers, whom all Africa came to hate from its guts', and ended by stating that it was India's duty to accept the expellees ('the original gold diggers') rather than Britain's at a time when it was 'saddled with one million jobless'.[7]

By the end of August, however, there was discernible a shift in the *Mercury*'s reportage of the crisis and of BAWS itself. By now the City Council had declared its policy (or rather non-policy) towards the refugees. The numbers of the Ugandan Asians actually arriving in the city during the month of September continued to be small, and the 'phoney war' atmosphere that had prevailed throughout August, when Central Government was simultaneously attempting to appease and bargain with Amin, was over. There were national and official policies as well as just local opinions on which the media could report and comment. The *Mercury* no longer had to rely on the pronouncements of BAWS alone; it now had official forecasts of the numbers expected to arrive, which it put at around 5,000. On 2 September its editorial ('The Tide Turns') praised the Resettlement Board and the Council for advising the refugees not to come to Leicester. It also praised the President of BAWS: 'To-day a member of our existing immigrant community gives his support to deter them coming to Highfields.' This was on the basis of an interview with Mr Ratoo who had stated that as a member of 'the National Co-ordinating Committee of Ugandan Evacuees' he would be telling Sir Charles Cunningham: 'Leicester must expect to get some Ugandan Asians initially. They need to recover from shock. But we shall try to persuade people not to settle here by giving them information on places where there are greater job opportunities.' The President of BAWS seemed to have forgotten the optimistic forecasts

about employment he had made earlier, and also the claims made by his association about housing all the refugees. From September 1972, though, BAWS
was being openly criticized by other organizations and individuals.

3. SEPTEMBER 1972 TO MAY 1973: ACCOLADES AND CRITICISM

After Harbans Ratoo's volte-face in September 1972, BAWS came to be seen
by other Asian organizations in Leicester as having accepted the City Council's
policy of advising the expellees not to come to Leicester. The local branch
of the Indian Workers Association (GB) repeated what its National Vice-President, Surjit Mann, had said: that the leaders of BAWS were 'scaremongers',
who had aided the City Council in its exploitation of the situation, with the
result that it had come to be viewed as a 'crisis'.[8] The IWA knew of only
70 families who wished to settle in Leicester, and it made a firm but modest
offer of free hospitality to ten small families. The IWA was outspoken about
its view that the sole responsibility for large numbers of Asians having to leave
Uganda lay with the British government, who had known that there was a
danger of expulsion since 1965 but had delayed over accepting increased applications for admission. The general meeting of the Leicester Branch of IWA
(GB), which took place on 5 July 1970, had condemned the Tory government
for acting in its usual imperialist tradition 'by bringing out two new laws:
the Industrial Relations Act and the Immigration Bill'. Subsequently the IWA
picketed a meeting at Melbourne Hall in Highfields at which Ian Paisley, MP,
was the chief speaker. According to a pamphlet issued at the time by the IWA:
'While this degenerate was preaching inside, his guardian lackeys, the police
were harassing and intimidating black workers who had come to protest. The
so-called "Council" and its black and white leaders whitewashed the case
and as usual betrayed the people and sold themselves.'[9]

In a series of subsequent pamphlets the IWA continued its attack on 'opportunist leaders' who purported to speak for Asians in Leicester, describing them
as 'do-gooders', who surfaced as leaders of welfare and social organizations.
The IWA took no part in the reception at the railway station for refugees.
Instead, it saw its role as primarily political: in the latter part of 1972 its main
activity was supporting the Asian strikers at the Loughborough Mansfield
Hosiery strike. But its particular political stance did not, in turn, appeal to
the majority of the moderate Ugandan Asian (and predominantly Gujarati)
refugees: a typical response from them was that the IWA were 'all Punjabi
and all communist'. The IWA summarized its view of politics and Asian leadership at the time of the Ugandan exodus thus:

> The I.W.A. (G.B.) has always openly preached that as far as the immigration acts
> were concerned the Labour and the Tories were the same. When Uganda Asians
> came to this Country a deputation from Leicester Labour Council went to Parliament
> House to say no more Ugandan Asians will come to Leicester. So if the Labour
> Councillors are racialist can the few black Labour Councillors stop the racialism?
> No they will bark for their imperialist masters and bark at their own brothers.[10]

But other opposition to BAWS was to come from sources very different from the IWA. At the end of August the *Leicester Mercury* mentioned that the Gujarati Hindu Association had decided to volunteer its services to incoming Ugandan Asians 'on humanitarian' grounds, and announced that its members 'would be willing to sit on any panel set up to help the Asians'. This organization, which was to have an offshoot called the Gujarati Welfare Society, claimed that it was the most appropriate group to be consulted about, and to be asked to help, the refugees. All its members were Gujaratis from East Africa. It had some women members one of whom had done social and welfare work. Another of its members was to become Leicester's first Asian councillor. But because BAWS had already established itself and had an office from which its President and Vice-President could issue press statements, the GWS never gained equal public recognition.

So few Ugandan Asians arrived in September that there appeared very little for any organization to do. Of the first batch of 500 Ugandan Asians who had been issued permits to enter the UK, only 70 gave Leicester as their destination. BAWS therefore called off its reception facilities at the railway and bus station 'for a couple of days'. It now forecast that the main exodus would begin by 8 September. But by 15 September only 39 families were known by BAWS to have arrived. They had been accommodated with friends and relatives, and Dr Seth was admitting that 'no refugee' had up to that point been put in the care of his association. Even by the end of September the expected 'main exodus' had not begun. The Uganda Resettlement Board had by then established its centre at Stansted Airport, but only 15 families had passed through it to Leicester.

All through September, 'guesstimates' of the numbers of the expellees from Uganda and when they might be expected to arrive in Leicester continued to be made. Though in retrospect they make for tedious reading, they do show that the city's policy-makers were without accurate forecasts on which to base their forward planning. The city's political leaders and its Asian voluntary associations (and an increasing number of the latter) had their approximate calculations faithfully recorded by the media. This added to the general confusion and the concern of the 'ordinary people of Leicester'. The leader of the Conservative opposition, Alderman Kenneth Bowder, estimated that Leicester might have to accommodate 15,000 Asians. The leader of the City Council, Alderman Edward Marston, talked of 10,000 coming to Leicester.[11] The Indian Social and Cultural Society reported that it was 'having surveys carried out here and in Kampala to find out how many were coming to Leicester'. It expected to have accurate information within a week, since 'a voluntary organisation in Kampala was undertaking a survey on their behalf' (the Society was later to refuse to give the *Leicester Mercury* any details of the survey). The Leicester Indian Art Circle (one of whose organizers became yet another critic of BAWS) told the *Leicester Mercury* that it had received a gift of £5,000 'to help the refugees', but it gave no further details of the donor or of how the money was to be distributed. On 12 September, in the public notices of the *Mercury*, appeared a display advertisement, its format a match of the notices which had appeared in the *Ugandan Argus* on behalf of the Council of the City of Leicester and the Resettlement Board. The advertisement was headed 'An Appeal to the Good People of Leicester'. The appeal was on behalf of the India Film Society of Leicester. It called upon the people of Leicester 'to ignore the statements made by some members of the Asian community of our City regarding the influx of Uganda-based British subjects'. It praised Her Majesty's Government for its right and timely approach to the good people of Leicester to allow these 'Ugandan based Britishers' to enter 'our City with dignity and respect, for it is known that there is a vast Wealth of Good Will' and this was to be found amongst 'the silent majority of people in this City'.

In a city 'waiting for the Asians', BAWS continued to present itself as the authentic negotiator with the host community. Its office was used as the Reception Centre by the Social Services Department, and it was officially recognized as the best agency to register numbers of refugees coming into the city. BAWS kept details of all from Uganda who contacted it, and sent this information on to the Town Clerk and the Employment Exchange. By this means, as well as the 'green arrival form' filled in at the railway station reception point, the authorities hoped to monitor arrivals and needs, believing that 'local Asians should meet the strangers being of the same race and beliefs'.[12] But when BAWS said that 500 empty houses due for demolition should serve as temporary accommodation, the chairman of the Housing Committee, Mrs Janet Setchfield, replied that this was impractical; and when Dr Seth said he had on file 200 jobs from knitwear companies, many of them owned by Asians, and that this should not give restless nights to Leicester people, the *Sunday Telegraph* (3 September) concluded that whether his optimism was well founded remained to be seen.

On 5 September Sir Charles Cunningham and other members of the Resettlement Board visited Leicester 'to see for themselves' the city that was asking £300,000 for dealing with the Ugandan Asian crisis.[13] They met members of the GWS who now claimed that they could provide homes for 500 refugees. The President, Mr V. Patel, said that his organization would raise money and keep a register of those who could offer temporary accommodation. But, unlike other organizations, GWS said it would not make any estimates about the numbers of refugees but instead would provide help for whatever number arrived in Leicester. Unlike BAWS it had no reception centre, nor did it have plans for a resettlement hostel. BAWS had announced that the old Co-operative Hall in Belgrave (owned by the Sikh estate agents Ramon Bros) would be made over to them free of charge. With this temporary accommodation 'a hundred refugees could find B.A.W.S. as their benefactor'. GWS did not even take part in the 24-hour manning to help the refugees when they arrived at London Road railway station. Whilst GWS never made public its views on whether the refugees should be discouraged from coming to Leicester, Dr Seth and Mr Ratoo of BAWS once again told Sir Charles Cunningham that Leicester should not be a 'dumping ground', and if the refugees could not be prevented from coming, then Leicester should only be a transit point. As Dr Seth told the press: 'We would like to see some dispersal in London, but if there is none, then for a short time we can cope. I think the host community has been very good to us so far, and we intend definitely to cope with them in the future.'[14]

On 7 September the Leicester City Council announced that it was to follow the lead of the Uganda Asian Resettlement Board and place advertisements in the Ugandan press advising Asians coming to the UK not to make for Leicester. The *Leicester Mercury* reported the Home Office as having sanctioned a telegram on behalf of the Uganda Resettlement Board to the British High Commission in Kampala to instruct them to put the advertisements in newspapers there. It also stated that Mr Harbans Ratoo of BAWS had given his support to the attempt 'to prevent large numbers of Ugandan Asians settling in this City'.[15] These attempts by BAWS to appease the 'host community' ('the atmosphere is bad, but not so bad now that Leicester will be used as a transit point') were futile, at least as was reflected in the letters page of the *Leicester Mercury*. On 14 September it printed 13 letters all of which were anti-Asian:

> With every post letters about the entry into Britain of the Ugandan Asians continue to pour into our Page Four letter box, making it easily the most controversial issue since the page was given over to letters. To-day our space is again devoted to extracts from a further selection of reader's views on the subject.

The next day BAWS was criticized by Asians for its appeasement and its earlier predictions about the numbers expected: 'I go along with a good many Asians, am appalled at the wild and unresponsible statements made by Asian leaders – self appointed and otherwise – on the issue of influx of Ugandan Asians in Leicester.'

On 4 October Dr Seth announced a sudden upswing in the numbers arriving in the city: 247 adults and 108 children had reported to him. He was expecting a final figure of over 1,000 but 'given co-operation, especially with education authorities, these people could be absorbed without difficulty.'[16] The same day Seth appeared on Midlands TV, and was most critical of Leicester's Education Department and its policy of 'wait and see'. He said that its officials should 'wake up'. Two days later Page Four was monopolized by a series of letters all attacking Seth.

> What right has Dr Seth to push around M.P.'s and Local Government? I do not think his remarks make for good race relations and in fact I find them infuriating.

> What right has Dr Seth to interfere with the work of the City Council – the sooner Asian leaders shut up the better. But when are our elected Councillors going to speak out?

Similar attacks were made on Dr Shakir who, though still nominally Vice-President of BAWS, had already broken away from its attempts at conciliation and appeasement with the city's political establishment and statutory authorities. In October Shakir wrote an article ('Leicester Lurches Right') in the journal

Race Today and criticized the Resettlement Board's lack of grass-root Asian representation. Above all he chastised the leaders of both Leicester's Labour and Conservative parties for being intimidated by 'a small number of totally prejudiced people'. The *Leicester Mercury* (11 October) reported these points from Shakir's article with a headline: 'Leader Hits Out as Asian Count Nears 1,000'. Predictably this led to a spate of letters against Shakir. Some complained of the continual Asian doctrinal (*sic*) outbursts:

> How many more Asian doctors are going to declaim their views before they leave the running of the City to the men elected to do so ... should the rantings of these doctors over the past few weeks be a foretaste of demands to come, I must come to the conclusion that Dr. Amin is not so mad.

Others complained about Asian leaders pronouncing on such problems as housing:

> About the claim by Dr. M. A. J. Shakir the Vice President of the British Asian Welfare Society that we have been told many times in the past year that housing is no problem in Leicester: We have put off our wedding, we queue for the accommodation lists every Saturday.

The next public challenge to BAWS came from a young Asian, Ramesh Jani of the Leicester Indian Art Circle. Jani had worked as a journalist in Uganda, and spent some time in prison there for criticizing the country's immigration rules. He had already received publicity early in September 1972, when he claimed that a letter he had written to the Ugandan millionaire Manubhai Madhvani had been responsible for the latter's arrest along with that of the British Managing Director of the Madhvani Sugar Company, Mr Donald Stewart. Jani and the Leicester Indian Art Circle decided that it was time to explain to Robert Carr, the Home Secretary, that trouble was being caused by the 'self-styled' Asian leaders in Leicester who were just 'a handful of the business minded'. The solution could only rest with a properly conducted election by Asians in Leicester of those who they would like to hear speak for them.[17] On 25 October BAWS held an emergency meeting to discuss this criticism. At the meeting its President revealed that Jani had plans for forming a group of Asian Freedom Fighters to fight in Uganda. BAWS planned a public meeting at their headquarters to expose this 'rash and irresponsible plan'. Harbans Ratoo challenged Jani to come along to the meeting, saying: 'We have been looking after the Asian community for a long time and this is hardly the time to start quarrelling about who should or who should not be leader.' A petition was launched against Jani and signed by people who, Dr Seth said, were worried that 'race relations would be hurt, and once General Amin heard about it there will be difficulties for people in Uganda.' BAWS dismissed Jani as 'seeking self glorification'. The Society had exact details on every refugee and had no knowledge of these 'Freedom Fighters'.

However, the debate over leadership went on. When the Indian National Club was founded in Leicester, Jani stressed at a dinner held to celebrate Indian Republic Day that the Club was going to be the organization which would 'find a proper leader for the Indian community in Leicester'. On the same day (20 January 1973) the Indian League also celebrated Republic Day. Ratoo in his role as President of its Leicester branch introduced the Lord Mayor, whose 'warm words belied reports that Leicester was unsympathetic to immigrants particularly those from Uganda'. Later, in June 1973, a Ugandan Asian refugee, Mr Gordhandas Kotecha (former Alderman of Kampala City), arrived in Leicester and was interviewed by the Leicester Mercury.[18] Kotecha's suggestion was that Ugandan Asians should form their own association:

> We want an association that can liaise with the Local Authority and other
> organisations, to discuss problems like education, the sick and the disabled ... Asians
> should be told exactly what is right and what is wrong. Then I think allegations
> that they abuse British hospitality will die down. A strong organisation is needed
> by Asians, to which they would pay a fee.

Ratoo replied that Kotecha had not troubled to find out what BAWS had done and would continue to do. Kotecha's views were not those of the majority of Ugandan Asians: most were thankful for the help Leicester had given them. All the expenses of BAWS had come from 'the income of Leicester people' and grants from the Social Services: 'In Leicester alone there are something like 40 different clubs, societies and associations looking after various aspects of Asian Welfare Matters. Along with these is the voluntary British Asian Welfare Society which was set up specifically to deal with difficulties faced by Ugandan Asians.'

Kotecha then said that the refugees should form their own organization: only thus could their problems be properly presented to the authorities. The help that was being offered tended to be short term. What was needed was a policy 'which looked into the future'. Ramesh Jani in his capacity as 'founder and president of the Leicestershire Indian Art Circle' backed this. He said that Ugandan Asians definitely needed an association run by themselves: 'The majority know each other and can work with each other. These Asians are well educated and businessmen. They can run their society well and there is no need for others to tell them what to do and how, when the others have not lived among them in Uganda.' But it was not until 1982 that such an association, or rather several such associations, emerged publicly.

The minutiae of these rivalries have been detailed because of the extensive coverage given to them by the *Leicester Mercury*, often to the exclusion of other more constructive activities of these voluntary associations. On most other issues, however, the various Asian associations were not reluctant to give interviews to the local media, particularly about their feuds. This stands in contrast to the fact, noted previously, that they failed to mount any sort of rejoinder to the hostile opinions expressed about the coming of and the help to be given to the Ugandan refugees. That these factions split the Asian community and engaged their leadership over a considerable time cannot be denied. Some of the Ugandan Asians themselves were more conscious of these factions than they were of anything else, frequently mentioning the leaders of the voluntary associations, just in their capacity as faction leaders. Indeed, some of the refugees interviewed preferred to side-step the benefits that they could have received, especially from BAWS, because they felt that as clients they would become involved in some way in this inter-faction activity.

The *Leicester Mercury*, despite its intensive coverage from August to October 1972, thereafter virtually stopped reporting on the Ugandan Asians, except for documenting attempts by the City Council to clarify the amount of grant aid it could expect from Central Government for the resettlement process. Moreover, from the end of November there was a new 'race relations' story: the strike of the Asian workers at Loughborough's Mansfield Hosiery factory. By then BAWS and its leaders' statements had almost ceased to be newsworthy.

4. BAWS AND ITS MAIN WORK PROGRAMME

What then of the actual work done by this voluntary association from November 1972 to the end of its existence, or rather of its public funding, at the end of 1973? This work fell into six major categories:

(i) the registration of the refugees who reported to its office;
(ii) public comments on local and national events concerned with the refugees;
(iii) the right to admit husbands of refugee women;
(iv) the administration of the Relief Trust;
(v) the dispersal of the luggage delivered from Uganda;
(vi) coping with the situation after the fire in its office.

By November 1972 the pattern of refugees arriving in the city seems to have altered. Large numbers of the refugees were contacting BAWS and being registered at its office: by 6 November 2,599 had done so.[19] The official 'Town Hall' figures were based on Seth's count, but it was argued that the real figure was probably higher. Seth admitted that not all were contacting him: he knew of 98 people who had left Transit Camps saying they were going to Leicester, but had not come to his centre. He was aware of no wish by the refugees to stay in the camps indefinitely or to return there once they had left.

He also revealed, in a report to the Housing Sub-Committee of Leicester Community Relations Council, that landlords – many of whom were Asians – were 'cashing in on the refugee situation', charging exorbitant rents and generally harassing and threatening tenants with further rent increases. Rents of £10–£12 per week were being charged for a few rooms, and there was often no rent book or proof that the money had changed hands. Seth had sent all the victims to the Housing Advice Centre since he thought 'that the Housing Department should know of these practices'.

BAWS never commented on the Mansfield Hosiery factory strike. In January 1973 Dr Seth said that employment, while hard to find, had not proved to be the obstacle once feared. BAWS had experienced no difficulty in finding jobs for the refugees in Leicester. As for racial discrimination and the labour market, he had found that it was the unions that were prejudiced: 'My people are willing to start at the bottom and they do, but sometimes they are not allowed to progress.'[20] However, when a survey by Bosanquet and Doeringer[21] received local publicity because part of their research had been conducted in Leicester, Seth was asked his opinion. Although the survey pointed to a developing split in the labour market, with coloured people more likely to find themselves located in secondary and less desirable jobs in a 'dual-market', Seth told the *Leicester Mercury* that he and other leaders did not totally agree with the findings 'although teachers and accountants trained in India and Uganda are said to be finding difficulty in obtaining suitable jobs in Leicester'. This prompted a predictable letter from an anonymous Asian: 'It would be interesting to know who these self-appointed leaders are, and whether they have the courage to challenge the findings with facts and figures.'

In January 1973 Dr Seth announced that he had been able to obtain accommodation and jobs for some 30 families in Peterborough, Coventry and Birmingham and even Swindon. This number hardly merited the *Leicester Mercury*'s headline, 'Ugandan Asians Are Leaving Leicester' (27 January). Seth claimed that there was 'a steady flow of people leaving ... I have had various offers ... but first I must be satisfied that the families are not going to be a burden and that there is adequate accommodation.' But in March, in one of the last references to the British Asian Welfare Society in the national media (*Guardian*, 17 March 1973), its President Harbans Ratoo reported that between 2,000 and 4,000 Ugandan Asians had come to Leicester and there might be as many as 1,000 families in the city needing homes.

The campaign to reunite 'split families'

When David Lane from the Home Office and Lord Belstead from the Department of Education and Science visited Leicester in February 1973, they made walkabout tours of Highfields and Belgrave. Schools figured predominantly on their list of calls. But the main aim of the visit was to get first-hand information on the settling in of Ugandan Asians. As well as meeting refugees and visiting the overcrowded and out-of-date Moat secondary school, they were confronted by the Leicester Enoch Powell Support Group with its banners ('Ugandan Asians had African servants. Now the citizens of Leicester carry their burdens').[22]

The visit ended with a meeting at the Town Hall with the Community Relations Council and immigrant leaders. Although Mr Ratoo and Dr Seth were mentioned by name, their organization, BAWS, was not. Ratoo and Seth brought to the ministers their growing concern over split families, who had not been united since leaving Uganda. The status of the stateless Asians, who had taken out Ugandan citizenship but had their passports confiscated by General Amin's government, was an immediate issue at the time. Lane promised to consult with the United Nations Commission for Refugees to see whether ways could be found of speeding up the resettlement of the men and their dependants in other countries. But in September 1973 Dr Seth said that there were still at least 27 women and their children in Leicester who had husbands 'stuck in India and Canada', and some of whom had been separated for 12 months. The wives all held British passports and had been allowed to come to the UK, with their children, but the husbands, who had no current British passports, had had to go to whichever country would have them. He had approached the Home Office and received the answer that the families should go out and join their husbands, to which he replied:[23]

> This is not practical as they cannot get jobs out there. I estimate that only about
> 150 people in the whole of the U.K. are in this predicament. It is the breadwinners
> who are not being allowed in, until they are given permission to join their wives
> and children, the families will not be able to support themselves or earn a living.

The Home Office informed Seth that each case was to be judged on its own merits 'in the light of special circumstances or undue hardship'. He therefore took up the cases on an individual basis. By the time that changes in the Immigration Rules making it possible for husbands to join their wives were put into operation BAWS had ceased to function except as a paper organization. Before this happened, however, it was the focus of two further news stories. The first was the arrival of 1,200 packages of luggage in March and the second was the fire which severely damaged its headquarters in June.

The fire at BAWS and the Ugandan Asian luggage

The 12 tons of luggage sent to Britain in various stages of disarray and even decay, belonging to the Ugandan Asians settled in the UK, and also those who had gone to Canada, consisted of more than 1,200 packages. Before they left Uganda the refugees had hopefully freighted all the material possessions they could. The handling of this luggage demonstrated how many agencies were involved in the resettlement process and its fate has entered into the folklore of the refugees. Every adult (and even some who were still at school) speculated on the rumours as to what happened to the contents en route from Entebbe Airport. Their most frequent stories concerned large amounts of jewellery that had been secreted in the base of cooking pots, all of which had disappeared, though some of the utensils with their empty hollowed-out bases were recovered.

The luggage had arrived at Heathrow Airport on East African Airways in November 1972, having been handled by Monoc Freight and then R & B Forwarding Company which had subsequently gone into liquidation. The press and the police were called in to witness the condition of the luggage the day after its arrival. A certain proportion of the luggage was destroyed and the rest stored in the warehouse of East African Airways. The Co-ordinating Committee for the Welfare of Evacuees from Uganda in the first instance approached Resettlement Board officials asking whether the Board could deal with the luggage. The Board (perhaps because of the state of most of the packages) declined to do so. Subsequently, though, the Board was to claim that it had not been consulted, but had been told that the carriers were themselves disposing of the unclaimed property 'to a charitable organization'. The Co-ordinating Committee then turned to BAWS and suggested they take it over, sell it and use the proceeds as a donation towards their Reception Centre work.

The luggage was delivered by two articulated lorries late one night in March 1973 at the BAWS Reception Centre at the Sangam cinema. Ninety-nine per cent of the 1,200 packages had no address; 95 per cent were damaged and 80 per cent were opened. Everything was piled into four rooms with packages spilling open and broken articles poured out. Had BAWS not taken the luggage over, it would have been destroyed. The *Leicester Mercury* (3 March) duly headlined its arrival as 'City Gets an Asian Luggage Problem'. But the city bore no burden at all. No statutory agency was called on to help – everything was channelled through the voluntary sector. It was BAWS who put notices in the Asian press telling people where the articles were and asking for claims to be made. In cases where the packages were addressed, the owners were contacted. By the end of May, Dr Seth stated that the greater part of the 12 tons of the luggage, which he valued at £1,000, was still unclaimed. Most of the packages had, he said, been pilfered during their journey to Leicester, which had added to the difficulty of identifying belongings. The absence of valuable contents removed in transit was also emphasized by Albrecht Turk, the Community Relations Officer, when he sent a list of unclaimed but named packages to all other Community Relations Councils. There were about 80 claimants. The cost of storage and delivery of the luggage was not borne by BAWS: the Director of the Co-ordinating Committee negotiated on its behalf with the Resettlement Board, which agreed to reimburse Seth via the Social Services Department. The letter confirming this ends with the Director of the Co-ordinating Committee thanking the Director of Social Services 'for all your assistance both to the Leicester Asian Community and this organisation'. It was decided to auction off the clothing, cutlery, crockery and bedding which had still not been claimed after all Community Relations Councils had received a list of the names or the Airway Bill number on the packages. But before this could happpen, a fire severely damaged the BAWS headquarters at the Commonwealth Community Centre.

The fire on the night of 31 May 1973 destroyed only the offices and did not spread into the Sangam cinema in the front of the building. Most of the unclaimed luggage was lost together with a pile of passports: Dr Seth was pictured in the *Leicester Mercury* (1 June) with a bundle of the latter which he had recovered from his office – why he was storing the passports is not clear. The *Leicester Mercury* reported that the cause of the outbreak was 'under investigation', but 'there were no suspicious circumstances'. However, the real cause was the subject of a great deal of speculation among the refugees and others. Dr Seth himself sent a photostat of a threatening letter to the Community Relations Officer and the police: 'What a Mess! You Get More Yet!! If some of your People DO NOT GET OUT of this Country! Too Many Here! – Britisher.' Whatever the cause of the fire, the rambling rooms heated by portable gas heaters became even less inviting to the refugees and to the volunteer from the Co-ordinating Committee employed there. And BAWS had to press hard for its grant to be extended for a further few months.

BAWS and the Ugandan Asian Relief Trust

The official reception facilities closed down at the end of October 1972. But the Director of Social Services, after consulting with the other organizers of Leicester's 'tripartite committee' (see p. 108 below), decided that public funds (recouped from the Resettlement Board) should still support BAWS.

> The present policy of paying £30 per week and keeping the Reception Centre open will continue until 31st January 1973, and after that until 31st March the Social Services Department will pay £7.10 per week towards the cleaning and will also pay the rental of the telephone and official calls.[24]

At the same meeting it was noted that there was continued need of such things as the distribution of blankets and 'social work help' with the Asian elderly; and that the Resettlement Board's decision not to let people return to the camps for a second stay, was likely to cause problems locally. BAWS had been officially recognized by the Co-ordinating Committee as the organization to which any enquiries from outside Leicester should be directed. In addition, it was working closely with the officers of the Social Services Department in receiving applications for aid from the Uganda Asian Relief Trust which had been set up in November 1972 as 'a special source of Funds on which local authorities could draw to meet particular needs such as tools for a workman and the basic minimum of furniture and household equipment'. The Trust believed that there were 'doubtless, many special cases where a small grant of perhaps £10 or £15 will meet a particular need', and would do something 'to ease the problems of a family trying to set up home for the first time in a wholly unfamiliar society'.[25] These cases became the special task of BAWS. Most of the refugees approached the Society for help as a second or indeed last resort, after they had exhausted the resources or indeed the patience of relatives, and when all other sources for help with employment and accommodation had proved fruitless. However, when Leicester's Community Relations Officer, Albrecht Turk, wrote to the Director of Social Services suggesting a plan for speedy allocation of the money from the Relief Trust, he mentioned the number of applications already being received and channelled through Dr Seth. He also involved BAWS in a small committee which he hoped would function as 'a neutral basis for vetting the applications', but which did not include any member of GWS or of any other Asian organization apart from BAWS. And in his official report on 13 January 1973 to the Community Relations Commission (in answer to their circular about the general situation of coordinating committees dealing with refugees from Uganda), Turk reviewed the work still being done by BAWS and the request made that it should continue to be funded:

The request made by Dr. Seth to the Director of Social Services in January 1973 appears then to be valid. In this he acknowledged that the number of people reporting at his Centre direct from the Camps has declined, but the inquiries from the various Camps for suitable accommodation has increased. This necessitates visits to many houses. He is dealing with lost baggage, recording assets left in Uganda and sending details to the Ugandan Property Record Section at the Home Office, and receiving more and more requests about schooling. He asks that he might retain clerical services until the end of March.

But he made no mention of the fact that the Community Relations Council now had an assistant officer, and in addition a temporary appointment of a young Community Service Volunteer, both of whom consistently contacted GWS when any specific request came from camp officials about Gujarati-speaking contacts. Neither did he mention that BAWS had taken on the task of coordinating the voluntary scheme to visit the refugees in their homes, which was a follow-up to the station reception.

Not only was BAWS backed by the Community Relations Officer but also by the Chairman of the Community Relations Council, the Earl of Lanesborough, who wrote in support of Dr Seth's application for financial support from the authority to continue at the same level until March. He added that he would go further 'and in view of the fact that his Centre is still very much in demand and will be used for the distribution of Trust Fund money there might be a very real need for a further extension'.[26] But when the request was sent on to the Resettlement Board, which was funding the BAWS operation through the Local Authority, the grants section of the Board was not so supportive, emphasizing that 'while appreciating all that Dr Seth has done – the Board at no time asked him to act as their representative', and suggested a reduction in the running cost to £7.50 a week.[27] The Board's view (with particular emphasis that BAWS was never formally nominated by it) was passed on from the Town Clerk to the Director of Social Services. The latter, perhaps because of the lobbying done on its behalf by the Community Relations Council, agreed to go on with its backing of BAWS. 'In view of the volume of work still being carried out, the Social Services had agreed to support Dr Seth until the end of February, on the understanding that he gives us a full report on his activities.'[28]

Even some of these activities were criticized, particularly the vetting of houses which was described as 'rather doubtful, this is now a task for the Public Health Officials', and the Director of Social Services emphasized 'the *claim* that Dr Seth has found jobs for 600–800'. So it was for its other tasks – dealing with 12 tons of unlabelled luggage, registering new arrivals into Leicester (often from refugee camps on the continent), handling cases for the Ugandan Relief Trust – that the Local Authority continued to fund the operation at £7.50 a week. This continued when Dr Seth was away 'on a visit to Canada and the U.S.A., to present the case for claims by the Ugandan Asians to the United Nations, as I feel that the British are not to be taxed further'.[29] The secretary and worker funded by the Co-ordinating Committee for the Welfare of Evacuees from Uganda continued to run the Reception Centre.

Most of the adult refugees remembered BAWS for the way in which it administered the Relief Trust, which they frequently felt to be inequitable. Under the terms of the Trust Deed, assistance could only be given to 'persons who shall have entered the U.K. in reliance upon passports issued to them by the Government of the U.K., and their spouses, relicts, children and other dependants being in each case persons who were ordinarily resident in Uganda on the 4th August 1972, and children of such persons born since that date'.

The initial amount of money allocated to Leicester was £6,325. The Trustees devised an appropriate claim form, on which the recipient acknowledged the payment. The form was printed in English only, with no translation into any appropriate Asian language. Applications as well as completed forms were all forwarded by BAWS to the Director of Social Services, and after final approval were passed to the accounts section for immediate payment. BAWS had, then, a fair degree of discretion as to who should qualify. Lord Sainsbury, the Director of the Trust, appeared on television to explain its limitations; nevertheless some of the refugees still assumed that each member of a family, not just the head of household, could qualify for £50. When they approached BAWS they were disappointed and blamed Dr Seth rather than the limitations of the Trust.

But the first complaint made to the Trust was not that BAWS was distributing the money unfairly, but too generously – to stateless persons not covered by the Trust Deed. BAWS replied to this by claiming that Dr Prem of the Trust had told them this was legal. Prem denied this, but because some of those accused of being ineligible had in fact documentation of entry certificates issued by the High Commission in Kampala, though valid only for three months, the Trust's legal advisers sanctioned the payments. The next concession was of advance funds from the Trust. On the recommendation of the Co-ordinating Committee, this concession was given to BAWS because its President and Dr Seth were 'paying out of their own pockets' in the case of the more urgent cases, and could no longer go on waiting 'several weeks to get it back from the Trust'. By March 1973, £5,000 had been allocated; and the Director of Social Services was told that a further allocation of two further grants of £2,400 would be made to Leicester. But in July the Trust had received several complaints that people had been asked to sign for the receipt of money before it had actually been given, and had either not received it or received only a smaller amount. There were also allegations that blankets purchased out of local authority funds had not been properly distributed, and that refusal of help had been through personal spite rather than any objective assessment. Throughout the time these complaints were being made, in some cases in the presence of the police, the Trust remained firm in its support of BAWS, who had done more work and dealt with more grants than anyone else in the country, and never had the slightest doubt that the amounts distributed to individuals were correct. The Trust had been holding up Leicester as an example of how its grants could help Ugandan Asians. However, it did suggest that in future no client should sign any document before receipt of money, that the receipt should be witnessed and that a separate bank account should be opened to handle the Trust money. By October 1973 the Trust was, in any case, about to complete its work, and it urged that outstanding cases be dealt with as quickly as possible.

All the allegations and counter-allegations were made public when in October Dr Seth circulated a letter to the executive members of the Community Relations Council which gave details of the whole affair (including all the correspondence), produced receipts for the blankets and pointed out that all the complaints had been made through leaders of the GWS. None of those who had spoken evil of him had been willing to take an oath at the Hindu Temple, and 'some of these people think that records I held have been burnt (in the fire of my offices) ... they are not aware I have receipts.'[30] To BAWS, then, the whole affair was seen as no more than yet another incident in the long saga of challenges to its leadership. But the events coincided with the withdrawal of its funding by the Local Authority and the cessation of the services of its full-time worker funded by the Co-ordinating Committee. The association continued in name at least until 1979, but by that time Dr Seth had died and its President Mr Ratoo was on a prolonged visit to India.

5. THE ROLE PLAYED BY BAWS: AN EVALUATION

Originally, BAWS was just an ad hoc group, hastily brought together at a time when both the local political leaders and local government officials, conscious of their own accountability, hesitated to act before accurate information about the actual expulsion of the Asians from Uganda was forthcoming. In such a vacuum, the national media in particular elevated this ad hoc group to a position in which it was described as a model for voluntary action in other cities in the UK: it was Asian, it was articulate, it claimed to know the current situation and what the future plans for Asians from Uganda would be. This almost instant 'media visibility' so enhanced the reputation of the group's spokesmen, especially outside Leicester, that they were led into making yet more forecasts and promises about their ability to organize a reception programme. The local media, however, were not reluctant to reveal the shortcomings of BAWS and to give publicity to persons from East Africa – and especially from Uganda – who claimed to be more truly representative of the refugees. And like other groups in other contexts, because BAWS was led by a few businessmen, who acted as guides to the newly arrived, introducing them through their own commercial connections to employment and housing, critics found it easy to accuse its leaders of making a profit out of their voluntary efforts.

Perhaps the most important feature of BAWS was that it, a voluntary association, was used by the Social Services Department: it served as an interpreter of the needs of the refugees and as a means for distributing the Trust money. These were both sophisticated and sensitive tasks which needed the input of trained social workers. But in 1972, after a decade of migration from the New

Commonwealth, there was not a single trained social worker from East Africa in the Social Services. There were some in clerical grades, and one of these acted as the liaison officer between BAWS and the Department. So when the Director of Social Services was asked, along with the other heads of the city's Housing and Education Departments, to report to the special meeting called to discuss an article in *The Times* (3 August) which estimated that in 1973 250 of the Ugandan Asians in Leicester were living below the poverty line, his report was almost entirely concerned with details of the work done by BAWS.[31] He stressed the importance of its work for the Relief Trust (it had processed 392 grants involving a total of £11,464 with the Social Services merely 'monitoring'). The section dealing with the work done directly by Social Services listed involvement with only 50 cases (homeless families; subnormality; mentally ill and police referrals). The Director concluded: 'It will be seen from the foregoing that most of the detailed day to day involvement with Ugandan Asians has been with the British Welfare Society Advice Centre ... and *praise should be paid to the magnificent work of Dr Seth.*'

There has been a growing literature on the practices by and attitudes of statutory services to the needs and perceptions of minority group members.[32] Mary Dines,[33] who was closely involved with the resettlement of the Ugandan Asians, contrasted the UK with the Netherlands where immigrant organizations were from the start not only trusted but substantially funded by Central Government. In the UK, too much was expected too quickly, and the authorities failed to grasp the diversity of immigrant groups. It is unfortunate that one result of the Social Services' use of BAWS was to create suspicion among sections of the Asian community.

The organizations – particularly BAWS – were operating on an idea of leadership generally found in the Indian subcontinent, where in the confines of intimate communities the leaders and followers are entirely dependent on each other. But however objective and unselfish this leadership may be, it is inevitably seen as opportunism, and is accompanied by speculations over its motivation. Moreover, leaders of voluntary organizations are often authoritarian and see no need to account for their initiatives. Yet when these concepts were transferred to Asian organizations in Leicester in 1972, they were challenged by the more radical and political groups (such as the Indian Workers Association), and the younger members of the community. To these, the leaders of BAWS were 'the chamchas' who in their attempt to gain respect from the white establishment actually became part of the colonial device of 'co-option of and divide-and-rule'.[34] Despite these criticisms, however, Dr Seth was almost invariably referred to by fellow Asians as 'a leader'. It sometimes happens that those thought to be minority group leaders by outsiders thereby attain prominence and power amongst their own community, even though there is in-group opposition. BAWS can also be viewed as a group of mediator-brokers. Such brokers are a familiar feature of the first phase of any migration. They provide practical help of various kinds to their fellow countrymen, who believe that they have the power to influence the local political leaders.[35] Moreover, they are seen as patrons, who have the powers to dispense favours themselves. In this case, these roles matched the preconceptions of the community leaders that the refugees had known in Uganda.

One factor is clear: ethnic leadership at the time of the Ugandan Asian arrival and afterwards had to do primarily with internal processes among the Asian community in Leicester. When there was gossip, it was centred on the theme that businessmen form associations to enhance not only their own reputations but also their business interests. Some of the refugees, indeed, denied that there was any element of altruism at all. Others, however, recognized the fact that Asian businessmen often have community service careers as well as their business careers: that for each step on the business ladder 'there was a corresponding step' in helping the refugees. The one resource that the refugees had to control those who purported to speak and work for them was gossip.[36] A young woman who worked in an office of a locally based national voluntary organization expressed concern about the accusations of 'jungle-drum messages' which are constantly made about Asian communities, but she pointed out that gossip provided 'a way of making leaders do the right things. They should have been grateful for fingers being pointed at them. It stopped them getting too big-headed, and forgetting that they themselves should live up to all those things they boasted they did.'

6. OTHER ASPECTS OF THE VOLUNTARY AND STATUTORY CONTRIBUTION

Although, then, BAWS gained the prominence it did partly because it was promoted by the Social Services Department, which could not itself provide specialized understanding of the needs of those newly arrived from overseas, there were other voluntary organizations which also aimed to help fill this gap. Their motivation is illustrated by an appeal for help for the refugees by the Leicester Progressive Jewish Congregation:

> Leicester is in the news in a big way, as some of our local Councillors have expressed the notion that we cannot cope with the great influx of Ugandan Asians. They may be right, when it comes to providing schools, housing and jobs, for a start, since any large number of people seeking scarce resources are bound to go short. But does this mean we should not try to open our hearts and purses and give some help? Those of us who came from Germany will remember that Britain and her people gave us a chance to live, and eventually contribute to the well-being of her people. If you want to help locally, why not get in touch with Dr Seth the Community Relations Officer [*sic*].

The Leicester Quakers also issued a statement:

> We all realise that there will be problems when the families from Uganda arrive, but feel that only a very practical approach by the people of Leicester and by the Local Authorities will meet this situation ... we are privileged, through God's grace, to live in our Country and our City. Each and every one of us has a human

responsibility to these unfortunate people, who have been effectively thrown out of their homes ... we will welcome those who choose to come and live in Leicester.

The Leicestershire Branch of the Red Cross published in its Newsletter:

Ugandan Asians: In the light of all the publicity in the media, the National Headquarters has made it clear that we will help readily and willingly. The precise nature of this help is difficult to foresee. We have been in touch with both the County and the City Directors of Social Services. We must be ready to act quickly, if and when the call comes.

The indigenous sector

It was the Rev Brian Taylor, the Secretary of the Leicester Council of Churches and responsible for its 'community relations', who took the initiative of calling the first meeting of representatives of those Leicester organizations which were anxious to know what they could contribute to a reception programme for the refugees coming to the city. Taylor wrote to the Town Clerk on 17 August to inform him about this meeting which was held at St Peter's, Highfields. On the basis of estimates from the national British Council of Churches, it was probable that 4,000 families from Uganda would come to Leicester. Therefore, there should be a local pressure group to urge the Local Authority to start making plans to receive the refugees. At the meeting the Community Relations Officer, Mr Turk, had said that the Leicester Community Relations Council had 'generally accepted' BAWS as the co-ordinating Asian voluntary organization, but:

The voluntary sector by itself cannot tackle the huge problem. The main decision must be made by Central and Local Governments ... but so far inquiries of the Local Authority had met with evasive replies, suggesting that no plans had been made and some were waiting in the hope that others would take on the burden.[37]

The first official plans were not disclosed, however, until the opposition Conservative group on the City Council made public their anger about the 'wait and see' policy of Alderman Marston and other members of the Labour group of the Council.[38] So Marston requested that the Town Clerk be asked to prepare costings per 1,000 immigrants for Education, Housing and Social Services and these had to be submitted to the City Treasurer within two days – in time for the emergency meeting of the full City Council.

In its reply the Social Services Department concentrated on the cost of temporary and emergency accommodation, which it regarded as 'the largest problem'. Despite hearing estimates from BAWS with whom its representatives had met, the Department assumed that only 25 per cent of the refugees would be accommodated by relatives. This would still leave 750 people (150 families) per 1,000. The Department had no existing resources to cope. The homeless unit at Hillcrest was able to accommodate a few, but no major reorganization there was possible. Some large-scale temporary accommodation might be required to keep the families together. There was nothing within the city, but east coast holiday camps might be the answer. If costs had to be met by the Council (although there existed no real basis for assessment) for every 750 of the 1,000 'immigrants', this would amount to £5,000 per week. The Director of Social Services concentrated on the immediate needs of housing the refugees. He sent a memo to the Social Services Committee of the City Council underlining his Department's fear that it would be 'totally swamped if numbers in excess of say 50/60 persons were arriving without any arrangements'. His Department was unprepared and it would involve securing staff especially: 'in fact the whole would be seen as a military transit camp operation.' He added: 'After absorption into the community, with all the problems which that would involve it would be appreciated that Social Services needs would be increased in all sections. But this would be minimal compared with the Reception exercise.'[39]

On the 31 August the Town Clerk requested the Directors of Education, Social Services, Housing and the Health Departments to report to him daily at 10.30 on any matters concerning the arrival of the refugees. On the same day came the first circular letter from the Uganda Resettlement Board addressed to the Clerks of Local Authorities. This outlined the functions of the reception teams at points of arrival, expressed the hope that Local Authorities would work closely with the Board, acknowledged the apprehension felt by many authorities and stated that it was to be appreciated that the Board had no powers of direction even though it agreed that it would be 'best all round for the evacuees to go to areas where problems were less severe'. The Board gave priority to how temporary accommodation could best be provided. It also led to a series of suggestions published in the *Leicester Mercury* that a local residential centre or a transit village of prefabricated bungalows should be set up so that 'Leicester could contain its own problem'.[40] Then the *Mercury* (23 August) reported: 'Wild rumours are circulating in the City over the issue and one has its funny side. Some have said that the tents now going up in Abbey Park are to accommodate the Ugandan Asians – completely forgetting that it is the Abbey Park Show next week.'

This idea of a prefabricated village was taken up as a matter of practical policy by the Leicestershire Social Services Department in November 1972, when it was faced with the problem of 19 families who had arrived and had nowhere to go permanently. A large country house, Beaumanor Hall, had been acquired by the county authority from the War Office. The Social Services Department worked out a detailed plan for temporary billets in the Hall itself, and planned to spend £6,000 on the purchase of 12 second-hand caravans. The establishment officer at Beaumanor Hall contacted the Uganda Resettlement Board, but was told that no grant aid was available for temporary accommodation. The November minutes of the County Social Services Committee record that 'The Authority received no further information from the Board on short term accommodation. Following the receipt of a Circular on the subject, a second Circular was received which almost immediately cancelled the former.'

Although these ideas of prefabricated villages and a caravan park never came about, the provision of such temporary accommodation within easy reach of Leicester where the refugees' relatives could have helped with long-term arrangements was something many of those who went to the more distant Reception Camps would have found more acceptable. However, when the city's biggest 'umbrella for voluntary agencies', the Council of Social Service, together with the Council for Community Relations, issued a joint statement on what they considered the first priority, finding accommodation for the refugees, they concentrated on registering individual offers.[41] This proved to be not very arduous: in the two months of August and September the register had 32 entries from a city of 279,000 people. Among these 'households' was a conference centre – Lindley Lodge in Nuneaton, three vicarages in the county area and Holy Cross Priory in the city. Only eight offers were for families, and all but six stipulated that the accommodation was to be on a short-term basis.

A much more radical plan of action was presented to the Town Clerk on 11 September. The signatories were from organizations such as Shelter, Inter-Faith, the Liberal Party, Holy Cross Priory and the Society of Friends. The petition began with a plea:

> What would the Leicester City Council do if there was a natural disaster in the neighbouring City? They would face the emergency and accommodate the refugees. The Ugandan Asians *are refugees* without money, property and resource . . . this is what the Corporation should do . . . present the plans to the Government and say *this* is what *we* are prepared to do. Now show how *you* will fulfil your promise of financial support.

It went on to catalogue the lead that Leicester should take: to use the university halls of residence, set up a reception centre with residential facilities, and to stop demolishing houses. There should be co-ordination with the county authorities; a single information centre with staff seconded from each appropriate Local Government Department; a single appeal for clothing and a register of accommodation. Schemes to enable refugees with special skills to receive orientation courses at local colleges and social work courses should be planned. The city, too, should send representatives to each refugee arrival point, so that proper warning of arrivals would be forthcoming. The signatories were 'confident that there were many people of good-will in the City'. The petition was also put to the General Purposes Committee of the City Council on 11 September. In his reply to the petition the Town Clerk stated firmly that the refugees should not be offered unfit houses and though most of the other suggestions were dismissed he added: 'We too wished for an early warning organisation. It is not good enough that the first information a Local Authority has of arrivals is when the children present themselves at schools.'

The 'three-pronged strategy'

On 6 September the Town Clerk wrote to both the Leicester Council for Community Relations and the Leicester Council of Social Service: 'Now that the pressure of our meetings with the Home Office and Resettlement Board has eased somewhat, I think it essential that I call a meeting of the representatives of the local bodies who are particularly concerned with the matter of Ugandan Asians.' Within a week a strategy had been worked out. This was thereafter always termed 'the tripartite, three-pronged strategy for the reception of the Ugandan Asians into Leicester'. It consisted of the LCCR and the LCSS in co-operation with the Social Services Department (the last appointed Major Wallis, an ex-Civil Defence Officer, as its representative). The three organizations met on 11 September and decided that there would be volunteers who would man the main railway station to greet refugees. There would be a small office in the station entrance where the refugees would be asked to report to BAWS at its headquarters at the Sangam cinema.

This reception was seen by the Community Relations Officer, Albrecht Turk, as having a symbolic as well as a practical function: a way of showing that indigenous and Asian groups could work together. In his view this was a vital way of fostering 'good community relations'. He also saw it as one of his main tasks to reconcile the rival claims of BAWS and GWS, both of whose leaders were prominent members of his own Council. He was anxious to show both nationally and locally that the refugees should be welcomed by all that was representative of a 'compassionate and friendly' Leicester. Turk, who had known at first hand the plight of refugees in post-war Germany, valued what volunteers could provide. Yet he felt as deeply as members of the Indian Workers Association that ultimately Central Government should be responsible. And in any case in August 1972 the LCCR consisted of just himself and a secretary. It was also largely due to his efforts that the indigenous volunteers were not really aware of the divisions in the Asian groups. On 8 October GWS wrote to the Town Clerk and the Director of Social Services that they had instructed all their members at the station reception to co-operate fully with other groups, but to take no orders from BAWS. Ten days later GWS wrote again to the Director of Social Services expressing their dissatisfaction about 'the manner in which the present co-ordinating team is functioning. We on this issue, represent almost the whole Indian Community in Leicester ... and are the authentic organisation to speak for the Hindu and Sikh communities.' However, BAWS continued to be supported by the authorities (the clerk who worked at its headquarters was paid £1,203 per annum and there was a grant of £30 'for extra typing and cleaning').

By November 2,000 Ugandan Asians had passed through the railway station. The Social Services Department had received notification of a further 350 from the Resettlement Board. The 'tripartite committee' of the Council of Social Service, Community Relations Council and Social Services decided to continue in being for a further three months. But it was decided to close the station reception on 10 November, but to retain the use of the office, so that, if necessary, it could be resurrected. This first phase of reception had cost just £636 – all of which was recouped from the Resettlement Board. A breakdown of this expenditure ('First Aid, Transport, Telephone calls') was given by the Town Clerk to a special meeting of the city's General Purposes Committee on 7 November. But the real significance of the goodwill and the practical help and sympathy shown by the station reception (coming as it did in the wake of the city's initial agitation about the influx of the expellees) was profound. Forty of the refugees offered their spontaneous testimonies about this. The 16 organizations which helped included groups from the College of Education, the Mothers Union and various churches (but not any representative West Indian group). Most who had volunteered often experienced 'hours of fruitless waiting. But there were also moments of fulfilment, when baffled travel-stained families were reassured . . .'[42]

The Social Services had asked a retired nursing sister to co-ordinate the project from a temporary waiting room. She was remembered by many of the refugees, particularly those who were ill (for example, diabetic). She herself was 'shocked to receive a cheque' for her service at the station from 20 September until mid-November. She registered all the arrivals and if necessary secured transport to take them to their relatives' homes.

> The refugees fell into four main categories. Most had come direct from the airport to stay. Next there were those who had come from camps to stay. Sometimes there were up to ten members of a family. Very vulnerable were the wives who had come separately from their husbands. They were the most lost of all. Then there were a number – mostly men and their sons – who had come to Leicester from London or the Camps to look for a job and accommodation. Then there were those who had just come to stay with relatives for a short time and then said they would move away.

She, and others, emphasized that no refugee, from September onwards, arrived at Leicester station without being met by someone, 'mostly their own people' but if not, a Leicester person. Another volunteer in this reception programme said that most people who participated did so out of sheer compassion. But there were some like herself who were motivated 'out of sheer anger mixed with a degree of disgust that a rich city like Leicester should become known as the place where homeless people could not be tolerated'.[43]

That this voluntary 'Welcome to Leicester' effort was seen by the Ugandan refugees as important is illustrated by one 16-year-old's account. Having spent one night at a camp, he and his family were phoned by a close relative who advised them not to tell the camp authorities that they were intending to come to Leicester: 'He said that we should say we were going to Kettering and get travel warrants for there. He told us that there was a lot of feeling against us in Leicester. But when we arrived, a British woman helped us off the train.'

It is very easy to dismiss statements like this as part of the trivia of the much bigger resettlement process, and mere gestures of goodwill when benevolent individuals were exploited by statutory agencies. But as was the case at the points of actual arrival in the UK, it is this which is still remembered. It was seen as reassuring, particularly by the women of the Leicester refugee group. One mother of three said:

In twenty-four hours I had left my life behind, seen my luggage taken from me and thrown on a heap at Entebbe; I begged for a drink for my children there. Then there was landing at Stansted, and waiting around. I saw London and the Underground and escalators and then the train terminus. Then Leicester – and a lady came up to me and said, 'You are welcome ... let me help with your children.'

PART TWO

The Longer Term

Chapter 6 Ugandan Asians and education

As our plane left Entebbe I said to the children 'our family is safe and soon places will be found for you at English schools – the best in the world.'

The official said to me that a Science degree from Nairobi and a qualification from the University of Moscow and being a headmaster of a school in Uganda was not sufficient for me to be allowed to teach in Leicester.

We called Wakerley School, 'wait-a long-time' school.

These recollections illustrate the aspirations of the Ugandan Asians and the frustrations and delays they encountered in their initial contact with the education system in Leicester. By contrast Mrs Dorothy Davis, the chairman of the Education Committee, emphasized that during these years Leicester had handled a regular influx of around a thousand children a year: 'not without strain, but certainly without fuss'.[1] The initial lack of clear direction by Central Government, however, especially about financial support to Leicester for the Ugandan refugees, led her to add that 'there should be a knocking together of the heads of the Treasury, Department of Education and Science and the Resettlement Board'. And when Dr Seth commented: 'I've found great difficulty in trying to fit them into schools. It's time the Department of Education wakes up and provides schools for these children', Leicester's Director of Education responded: 'it's not Dr Seth's job to find them places anyway.'[2] Whose job, then, was it? And how successfully was it done?

1. THE LOCAL AUTHORITY PROVISION, 1966–1972

The task of absorbing a large number of Ugandan Asian children into the schools of the city has to be considered in the context of the wider and the longer-term issues. A national building strike took place in 1972 which added to the three-year backlog in building programmes, and this was also the first year of the raising of the statutory school-leaving age to 16. There was, too, a long-running controversy over the reorganization of secondary education in the city. Although the total population of Leicester remained static at around 281,000 from the mid 1960s, the child population grew steadily.[3] A second post-war bulge in the number of births reached its peak in 1965, when the number almost equalled the total of 1947, and this coincided with large-scale immigration into the city. In one inner city secondary school a special group for teaching English as a second language had been initiated in 1957. But apart from special language provision, the Local Authority adopted an assimilationist stance and decided to make no administrative distinction between immigrant and indigenous children.

There was no count of immigrant pupils until 1966 when a return was demanded by the Department of Education and Science. This forced the authority to abandon its view that the only statistic of any value was just the one that Government Departments could not give: accurate forecasts of future numbers of immigrant children. In the first year of 'the count' (as defined in Form 7(i) of the Department of Education and Science), Leicester had 6.4 per cent of immigrant children in its schools. This figure did not include the number of 'internal' immigrants – those children moving to Leicester from their place of first arrival in the UK. But because of the 'exporting factor' – indigenous children moving with their parents into the suburbs and the rural areas of the county – the authority said it could cope, at least as far as the basic legal and administrative obligations of providing actual school places. Officials regarded the manageable figure for this as up to 40 children a month, and it was only when this equilibrium could not be maintained that children had to wait for school places.

The Kenyan Asian immigration from 1968 to 1971, and its effects on Leicester's schools, provided a rehearsal for the Ugandan intake in 1972. In 1965, as part of its Africanization policy, Kenya (followed by Uganda and Tanzania) introduced its Immigration Act and the Trade and Licensing Act which had serious economic and social consequences for Asians. More importantly, the restrictions placed on entry to the UK by the British government's 1968 immigration legislation led to a rush to gain entry before the Act became enforceable. By 1968 the number of children from Kenya in Leicester schools was 1,077 out of a total of 5,884 immigrant children, whereas previously there had been only 337 from Kenya and all other African Commonwealth countries. In addition there were numbers of immigrant students in Colleges of Further Education in the city and in the county, and also at Kettering in Northamptonshire.[4] By 1972 there were 2,321 Kenyan Asians at school in Leicester. Leicester's official view in 1972 was that 'we are used to dealing with pupils from overseas', and at the time of the announcement of the Ugandan Asian expulsion, in a series of press, radio and television interviews the Director of Education constantly referred to the entry of immigrant pupils 'as having been on average 100 a month since 1967' – an advance of 60 on the 'manageable figure'. To help with the increased numbers the Leicester Education Authority had in 1968 established its Immigration Education Fund which provided equipment and resources at short notice. In addition there was a Development Fund which gave immediate help to a school without waiting for normal estimate procedures, and a double capitation allowance for the first year to schools admitting immigrant children. The actual money allocated to the special Immigrant Education Fund was very small ('in the order of £3,000 to £4,000 a year'). But Mr A. Davis, the Director of Education, frequently made reference to it. In January 1973 he said: 'We are helped by an Immigrant Development Fund set up two or three years ago, to draw on.' He also commented that Leicester's schools had gained such expertise since 1967 that members of the Select Committee on Race Relations and Immigration who had visited Leicester in May 1973, suggested Leicester should publish a book about its pioneering efforts for immigrant pupils.[5]

2. COPING WITH THE CRISIS: EDUCATION PROVISION AFTER AUGUST 1972

Given this background, how far was the Ugandan Asian refugee entry responsible for creating a 'crisis'? How sudden was the actual influx? What were the numbers involved? Did these factors bring an entirely new situation to

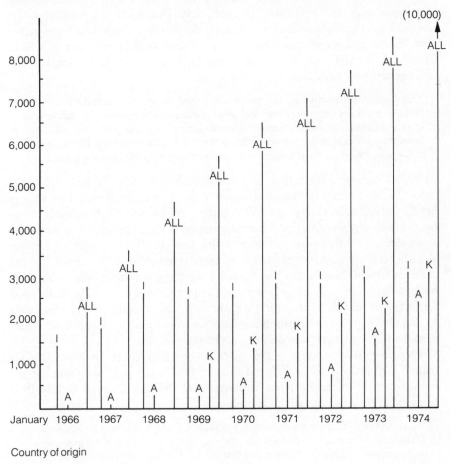

Country of origin

I India
K Kenya
A other African Commonwealth
ALL all immigrant children
The 'other African' group includes Kenya before 1969 when separate figures are not available

Figure 2   Immigrant children in Leicester schools, 1966–74

the city's schools? The Director of Education said that what distinguished the Ugandan Asians' impact on Leicester's schools was the 'unexpectedness of the influx'; the expulsion came in mid-August 1972, which was the school holiday period, and this made it difficult to recruit additional teachers for the new academic year – 'they have all got jobs, but we have managed to recruit 35.' It was also the worst year that it could have happened from the point of buildings; and the most worrying thing of all was 'the numbers seeking admission to inner city schools already full to their capacity'.[6]

But there was a breathing space between Amin's expulsion announcement in August and the time when the refugees actually arrived in substantial numbers. Even in early October 1972, the British Asian Welfare Society claimed that there were only 493 refugees in the city. But, more importantly, it was not the Ugandan Asians alone who caused the strains on local education provision. These had accumulated over the years and would have come to a head in any case in 1972. In October 1972 the local branch of the National Union of Teachers gave their view:

> The Association utterly and unconditionally repudiates the view that the continuing crisis confronting the educational and other social services is caused by immigration in general *and the arrival of Ugandan Asians in particular... This just is not true.* The immigrants do add to the problem but it is there not because of them but because of the way the educational system finances have been restricted for many years.

In 1970 Leicester schools had been described by the *Times Educational Supplement* (27 November) as 'bending under a flood of immigrants'. The waiting list for school admissions was 200 children, the six secondary schools in the heart of the city were full, and 'bussing pupils to the periphery' was becoming a problem. Children were arriving at the rate of '81.4 a month'. Leicester already had the highest proportion of immigrant children at school (14 per cent) outside London. Yet the school building programme was being held back because of lack of decision by Central Government. The Education Department told the journalist: 'We are in a bad situation to put roofs over heads. On the present flow of immigrants we would have to put up a secondary school and two primary schools every six or seven months.'

The promised increase in the quota of entry vouchers for East Africans from 5,000 in 1971 to 18,000 and then 12,000 in the next few years led the Finance and General Purposes Committee of the City Council in July 1971 to warn Leicester's Education Committee:

> The effect of this announcement on the schools of Leicester cannot be assessed. It could mean that at very short notice, the number of children seeking admission will increase ... Your Committee feel that any further increase in the continuing heavy demand for admission to schools cannot be met at short notice and will be met with only great difficulty and some delay in the longer run.

Mr Tom Boardman, MP for North East Leicester, asked a question in the House of Commons on 29 July 1971 about extra help from the government for Leicester. Mrs Margaret Thatcher, Secretary of State for Education, admitted she could not estimate the number of immigrant pupils that Leicester could expect. Boardman's reaction was to say that if the government could not estimate the number of Kenyan children likely to want school places in Leicester in 1972, how could the Local Authority be expected to cope? Another indication that the Ugandan refugees did not *cause* the problem are the letters from indigenous parents to Page Four of the *Leicester Mercury*:[7] 'My Child in a Wooden Hut'; 'No Schooling for our White Children'; 'Teachers Mesmerised in Accepting the Problems of Immigrant Children', which predate the Ugandan Asians' arrival. In 1971, too, there was a move to provide a secondary school in hutted accommodation in Humberstone Drive. The aim of the school was the same as that of the subsequent Wakerley ('the Ugandan refugee') School: 'to bring immigrants of secondary age as quickly as possible to a standard of written English, to enable them to transfer to further education and the British way of life'.[8]

Labour Councillor the Rev Alan Billings (who was to be one of the group of nine Labour councillors who 'welcomed' the Ugandan refugees) regarded the move as 'an act of segregation, a dangerous precedent for the solution of other problems'. The idea was dropped and the 'school' became a unit of the Southfields College.

The total number of Ugandan Asian children who were accommodated in Leicester's schools was in the end lower than that of those from Kenya. The memorandum submitted by the LEA to the Select Committee revealed that between January and August 1972, 1,126 immigrant pupils were admitted; for the period September to December 1972, 930 were admitted. In other words, fewer admissions are recorded *after* the main Ugandan Asian exodus than before. There are several explanations which may account for this. For one thing, the figures show only those actually admitted to schools, not those for whom no places could be found and certainly there were refugee children of whom this was true. Another explanation was offered by several of the Ugandan Asian parents. Even after all the publicity about the Ugandan expulsion, the schools continued to assume that all immigrants from East Africa came from Kenya. When parents went to register their children, they often did not contradict the teachers' assumptions.

Neither, though, was there a dramatic fall in the number of immigrant pupils arriving in the city after the 'Ugandan crisis' of 1972–3 was over. In 1974 A. J. Davis, who by then was Deputy Director of Education for the reorganized Leicestershire Education Department, stated that there had been 'no indication that there has been a falling off in the inflow of immigrant pupils to the City's schools... Immigrant pupils have continued to arrive at the rate of 90–100 a month.'[9]

Further evidence that the increased pressure for school places cannot be attributed to Ugandan refugee children alone is to be found in the official count by schools. These show that:[10]

(i) the number of *Kenyan* Asians in city schools between January 1969 and January 1974 increased by 2,029 (i.e. 1,077 to 3,106);

(ii) the number of '*other African Commonwealth*' children in schools for the same period increased by 2,113 (i.e. 342 to 2,455).

Although Ugandans must account for the greatest number of those listed under 'other African Commonwealth', Asian children from Tanzania and Malawi are also included in this category. But, as already related, teachers might have included some of the Ugandan Asian children as 'Kenyan'.

In November 1973, when Central Government accepted the recommendation of the Select Committee that the collection of figures of immigrant children should cease, both the Director of Education and the City Medical Officer announced that they would continue to collect these figures. One of the reasons given was the continued influx of Kenyan Asians, which was then estimated at around a hundred a month. The Director of Education stated: 'I think we have certainly got to continue collecting them ourselves if only because of placing immigrants in schools . . . One immigrant child with a special problem is not a big educational problem: but if we get 50 it is.'[11]   But Councillor Barrie Clayton, Chairman of the newly formed Leicestershire Conservative Monday Club, was emphatic that 'without any form of statistics we will know nothing and this is particularly important to a city like Leicester, where there should be extra payments to deal with the influx of immigrants. *We are faced with a further influx from Kenya.* Are we to pretend there will be no future problems?'[12] David Lane from the Home Office, and Lord Belstead from the Department of Education and Science, visited Leicester in February 1973 to see how the Ugandan Asians were coping with resettlement. The visit coincided with an announcement that 15 per cent of children in Leicester's schools could be classed as immigrant. But neither of the leaders of the city's two main political groups made any specific mention of Ugandan Asians when asked about these numbers. The *Leicester Mercury* in its editorial on the topic confined itself to criticizing 'City Councillors who merely said "Leicester had coped and should continue to cope."'[13] This was just five months after the *Mercury's* alarmist treatment of Ugandan Asians and their demands on the city's educational resources. The Ugandan refugees no longer commanded special attention. It was how to accommodate the numbers of Asian children who continued to come from Kenya which caused concern to the city's officials and elected members. But at the same time the main concern of the Ugandan Asian parents was that their children should resume their education as soon as they arrived from Africa.

Yet most observers, both nationally and locally, compared the comparative ease with which the refugees were absorbed into schools and colleges with their progress in obtaining houses or employment. In his account of Leicester, Wilkinson commented: 'Education has proved to be a small problem . . . the only problem is a shortage of teachers.'[14] And the CRC claimed: 'Only 7 areas of the 46 in our survey, mentioned education as a major problem of resettlement.'[15] The Uganda Resettlement Board's confident statement in its 1973 Interim Report that 'to the best of its knowledge all children and young people who needed them, have in fact been found places in schools, colleges and universities', did, however, prompt a reply from Leicester's assistant Town Clerk. He rejected this view as 'over confident'. In Leicester between 260 and 248 secondary children, together with a dozen or so primary children, were still unplaced. But since the opening of a refurbished primary school, the situation for younger children had eased.[16]

The numbers of schoolchildren needing places were highest in November 1972. At that time the Co-ordinating Committee had reported: 'Asian families in the quest for educational opportunities for their children are themselves leaving Leicester where school places are short and are moving into small towns.'[17] In May 1973 the Director of Education said that 250 secondary pupils were still unaccommodated. This was because of staff shortages. He pledged that 'all Ugandan Asian children in Leicester will be found places by the end of the present year.' But despite the official statement that the 'battle for school places' had been won by September 1973, in January 1974 a governor of an inner area school and District Councillor, Mr Jim Wintour, alleged that children still had to wait up to five months for a school place, and that sometimes the wait could be as long as a year: 'this is a disgrace to a civilised society. The Leicester Education Authority has a clear legal and moral duty to find a school place for every child of school age in Leicester (Section 8 of the 1944 Education Act).'[18] Wintour disputed that there was a 'crisis' in Leicester and produced figures to support his view that Leicester was 'not faced with an unexpected increase in the number of school children or with a severe shortage of teachers'. The Director of Education's reply was that Wintour's view was 'totally unacceptable, unwarranted and untrue'. While admitting that there were 50 children both Asian and indigenous unplaced, he added that 'this is a remarkable achievement considering the immigrant intake that the City has had to absorb in the last two years'.... 'Leicester has had to deal with more than 8,000 immigrants since 1967, 1,100 in the past year [1973], after the main influx of 2,000 Ugandan Asian children in 1972.'[19]

Emergency schooling

How then did Leicester's education officials meet the challenge of absorbing the refugees into its schools? Like other Local Authorities it bussed some of them from their homes to schools on the periphery of the city; and it provided two 'emergency' schools. But for some time for some of the children the only form of schooling they received was in two voluntary part-time schools. Above all, Leicester's Education Committee looked to Central Government for extra finance.

On 15 August 1972 it was reported that the Department of Education and Science (DES) was working on a figure of 19,000 school-age children arriving from Uganda. Brent's Chief Education Officer said that the borough 'would be happy to welcome the Asians so long as Central Government authorised the spending on emergency building'; Leicester's Director of Education said that he was not going to get dramatic but he hoped that the authorization for building and the employment of extra teachers was to be given quickly: 'In Primary Education, we could put up a systems built school in 2–3 months. The site is available.'[20] In another interview he told the *Guardian* (15 August 1972) that he wished to avoid a 'few schools having a high percentage of immigrants', although in fact in the inner city that had already happened. He spoke of 'preserving the kind of integrated society that Leicester had built up so far'.

The first move was to plan the reopening of the old Belper Street primary school, which had been closed down in July. The school, which was in High-fields, was to be renamed the Hugh Latimer. But when these decisions were made (on 28 September), the official minute recorded: 'it is not known what financial assistance will be received from the Government towards the cost.'[21] The only reassurance was that at an informal meeting with the Department of Education and Science on 25 August, Leicester and 12 other Local Education Authorities were told they could 'fly an SOS' to the Government Department to sanction extra expenditure through the rate support grant 'at short notice, provided the LEAs state a clear case for the need'.[22] But the Central Government Departments had no precise information about the financial arrangements.

The first detailed indication of what money Local Authorities could expect to receive for educational provision was given by Robert Carr, the Home Secretary, in a speech to the Association of Municipal Corporations in the last week of September: 'LEAs will be able to get a full 100 per cent grant for certain items of expenditure, such as hiring rooms, refurbishing temporary accommodation, and laying on school transport. When it comes to more substantial items, temporary classrooms for example, grants will be at the 75 per cent level.'[23] And the LEAs were told that they could start applying for grants as soon as they knew how many immigrants they were going to get. This meant that applications were really based on complete guesswork. Leicester's Education Committee now planned an emergency secondary school. Unlike for the primary school there were no vacant buildings in the inner city suitable, so the school had to be in temporary mobile cabins (for which only 75 per cent of cost would be given by the government). Neither of these schools was planned exclusively for Ugandan Asian children. Councillor Dorothy Davis wrote to *The Times* (20 October) and again emphasized that Leicester had for years handled an influx of around a thousand pupils a year 'without fuss'. Now with 516 children from Uganda and 240 from elsewhere, it could no longer continue to do so, unless there were clear guidelines to the Leicester Education Committee:

> Two months after the Ugandan Asian crisis began there is no indication whether
> any Government agency is going to give permission for the Authority to spend money
> on refurbishing the Hugh Latimer school or the planned systems built secondary
> school. Moreover, it is not clear whether these schools would qualify for

reimbursement, if having overfilled local schools with Ugandans we admit a few English or non-Ugandan Asian children.

She also wrote that the DES had delayed two months before granting written permission for the authority to lay out a preliminary sum of £85,000: 'In a Government-proclaimed emergency, and in spite of being labelled a "Red Area", we can get no hard information about the extent of, or conditions for, Government assistance with our additional Ugandan problems.'

Mrs Davis's criticisms were not backed up by the Director of Education, who said that he had received 'every co-operation' from the DES.[24] The Chairman of the Resettlement Board wrote to *The Times* on 2 November saying that he was sorry that Mrs Davis was unaware of the financial help available to Local Authorities, but that the Board's directives to the Local Authority on 18 September were clear enough, and would be expanded in a further directive; a member of his Board had visited Leicester on 27 October to discuss plans to reopen the primary school. Despite this, there continued to be fears among the city councillors about whether the extra money would be really sufficient. Leicester's 'complaints' were contrasted in the *Guardian* (3 November) with Brent's Alderman Philip Hartley's 'congratulations to the Board on having fought the Treasury so successfully'. Later, though, Hartley agreed with Leicester's Alderman Marston: if permanent school buildings had to be built then 'an indemnity of 100 per cent, not 75 per cent, should be given.'[25] Alderman Marston said that 'deep alarm' was felt in Leicester over the reimbursement being for just 12 months: Leicester with its 807 children out of school (only half of these Ugandan Asians) was faced with the possibility of building a new school at the cost of £150,000 of which 25 per cent might have to be spent by the Council. At the City Council meeting on 7 November it was decided to send a delegation to the Home Office, to argue for the 100 per cent reimbursement on all spending on Ugandan Asians.

The 'complaints' from Leicester brought the desired result. When in September 1973 the City Treasurer reported to the City Council he announced that there was a 'credit balance' a year after the Ugandan Asian emergency. He said that the Resettlement Board had 'done all it could for the special situation in Leicester'. No proposals put forward by Chief Officers had had to be shelved for lack of grant aid. Even the period of reimbursement for just 12 months was not as unsatisfactory as it might have been, since the Association of Municipal Corporations had protested on Leicester's behalf and the government had agreed to extend the cut-off date until 16 July 1974.[26] This financial assistance came through a special supplement to the Rate Support Grant (which affects other services as well as education), and the allocation to individual local authorities was based on the numbers of Ugandan refugees. Ironically enough it was the controversial figures compiled by the Medical Officer of Health which were accepted rather than the other official estimates of Ugandan Asians arriving in Leicester. So whilst the Ugandan Resettlement Board had quoted 2,307 for early 1973, the Medical Officer of Health's records indicated a total of 4,133. The City Treasurer and the District Auditor were convinced of the reliability of the latter figure and arranged for a senior official of the Registrar General's Department to visit Leicester in April 1973. After examining the MOH's statistics he agreed that his figure, which by then stood at 4,549, should be incorporated as the official mid-1973 population estimate for the city, and it was on that figure that the Rate Support Grant was based. The City Treasurer regarded all this as 'a very satisfactory outcome and the fact that a Government Department is prepared to accept the corporation figures in the face of alternative figures supplied by the Resettlement Board bears testimony to the accuracy and care with which the figures were compiled by the Medical Officer's Department'.

The opening of the two schools, Hugh Latimer for primary school children and the Wakerley for secondary students, proved to be two success stories from the point of view of the Ugandan Asian pupils and their parents. When the Director of Education announced the recommissioning of the Belper Street premises for use as a 'County Primary School to cater for 420 children aged 5–11', he again emphasized that the accommodation was necessary for *all* children in the area 'when all the dwellings are ready for occupation in July 1973', and also for the further anticipated arrival of immigrant children throughout the City.[27] The financing of the school was discussed at the November meeting of the Finance and General Purposes Sub-Committee, and after 'lengthy discussion' it was resolved to accept the proposed expenditure (with two members voting against the motion). The school opened in December 1972, a month earlier than scheduled, with an initial 98 pupils.

The *Leicester Mercury* editorial (ignoring the facts in its own news columns concerning 541 children waiting for school places) opposed the opening, saying that the school would 'inevitably be labelled and stigmatised. Asians who come here should not be isolated or accommodated in buildings which have been labelled unsuitable for use by indigenous population... if this school can now easily be made fit for Asians, why did it ever go out of use ...?'[28] But by February 1973 the *Mercury*'s educational correspondent described Hugh Latimer as 'a perfectly normal school'. Five- and six-year-olds were writing and drawing ('all about myself') and their 'happy faces belied the sad story of events leading to their coming to Leicester'. All the children were, however, Ugandan Asian refugees. The Headmistress commented that they were unable to grasp the cruelty and injustice which had so affected their lives: 'to them it is only a story. It's like another child coming and telling you about a visit to Abbey Park.' There was a staff of five, one of whom spoke Gujarati. The problem of language was there, but it was 'not serious... it will be overcome.' As for the children's showing any psychological reactions to their refugeehood, the Headmistress said that this actually helped in their settling down in school compared with the general run of infant children. She explained: 'this may be because they are settling down in a new home at the same time as starting a new school. This has the effect of helping them adapt to a new way of life altogether, rather than adding to their problems.'[29]

In 1974 Mr A. J. Davis, now Assistant Director of Education for the County Council, stated that because there were 'spare seats' at Hugh Latimer School the school had no long-term future, but there were 'no plans to close it at the moment'.[30] In 1980 the County Education Director, Mr Andrew Fairburn, announced that the Hugh Latimer School was to be closed. There had been a very rapid decline of children in other infant schools in the area, so pupils could be transferred from what had always been regarded as temporary accommodation 're-opened in the main because of the Ugandan Asian influx'.[31] But the *Leicester Mercury* which in 1972 had described it as a 'stigmatised school', now carried headlines: 'School Parents Protest Over Closure Notices' and 'Angry Parents Fight to Save School'.[32] A group of mothers (some indigenous, some Asian) complained to the Home Secretary over the way in which the official notices announcing the closure were published: the Section 12 Notices, they said, were published in English only, but 80 per cent of the mothers who took their children to the 200-pupil school did not regard English as their first language.

The Headmistress, Miss A. E. Watson, looking back on the short but significant history of Hugh Latimer, described it as having developed from a 'refugee to a community school'. She remembered the school

> providing colour, warmth and security to those Gujarati children from Uganda of whom very few were fluent in English. But that was not our main worry. What we found that we could not overcome or make up, was the fact that children start school at the age of 7 or so in Uganda, and had not learnt how to play in the educational sense. We could not make the parents understand this lack either. But in those days of the first refugees, we let them do all the mathematics they wanted. A page of 'correct' ticks was one of the best therapeutic aids we had ... Our Ugandan Asian refugees have moved on to their secondary schools and one has gained 10 GCE passes.[33]

Despite all the protests, Hugh Latimer was closed and in April 1982 advertised for sale. The school was bought by the Shree Sanatan Mandir ('Honourable and Pure Hindu Temple'), an international religious and social organization whose leader on a visit from India urged that it 'become the Headquarters of all the Hindus in Britain'.[34]

The decision to open Wakerley secondary school in mobile classrooms in a field off Ethel Road in the Evington area of the city also met with scepticism and misgivings. Two Conservative elected members spoke of a 'makeshift school' being seen as a 'dumping ground', and as being 'the wrong solution'. 'The playing field site was needed for recreational use ... The Council should invest in bricks and mortar. It should be built in Spinney Hill Park.'[35] At a later Council meeting other Conservatives suggested the use of the Hillcrest Geriatric Hospital or a large factory warehouse for the school.[36] Two of the Conservative group voted against the emergency school altogether:[37]

> As an Authority we are simply passively and lamely allowing ourselves to carry the burden by absorbing the Ugandan refugees. The Government nationally has gone through the motions of getting aid through the Ugandan Asian Resettlement Board,

but this has not amounted to much. We should take a firm position and say to
the Government that we just cannot cope under the existing circumstances, and
tell them to treat it as the emergency it is. This is where our loyalty to the rate
payers should be.

Councillor Dorothy Davis replied that the Education Committee was equally
unhappy to resort to a temporary school: it would be far better to have a permanent building and it was hoped that the school would no longer be in use
by 1975.

By March 1973 the staff of the school had been appointed, and despite
delays because of flooding of the site, the school was opened in summer 1973.
The Director of Education had again blamed 'the shortage of teachers...
we have tried every procedure to recruit more staff', but he made no mention
of trying to recruit from Ugandan Asian teachers who were jobless and anxious
to be back in employment. For the three years of its existence the school continued to be controversial. Left-wing groups opposed it on 'apartheid' grounds,
and when a local man complained that it was unlawful for it to be used just
for Asian children, the case was taken up by the Race Relations Board and
rejected. Thereupon the National Front issued a statement that it agreed with
the Board's findings:[38]

> It will be a relief to English parents whose children are at schools where they are
> so numerically overwhelmed by immigrants to see the Race Relations Board go along
> with us on the policy of racial segregation as at Wakerley school... We trust they
> will waste no time in effecting this policy in other schools where there is a majority
> of coloured or whites.

Contrary to the wishes of the National Front, in 1975 the school merged
with the adjacent secondary-comprehensive school. There was no organized
protest as there was over the closure of Hugh Latimer, for its temporary huts
were very different from the solid Victorian Gothic of Hugh Latimer, and
its first Headmaster became head of the comprehensive school into which it
was absorbed. Eventually the huts were demolished and its function as a reception centre for non-English speaking immigrants was transferred to a vacated
school building and attached to the Rushey Meads secondary school.

A school which lasted just three years can be easily forgotten. But for its
500 or so refugee pupils who passed through it, Wakerley School was their
'own school'. All still remember the stability and the return to some form
of normality that it gave. Mr Roy Pennington, the first Headmaster of the
school, realized that the views of both parents and pupils about schooling had
to be taken into account. After the first term, he told the *Leicester Mercury*:
'The school is running immaculately... the Ugandan Asian children are very
examination conscious, *they prefer a more formal type of education* and want their
G.C.E.s.'[39] His pupils agreed. One of them (when talking to the author) said:

> Our parents did not march up to the school and tell the teachers how we should
> be taught... but the school met us halfway and because there were 13 teachers

they really got to know what we wanted. I think it was right to put us in with another school after three years . . . but before this we even designed our own school badge.

The report on the school given by its second Headmaster, Mr Brian Piper, at its final Governors' Meeting on 21 May 1975 sums up the importance of the school to the Ugandan Asian children:

> This school could so easily have 'gone wrong' to the eternal embarrassment and shame of the Authority and the City. If it has succeeded at all it is in no small measure due to the quality and dedication of the staff of this school.
>
> What has it achieved? The most significant, if intangible result has been the rehabilitation of the students in their own eyes. They have become intensely proud of the school as each venture in competition with other schools has brought the reassurance that they can cope like others. We have also succeeded, I think, in healing the scars of their refugee status and they seem to have come a long way emotionally from the rather tattered and apprehensive group which first joined us in May 1973. Successive Governors' Reports indicate how we have measured ourselves alongside our contemporaries in other schools.
>
> What has it not achieved? We could list endlessly the things we would have liked to have done better; in examinations, in discipline, and in the welfare and guidance of students. I note too that in the first twelve months 109 of our 300 students changed their address at least once.
>
> Over the years a large proportion of the school have still needed welfare grants and free school dinners. This indicates to me that the resettlement of Ugandan refugees in the City generally is still far from complete, but that the school has in some measure been an island of normality in an otherwise uncertain stormy sea. An average of 45% have free school dinners. Perhaps the best way to look at it is to ask another question. What would have happened if Wakerley had never been?

But in the months before Hugh Latimer and Wakerley opened, voluntary part-time schools were the only source of education for many of the refugee children. The first of these projects was organized by the Students Union at the then City of Leicester College of Education, Scraptoft. A move to insert a 'Welcome to Leicester' notice in the *Ugandan Argus* and local papers had been defeated at a meeting of the College Union, but the students resolved that they should do something to help the refugee children in the inner area of Leicester.[40] For three months from November 1972 children, all of whom were of junior school age, were contacted through the Council for Community Relations. The children were 'bussed' out of the town to the pleasant rural surroundings of the college; one girl remembered that 'When we went to the College, we started learning again after months away from our books. I had my first reading lesson in England from one of the College lecturers.'

The second temporary school scheme was run by the Rev E. Carlile, Chairman of the Leicester Council for Community Relations, who was also Vicar of St Peter's in Highfields. For three half-days a week, ten volunteers taught classes of children aged between 6 and 15 years. In the first week 20 children enrolled, by December 1972 there were 50 and there was a waiting list. Mr Carlile spoke of it as a 'school on a shoestring running in a church vestry', but saw it as a substantial contribution to meeting a very acute need: 'many of these children would have no school for three to nine months otherwise.' The scheme was approved by the LEA, who provided books and materials, but there was a desperate shortage of any type of textbooks. Most of the children came from the Highfields area, though some came from the Narborough Road several miles away. The children were described as 'speaking reasonable English – the language of education in Uganda. But they start school at 7, and so are behind English children and they have no knowledge of English history.'

Though the Community Relations Officer had kept the Ugandan Asian Resettlement Board in touch about the teaching scheme, the St Peter's scheme received no financial help even in the form of a token grant:[41]

> there are 50 children attending classes and they are in desperate need of funds. This would enable us to cope with more children . . . Similarly Centres could be set up in different influx areas if money were available. Sorry for pushing this issue but housing and education are our two main problems where it is difficult to find a short term answer.

The project ended at Easter 1973, but one of the children involved remembered that 'going to St. Peter's meant we were not just left in our crowded home, with a bewildered mother and no definite news of whether we would ever get back to school.'

Students from Leicester University also ran a project for Ugandan Asian children who in January 1973 were still out of school,[42] and a special summer school was arranged at a local Further Education College in July and August 1973 to teach English and mathematics 'to older pupils not yet at school'. Three-quarters of these were Ugandan Asians, so the Uganda Resettlement Board agreed that the scheme should qualify for a 75 per cent grant; the *Leicester Mercury* (7 July) recorded that 'the cost to the rate payers was therefore only £845.' All these projects helped to 'fill the gaps' until all the refugee children could be absorbed into the education system.

Bussing

Although Leicester received almost as many Ugandan refugee children as Ealing and Southall, and there was similar pressure for school places and a resultant increase in 'bussing' away from the children's own neighbourhood to schools which could accommodate them, this never became a subject for controversy as it did in the London boroughs. Leicester's avowed aim was to restrict the volume of dispersal of children, and the Director of Education always emphasized that it was not just immigrant children who were bussed, but 'white children have to fight for places in their neighbourhood schools'.[43] In contrast to the protests made by community leaders in Southall and elsewhere, the one Leicester Asian who submitted written evidence to the Select Committee advocated the redesigning of the schools' catchment areas and increased bussing in order to avoid ghetto schools.[44]

None of the parents involved raised any objections to bussing, including even parents of primary school children, some of whom travelled daily from the Melton Road area to Hugh Latimer School in Highfields. To them the fact that their children were back at school was all that mattered: the more abstract debate about the desirability of ethnic mixing and contact with the 'host' culture in suburban schools was never mentioned. Instead, when talking about their children's schooling parents went into detail about how they had had to pay fees for secondary education, which outside the large towns meant boarding fees as well. In Leicester they were glad that there was 'a secondary school in every district'.

Some of the older secondary students and their parents would in fact have welcomed even longer-distance bussing, out to the county areas. But as in the provision of housing, the surrounding shire authority regarded the Ugandan Asians as the City of Leicester's problem. So though there were some vacancies in the county's upper schools, there were no offers of help. Because these schools had 'A' level courses, they were very attractive to the refugee students. In an interview, one of the parents, who had been a teacher himself in Uganda, argued that when the city and county were combined into one Education Authority in 1974, there was even less reason for rigid catchment areas. He said: 'There are no longer boundaries between the City and the other schools. Why could not our children go there for their "A" levels? We would have arranged our own transport.' His son, however, had a different view of the situation. He felt that there had been little opposition to bussing in Leicester because it had taken place within the city. In 'the target schools', Asian children often outnumbered the indigenous. He insisted that 'when a few of the Asians including Ugandans went to Further Education Colleges distant from Leicester, there was opposition and fights – literally.' The Education Authority admitted that there were pockets of resistance even within Leicester itself: in 1975 there were two schools, both on council estates, where 'because of overt racial prejudice, the decision had been made not to send children.'[45]

Bussing became an issue too, albeit for a brief time, at Judgemeadow secondary school, which was highly popular with Ugandan Asians. Opened in 1972, and situated in a pleasant Evington residential suburb, from the start it received a substantial number of Ugandan Asian pupils. The headmaster had consistently refused to refer to them as 'bussed' students, insisting that they were 'commuter pupils'. In 1975, as part of the secondary schools reorganization debate, a plan was mooted to convert this school from being an 11–16 to a 14–18 age school, accepting pupils who would come from outside its immediate catchment area. The Parents Association opposed the plan: '1,200 children could be bussed from the direction of Highfields... the school would become 98 per cent black... a very awkward social balance would be created.'[46] But the plan was dropped and the Ugandan and other Asian pupils continue to 'commute' to this 11–16 school.

Discussing the decision by Ealing to phase out its practice of bussing Asian children by 1981, an editorial in *The Times* argued: 'Whether bussing is in the interest of the children concerned is always a delicate question, with the answer depending very much upon local circumstances and attitudes.'[47] Would the Ugandan Asian parents have protested about the bussing of their children in Leicester if there had been channel for such a protest? Although the Select Committee was told there was not a 'single responsible immigrant citizen or parent on governing bodies in Leicester... this has given the impression to the immigrant community that they are not given a due place in the running of schools',[48] this was misinformation, for there were 19 managers of primary schools from ethnic minorities and four of these had lived in East Africa.[49] They were presumably in touch with some at least of the Ugandan Asian parents, and could have protested against bussing had this been necessary.

The Ugandan Asians' own expectations

In May 1973 Leicester's Director of Education gave the Select Committee his opinion that

> many Ugandan Asian pupils are already highly educated. Most Asian pupils are motivated by an intense ambition and by an appreciation of the values of school education. Their aspirations and their excellent behaviour are examples to us all. The danger is that some indigenous pupils regard such model pupils as targets for criticism.[50]

But he offered no explanation why in the light of this there were so few immigrant pupils in the city's grammar schools (there were only 3 per cent in 1973). A clue may be found in the report by the Leicester and Leicestershire Schoolmasters Association:[51]

> Indians from East Africa produce another kind of difficulty. They cannot follow English as spoken by the English. Yet they always think they can speak English. They learn by rote ... they cannot believe that anything in their own words can be a better answer than a question from a book.

And the Select Committee was told that 'Asian parents did not appreciate the broader curricular approaches and the acceptance of different ways in which learning can take place, which are characteristic of English schools.'[52]

All parents tend to judge and influence their children's education in the light of their own schooling, and for the Ugandan Asians their educational goals formed part of the 'cultural map' transplanted from Uganda to Leicester. If Ugandan Asian parents in Leicester subscribed to the idea that education can accomplish anything, they did so because that was what they had believed in Uganda.[53] There the educational selection at the end of primary schooling had been all-important, for secondary schools had functioned as key channels of social mobility. In the last phase of colonial rule in Uganda, an attempt was made to initiate schools of the 'secondary modern' type (as established in the UK by the Education Act 1944), and 'modern' courses were recommended for those failing to gain entry from junior to senior secondary school; but Asian parents refused to send their children to these schools. They were criticized by educationalists for not accepting their children's limitations and having unrealistic aspirations, for generally Asian candidates had a high failure rate in the School Certificate examinations. One of the legacies of colonial rule was the demand by Asians for traditional British education, with examinations and paper qualifications. And it was just this type of education that the Ugandan Asians looked for in Leicester. No wonder, then, that teachers expressed reservations about the refugee children's ability to cope with the more progressive British schools. 'They will have to face the hard and subtle challenge – to learn to relax, to explore for themselves and set their own pace, rather than doing what they are told.'[54] And in the speedily produced pamphlets[55] distributed in the camps, emphasis was laid on the need for play and free activity in primary schools. But what the Ugandan Asians wanted was more, not less, of formal and traditional schooling, because 'in a society... where, in the colonial period the ruling class was British... British ways became for the Asian middle class, a mark of status. The acquisition of British speech, manners and education were all valued.'[56]

In 1972 the involved debate about the need for Leicester's schools to recognize the cultural backgrounds of all their children was just beginning. But the refugee children and their parents were not concerned with it: 'We were anxious just to get back into school. I know it would sound good to say I was interested in the history of India... but all we wanted to do was to pass examinations.' As another explained:

> At that time we wanted nothing but to be out of the house and back at school.
> But I always said I wanted to do subjects that would get me a job. Indian things
> don't teach you car maintenance. It was bad enough being called a refugee outside
> school. Inside we just wanted to be normal pupils and not different.

Looking back, however, others felt differently:

> I know now that our Ugandan children missed out on a lot. But our parents didn't
> see anything wrong with paying for a 'British' education in East Africa and they
> were too busy or too crushed to start complaining about having the same curriculum
> here. The only thing they complained about was if we did not do well, they didn't
> care about what we were learning. It was only when many of us began to fail 'O'
> levels that they began to ask questions. Besides we did have our own 'hidden
> curriculum': we went on talking Punjabi or whatever and we knew about folk stories.
> And at that time, I wanted it to stay hidden: it was our private world that we had
> brought with us.

There was yet another reason why the refugees concentrated simply on gaining access to Leicester's schools and colleges. Before the expulsion pupils and students in Uganda were the most disadvantaged of the British Asian community. Because of government restrictions on their trading and other employment activities, parents were unable to pay school fees and so their children had been compelled to leave before completing their Cambridge Certificate Examination. Non-citizens were unable to enter Makerere University. And by 1970 the situation was that 'Parents and younger children receive their vouchers for the U.K. in advance of their older sons and daughters, so that a young teenage boy or girl is left behind in Uganda, lonely, penniless, unemployed and forbidden to study.'[57] British education in Britain was for many a longed-for ideal. The most prestigious schools (including those established by Asians) in East Africa were exported versions of the British public schools staffed by expatriate teachers. Education in the UK was considered superior to anything that East Africa could provide especially when the African governments began a determined attempt to 'Africanize' the curriculum of the schools and favour the admission of African students to the higher levels of secondary education. Asians did not approve of the well-respected Cambridge Overseas Examination Board being replaced by a locally administered secondary schools examination. Even before their enforced expulsion, Asian parents were sending their children to the UK for education and they had been condemned for this by Amin in December 1971. And earlier, in 1968, a Leicester teachers' survey had commented on the fact that in one inner city girls' secondary modern school 17 per cent of Kenyan Asian girls were separated from their parents who were still in East Africa. The girls were living with older brothers who had themselves often come to the UK to complete their education.[58]

A wasted asset: Ugandan Asian teachers

In contrast to curriculum content and bussing there were other Central Government policy decisions which, when applied to Leicester, were resented by the refugees. First, there was the non-recognition of the professional qualifications of Ugandan Asian teachers.

It has been estimated that 5 per cent of the Asians from Uganda were teachers.[59] Locally, the British Asian Welfare Society was able to produce from its register of refugees a list of 14 male and nine female qualified teachers, all of whom had been in posts in Uganda in 1972, and of whom four had been headmasters. All of those listed had degrees or recognized teacher training qualifications acquired before Ugandan Independence. BAWS campaigned on their behalf and its spokesman Dr Seth asked: 'Why aren't we using them... They are doing menial jobs... there is a chronic shortage of teachers. Why should they go on a one year course when they have worked under British rule in East Africa and were British trained?'[60] In 1973 (10 May) the Education Authority was placing half-page advertisements in the *Leicester Mercury* for 'Teachers: suitably qualified and experienced required to teach immigrant pupils of secondary age', yet six of the 23 teachers who had taught in junior secondary schools in Uganda were employed in semi-skilled factory jobs. The problem was that these teachers, like other professionals, had not bothered with the administrative nicety of applying to be 'recognized' by the DES when they had qualified, since they had envisaged no career outside the Ugandan teaching service. The DES recognized East African teachers if they had applied before 1968 (the date of Ugandan Independence), irrespective of the year that they had qualified. Only those who had had the foresight to have made this application were entitled to teach in the UK and also to claim full credit for service in Uganda. Thus a situation arose in which Ugandan teachers could not teach, although in places like Wandsworth children were being sent home from school for lack of teachers.[61] A further irony was the fact that in Uganda itself a recruiting drive was launched to encourage Asian teachers in Singapore and even from the Indian subcontinent to come to Uganda to replace those who had been expelled.

One of the Leicester teachers did in fact contemplate going back to Africa and was interviewed at the Nigerian High Commission in London by a recruiting agent sent from Lagos to woo Ugandan Asians to enter the Nigerian education service. An editorial in the *Times Educational Supplement* (28 December 1973) suggested that General Gowon of Nigeria was more astute than the DES:[62]

> Is the quality of our own teachers so good at understanding the problems of immigrant children and communicating with them, that we cannot find some useful role for Ugandan Asians in our Schools? Or is it that the racist stereotype of the B.A. Calcutta (failed), still haunts the minds of our education establishment?

Neither the City of Leicester College of Education nor Leicester University's School of Education responded to the plea for special crash courses made by Professor J. A. Bright, a former Dean of Education at the University of Makerere.[63] There is no doubt that these teachers could have been used to help the Ugandan Asian children settle into schools. They wanted a job straight away rather than having to spend three years following the same training route as 18-year-old girls which was what the DES advised. Brian Jackson of the Advisory Centre for Education continued to campaign for teachers to form a 'flying squad' who would go into areas like Leicester 'where despite the Resettlement Board, the refugees are settling with the friends, cousins, curry shops and Indian cinemas'. Nationally only 14 teachers had begun the three-year course: they had enrolled in January 1973, and it was reported that the handful were unlikely to complete the course, because of the difficulties of keeping in touch with their families, the cost of buying school books and other hardships.[64] None of the Leicester Ugandan Asian teachers resumed their careers despite the Director of Education's claim that the 'city is ahead on ideas about migrant education'.[65] A decade later, much greater sensitivity was shown to teachers among the Vietnamese refugees. A special short course was mounted for them, although they were faced with a much greater task in becoming competent in English than the 'wasted' Ugandan Asian teachers.[66]

Student grants

As well as being involved with refugee teachers and children of school age, the Resettlement Board was also concerned with helping Local Authorities with their British Ugandan Asian students. The first group were those students following courses or who had been about to start courses in Uganda. They faced severe interruption to their education, unless special arrangements could be made for them in the UK. The second group were those who were already embarked on courses of study in the UK. Unfortunately the Resettlement Board's power was restricted to British passport-holders domiciled in Uganda on 4 August 1972, and to the children of British passport-holders who had come to the UK. So, as the *Guardian* (29 September) pointed out, 'there will inevitably be hardship cases falling outside of the categories so defined: so far as the students are concerned, we would urge a humane rather than a legalistic approach.' By 3 October 1972 the Resettlement Board announced that they had been authorized to say that Local Authorities 'will be invited to waive existing resident requirements in respect of Ugandan Asian students and to consider them for grants on the same basis as ordinary students. The Board will reimburse Local Education Authorities for the full cost of grants to Ugandan Asians in the present academic year.'[67] But even this did not help all the Ugandan Asian students, particularly those who were in Further Education Colleges. Term had already started, and the colleges, unlike the universities, did not have the freedom to waive the payment of fees. There was the case of one Leicester student who was half-way through his 'A' level course. The money his parents sent when they were in Uganda was frozen; then they arrived in a Resettlement Camp, and as the eldest son he felt it necessary to take a factory job:

> I couldn't hang around not having fees or anything. My family wanted me to stay on, but I had no peace of mind, or money. If I had known by mid-September that I could get a grant then it would have been different. The government knew about this condition since the beginning of August 1972.

The Co-ordinating Committee worked with the United Kingdom Council for Overseas Student Affairs to compile a register of Ugandan Asian students already in the UK who had been deprived of financial support hitherto. By late September the number on the register amounted to 263 described as being in 'dire financial straits'.[68] Some of these were Ugandan passport-holders, some were British passport-holders. For the first category there was a further hardship. Many of them had visas which were due for renewal, but this depended on their being able to prove themselves financially self-supporting. There were Leicester students who, by the beginning of October, were totally dependent on the generosity of fellow students. The majority had received no money since August: 'They paid £3.50 each week for rent in their Jermyn Street, Leicester house, £2.50 a week on food... two brothers have just £30 left until they receive aid.' Another student was keeping himself and his brother on £4 a week social security. Some students paid 60 visits to the local DHSS: 'We queued for hours, only to be told that we were entitled to no money at all.'[69]

In October, a letter from the Secretary of State finally allowed LEAs to use their discretionary powers to make awards to Ugandan Asian students. Leicester, having been invited to be sympathetic, appears to have responded positively. Grants were given to both university and further education students whether they were British passport-holders or not. However, not all the students could be accommodated in the city's colleges, and some found places at Kettering College. The Principal of the college claimed in a controversial debate over the number of Asians at the college: 'We have been absorbing an "overflow" of immigrant students from Leicester, and this number has increased with the Ugandan Asian situation.'[70] Leicester found that it had to pay substantial 'out of county' fees for these students, and after 1973 the students who had arranged their own entry to Kettering College were placed in Leicester's colleges. Leicester paid a travel subsistence in cases of 'extreme hardship', and BAWS approached the Ugandan Asian Relief Trust for help towards the cost of meals and transport.[71] Most of the students, however, found gaining a place in either further or higher education was difficult, even if they had passed a qualifying examination, and for most it meant waiting until a year after they had arrived. To avoid this the President of the National Union of Students, Digby Jacks, suggested that Student Union buildings could be used as day centres. 'These people are British citizens. We cannot give them that right and as soon as they need to use it, dole it out so grudgingly, with such bad grace that they will feel like intruders here.'[72]

At university level, the Committee of Vice-Chancellors and Principals made an official approach to the Ugandan Resettlement Board stating that it was confident that universities would be sympathetic towards expelled Ugandan students, and would circulate information to the universities through a special section set up at the Universities Central Council of Admissions. Leicester University along with others said it would welcome Ugandan Asian students subject to the necessary finance being found from governmental or voluntary sources. One of the most positive statements was made by a representative of St Andrews University:

When there were Czechs and Hungarians there was a centrally inspired policy [for dealing with refugee students]. There will be some young men and women who have already begun their studies in African Universities ... there will be others too, with the ambitions of their family behind them who will have been training with University education in view ... Scotland has unemployment, but Scotland can profit from the arrival of a small number of alert, hardworking and ambitious men ... the students could be drawn from this community ...

He also said that Ugandan Asians had the same frugality, sobriety and industry as the native Scots. It is something of an anticlimax to note that St Andrews could only admit 'six refugees' at the most. In general, institutions of further and higher education were only too happy to bend the rules, so long as the finances were taken care of. And once they had gained admission the refugee students, with very few exceptions, successfully completed their courses of study even though this meant for many of them that they had to start from the first year of the course. Often no recognition was given for parallel courses that the students had already completed in Uganda.[73]

3. EDUCATIONAL PROVISION IN THE RESETTLEMENT CAMPS, 1972–1973

A suggestion was made early in 'the emergency' that the Royal Army Education Corps (with its 'unrivalled experience of dealing with boys and girls whose education has been interrupted by parental migration') should be employed in the Resettlement Camps and reception areas such as Leicester, to counteract what was perhaps the biggest educational hazard, the psychological effect of being uprooted; but this was nowhere initiated.[74]

The accounts gathered from those Ugandan Asians of school age who received some of their education whilst in the camps, or who went to local schools or colleges near the camps before settling in Leicester, are vivid and revealing. The most abiding impression was that they were, indeed, being taught in a transit situation. Different camps adopted different strategies. Some relied almost entirely on resources within the camp, volunteer and Ugandan Asian teachers. But Stradishall, the first centre to receive the refugees, worked from the start with the local LEA.

In 1972 scant regard was given by educationalists to the importance of children retaining their own community language during this period of great psychological uprooting. One of the refugees, who later came to Leicester, recalled Sradishall and its rules:

> There was the rule of no Gujarati speaking in the classroom for anyone over nine years old. Our secondary school was called 'The Flying Wing School'. There we had lessons about British life styles. We were told about the rules for 'O' levels, which sounded much easier than our School Certificate! We came into contact with English teachers, and we thought that they too were easy on discipline.

But others who had been at the same camp remembered their parents' pleasure at receiving the pamphlets on the British school system, produced by the Advisory Centre for Education, in Gujarati as well as English. The Centre produced these within 48 hours. They were funded by the Rowntree Trust and copies were distributed to all the camps.

At Tonfanau Camp in Merionethshire the Advisory Centre for Education team used expertise previously acquired at a different type of camp – a Butlins Holiday Village where they had run an Education Shop. They organized a parents' centre where adult refugees could come in and talk about education matters.[75] One young married woman remembered her stay there:

> Remote it may have been, but I arrived with my brother and his family the first week of October. Thanks to the advice, guidance and help in the camp and a local education official who visited us, within two weeks I had started an Education degree in Birmingham. Perhaps the advice came too quickly: I left here after the first terms. A Church of England Training College was too much for me, a young Muslim refugee.

And at the Greenham Common Camp there was praise for the help received from Berkshire Education Department, who re-established a school formerly used for the children of service personnel, staffed by two ex-RAF education officers, in a corner of the camp. By November 1972 all those of school age in the camps were receiving at least some tuition. Some of the camps were using their Ugandan Asian teachers. The older pupils had started on 'O' level courses and students were receiving advice over their admission to further education or university. There was even the hope that some would be sent to top-rank boarding schools.[76] There was general agreement among the Leicester refugees that those of them who had been in the camps fared better with regard to immediate facilities than those who came direct to the city and might have been without a school place.

4. CONCLUSION

Many of the refugee children of 1972 did not 'miss out' or fail to achieve in terms of formal education despite the formidable obstacles that they had to overcome. Of 79 secondary pupils followed in one study,[77] 28 had attained a degree by 1982. Of those who were among the first to obtain degrees, the majority did so through originally availing themselves of full- or part-time 'A' level courses at local Colleges of Further Education. After 1976 an increasing number went to the city's Sixth Form Colleges (based on its former grammar schools). Those who have gone on to higher education have followed the pattern of others from East Africa and the subcontinent, mostly choosing science and business courses. Examination successes are particularly important to refugees. As a Jewish refugee student in the 1930s had noted:[78]

> If one is to attempt at all to pinpoint the moment I stopped being a refugee this was probably it: the day I passed my School Certificate. From then on I had increased confidence and security and looked forward to the future with a reasonable amount of optimism.

And as far as Leicester's education system was concerned, it was Councillor Dorothy Davis who put the Ugandan Asian 'crisis' in perspective. Just a year after the expulsion had taken place, she said:[79]

> In spite of the apprehension of a year ago, when the Ugandan Asian crisis broke, *we are relatively better off now for school places than we were then.* The log jam has been broken ... Government grants and permits in connection with the Ugandan crisis have helped in the overall situation considerably.

Chapter 7 The housing question

1. INTRODUCTION

The access by ethnic minorities to various categories of housing stock has been much researched. One of the major themes has centred around the notion of 'housing classes'. A highly theoretical debate has been conducted by urban sociologists into interpreting the underlying structures and processes of industrial cities, which has its base in the accepted fact that housing, though essential, is a scarce resource: thus groups who have different access potential are 'classes' in competition with each other.[1] Black immigrants are seen as the most disadvantaged in this competition, and especially those who are newly arrived: generally, it is said, immigrants are in no position to acquire public sector housing. At the same time immigrants lack the necessary finance to own good quality owner-occupied accommodation in the private sector.

Interrelated with these continuing debates are theories which concern the status of properties. In most British cities the status of properties in the suburbs is higher than that of accommodation in the central zone. If an ethnic minority takes part in the drift out to the suburbs, this is seen as indicative not only of their increased prosperity, but also of their adaptation and acculturation. However, there are sometimes positive reasons for ethnic minorities 'clustering together' and this can happen outside the area where they first settled in the inner city.[2] Sometimes this residential clustering has been actively encouraged by Asian businessmen for their own interests (allegedly this happened among Pakistanis in Bradford).[3] Some observers have, then, concluded that 'the ghetto must now be recognised as an established feature of our inner cities.'[4] All the surveys directly relevant to Ugandan Asians and their access to housing in Leicester relate to the private housing sector.[5] Because Leicester has traditionally very little private-rented furnished accommodation it was 'inevitable' that the refugees would share houses (particularly as owner-occupiers). A fairly accurate count of immigrants arriving was 3,900 by March 1973 and 5,000 by August 1973,[6] and this caused an enormous rise in the incidence of shared housing – a phenomenon not previously common in Leicester. The newcomers were of necessity forced into the 'ethnic rented sector' for the first years, taking up housing in the Highfields area of Leicester, where houses were generally in a poor state. However, the majority had achieved owner-occupier status within five years. They found the Belgrave area, already developed by Kenyan Asians, particularly attractive.[7]

2. HOUSING: 'OUR BIGGEST PROBLEM'

Asians still left in Uganda when Sir Charles Cunningham visited Kampala early in October read a local newspaper interview in which he stated that the 'Resettlement Board's job would be much easier had it just to find employment rather than accommodation'.[8] The Board had received offers of help from some private landlords, but this accommodation was always on an unsatisfactory temporary basis. If the Asians read the few job advertisements by UK employers which appeared in the *Ugandan Argus*, they would have noted that the firms always added that 'no accommodation can be provided'.

In Leicester the most frequently discussed of all the crucial problems involved was how to balance the existing housing stock against the unpredictable numbers who would arrive from Uganda. Having tried first to discourage the Asians from coming to Leicester at all, the city's officials and councillors decided that only those refugees who fell within the designated official category of being 'temporarily homeless' would become their responsibility and would qualify for an offer of council-owned accommodation. But the Social Services and the local Shelter Group pointed out that this was futile: the existing facilities could at a stretch accommodate just 20–30 individuals. Official policies varied: one was to encourage 'people of goodwill' to register their offers of accommodation; another proposed the setting up of special reception centres, offering temporary accommodation, which would be run by BAWS.

The Council did indeed have a problem. Leicester was then building 1,000 new homes a year, but there were around 10,000 people on the Council's housing list, and the average waiting time for a council house was 15 months. Leicester had had plans to improve its inner city area since 1964. This had meant initially a large-scale clearance, and in the five years before the Ugandan Asians arrived 4,000 properties were demolished but only 3,000 built. In effect, without government aid the Council could provide little help on the housing front. Alderman S. Bridges said at the time that 'if we just had Government co-operation then Leicester could accommodate 20,000 ... trying to prevent them coming here is like spitting against the wind.'[9] In these circumstances the Council was firm on one policy in particular: no concessions would be made to the rule that one year's residence within the city was necessary before an applicant was considered eligible for a council house. Also, because immigrants had apparently entered the private housing sector because that was what they wished to do, initially this was assumed to apply in the case of the Ugandan Asians too. No one from the Asian community spoke against this presumption; BAWS actually confirmed it; and there were optimistic reports about the Kenyan Asians, who had been well able to care for themselves and were now to be found in suburban housing on the city's ring road.[10] But by September Council members were reporting to the Resettlement Board that there were '14 Asians under one roof'.[11] Alderman Bridges pointed out that there were sometimes as many as '24 to a house', but said that while it was true that use could be made of unoccupied properties, this was not a practical proposition. Other alternatives such as erecting prefabricated houses or using church halls had been considered by the Council, but these 'were just not on'.

There was also an unforeseen factor that complicated the situation still further: even if the councillors had been correct in assuming that the refugees would be able to move into private housing (and by their council house allocation policy they made it impossible for them to do otherwise), what they did not take into consideration was a sudden change in the house market. There was a housing shortage and a sudden escalation of house prices in 1971–73 which affected the East Midlands region, traditionally not an area of high-cost housing, so that inner area terraced housing in Leicester increased in price by at least one-third and better properties by two-thirds. The President of the Leicester and County Estates Agents Association spoke of the city 'facing a nightmare housing problem'. He pointed out that usual lethargic Local Government procedure entailed a three-year lapse between the planning stage and the erection of houses; that the delay in the proposed Beaumont Leys housing development had 'robbed the City of about 1,000 new homes', and that the situation was 'aggravated by the sudden influx of Ugandan Asians'. Unless the Council embarked on a crash housing programme he foresaw that 'there would be the threat of racial trouble of a kind which has already occurred elsewhere.'[12]

One result of this rise in house prices was that the slow trickle of ethnic minorities from the Highfields area into better housing stock in neighbouring Evington slowed down, as did the buying of semi-detached housing on new private developments on the outer ring of the city, particularly Rushey Mead and the suburbs of Wigston and Oadby.

And there was yet another temporary, but immediately important, factor: that for furnished rented accommodation the refugees were in direct, but unequal, competition with local students beginning their academic year in late September and early October. The Leicester Polytechnic students, in particular, were unwittingly competing for the same accommodation as the refugees. The Polytechnic was a rapidly expanding institution, which had late enrolments and could provide very little purpose-built student accommodation – in 1972 the Polytechnic with its 3,770 students had only 320 accommodated in halls of residence. Students snatched up and shared between themselves any cheap and furnished rented accommodation in Highfields and Westcotes, two of the areas where the refugees were also hoping to find housing.

A report[13] by the Manager of Leicester's first Housing Advice Centre (which had been opened by the City Council in October 1971 in the middle of Highfields, 'it being Leicester's policy to operate from centres in housing stress areas rather than from centrally situated premises') described how at first very few immigrants came for advice. 'At the height of the intake of refugees, most of the 782 enquiries at the Centre were from students.' The few Ugandan Asians who did come were the tip of the iceberg: victims of city landlords 'cashing in on the Asian crisis' and charging exorbitant rents for rooms. The landlords were generally believed to be 'often a friend or a relative', and 'the Ugandan Asians who had come to the Housing Advice Centre had refused to take legal action because of the family ties with the landlord and because they did not want publicity.' There were also those landlords who were actually living in the same house and would not accept that they had made a subletting, but merely 'charged' for a room. The Centre's Manager believed that intervention by the Local Authority would simply have made matters worse: the refugees would have been evicted. Stories of malpractices were repeated by many, especially high rents and lack of rent books. By contrast there were frequent evictions of their former tenants by the kin of newly arrived refugees. The Housing Sub-Committee of the Community Relations Council (on which BAWS was represented) concluded that 'in view of the delicacy of the situation the Committee would be wise to leave the matter alone for the time being.'[14] However, no one questioned publicly the practices of indigenous landlords in inner city areas and their preference for students rather than the refugee population.

3. LEICESTERSHIRE'S 'GREEN AREAS': A POLICY FOR NON-COOPERATION

In September 1972 there was a fairly optimistic forecast of how Local Authorities where there were few immigrants would respond to the Ugandan Resettlement Board's circular asking for offers of accommodation:[15]

Despite a general reticence to discuss this contentious subject, most local authorities, away from the stress areas, gave the impression that they would provide a limited amount of housing accommodation if asked ... There are fears of conflict between black and brown races in areas with large numbers of waiting list applications for housing.

Despite this optimism, neither Councils nor private landlords in the county and suburban areas surrounding Leicester, with the exception of Loughborough, offered any such help with accommodation. Yet there is evidence that at least some of the refugees would have settled in places where there were no previous immigrants. And previous immigrants from East Africa had found the smaller towns, within easy reach of Leicester, attractive places for settlement.[16] Liaison officers in the Resettlement Camps observed that 'Asians are discovering that small towns in Britain have all the amenities of large towns (this was by no means always so in Uganda) and at once, the ideas of settling into a smaller town becomes more attractive.' The Regional Officer of CCWEU, Himat Lakhani, pointed out that other smaller towns within travelling distance of Leicester had vacant school places:[17]

The reasonable strategy of getting groups of families to go together to places only a short journey from the dozen or so locations where they had contacts, would have fulfilled the nice distinction between persuasion and pressure, especially, when dealing with people who were tired and distressed.

The Shire and District Councils decided, however, that the refugees were

Leicester's problem, to be settled with Central Government support. Oadby was the first to announce it would provide no council housing,[18] followed by Market Harborough, Hinckley ('there is a lack of houses and education for such people'), Melton ('Asians must not have preferential treatment – they could be put into stately homes ... but let's put our original problems to rights first, before accepting more responsibility') and Market Bosworth (though here one member did oppose the majority, pointing out that 'this type of district is one which could accept them'). Lutterworth followed the other authorities in indicating that it had 'its own particularly acute housing problem', whilst Barrow-on-Soar decided in December 1972 that since no grant was available, it could not refurbish a church cottage. The chairman of Barrow Council rejected the suggestion that the rural councils in the area around Leicester should have a special obligation to 'lean over backwards' to help both the Asians and the people of Leicester, and also disputed the accusation that the housing list had been 'artificially inflated by 400'. The County Council Housing Committee opposed the use of Beaumanor Hall for the refugees because teachers needed it as a 'centre for conferences'. Barrow Council claimed that it had to look after its own, and that meant the people on its own housing list, not Leicester's Ugandan Asians.

In September Oadby District Council agreed in response to a second request from the Resettlement Board to open a list of people who were prepared to offer accommodation, but no offers came. Market Harborough stated that it 'would be nice if someone came forward', but no one did. A Blaby resident complained that new flats at Stockton-on-Tees had been offered to the Resettlement Board below their cost price. However, no such scheme was planned in Leicester.

Some of these housing policies were challenged, particularly by Liberal councillors. In Hinckley one councillor pointed out that the Home Office had said that if each Local Authority were to take seven families, all the refugees' housing problems would be resolved. What haunted these authorities was what would happen in the future and particularly with regard to policies about other immigrants. An Oadby councillor asked: 'Leicester's view is well known, but what of the Shire? With Local Government reorganisation in 1974, the County Council would become the first tier authority and become responsible for these problems.' Leicestershire's Alderman George Farnham, speaking for the Council for the Protection of Rural England, emphasized that the Structure Plan for the County was at risk:[19]

> the influx of any large number of people, particularly those who are to all intents
> and purposes foreign nationals, is not in the interests of Leicestershire and England.
> It is to be noted with alarm that such people have no wish to absorb the English
> way of life but prefer their inward-looking communities.

What this statement did not recognize was that the shire's housing authorities were not encouraging them to do anything else.

It was only in Loughborough that the Council decided to house a few families in property scheduled for demolition. There were several hundred Asians from East Africa already living in the town, and it was thought that 70 families would wish to join them. There was one refugee family already housed in the Shree Ram Krishna Centre. Loughborough's decision was immediately condemned by the *Leicester Mercury*: the Council's policy was the 'wrong kind of help'. Putting people into slums was no answer. Leicester had many such properties standing empty and rotting, but far better for the Asians to spend longer in Resettlement Board Centres than move into these. So the *Mercury* said it had been right all along:[20]

> Now people who scoffed when certain Councils said 'we can't take them' will realise that there was nothing special or inhuman behind the statements ... We have said from the outset that this area cannot cope ... We have also said that those who do come here must be cared for properly.

By October, Loughborough had refurbished 24 houses and its Health and Housing Committee had recommended a broadening of the Council's mortgage advance scheme so that Ugandan Asians could qualify. Apart from Loughborough, the only other housing authority in Leicestershire to grant a house to a refugee family was Ashby Urban Council; this action provoked public protest about 'queue-jumping'.[21] Loughborough was about to extend its refurbishing scheme to another ten properties when in November 1972 financial aid from the Resettlement Board was clarified. The Board was prepared to reimburse Local Authorities in full for the refurbishing of temporary accommodation which was under their control. But refurbishing meant 'the reconnection of main services and work necessary to make the accommodation habitable, but not necessarily to improvement grant standard'. Loughborough (as well as Redbridge and Harrow) protested about the Board reneging on earlier promises, and dropped schemes for providing further refugee accommodation.[22]

4. OVERCROWDING

Unless then the Ugandan Asians were 'homeless', in that they had physically no shelter at night, Leicester as a housing authority took no definite action at all to provide accommodation. It did suggest that there was always a place on the Council waiting list and the Rents Investigation Officer would help in cases of alleged malpractice. The result was what Baroness White described in the House of Lords as 'some really horrific figures of overcrowding'.[23] The true picture of what accommodation in Leicester was like for the refugees emerged in an interview in the *Leicester Mercury* of 22 September 1972. A husband and wife, their children and a grandfather were living in a 'small and dingy' house off the Melton Road (the grandfather, 'though thankful, thought his room was a prison'). Leicester's two Labour MPs, Tom Bradley and Greville Janner, also spoke in the Commons about the city's housing shortage and 'the shocking overcrowding causing hardship to the refugees themselves and resentment among neighbours'.[24] The research of the local Shelter

Group,[25] which was based on the 1971 Census, showed that overcrowding was already a feature of Highfields (in the Spinney Hill area it was estimated at 17.5 per cent of the population). The *Leicester Mercury* and the city Housing Committee's vice-chairman chose to comment on this, but they ignored the fact that research showed that the worst overcrowding, however, was in north Braunstone: in local authority housing and where there were few immigrants.[26] So the Ugandan Asians were not originally responsible for overcrowding, nor did they go to where it was worst.

In 1972 Brent Borough Council announced that it intended to waive its regulations about multi-occupation for a few months in the case of Ugandan Asians. Leicester, however, directed its Medical Officer of Health and Public Health Inspector to continue their normal inspection, but to take no legal action unless given the authority to do so. By 1973 BAWS was fighting 'to reduce the estimated 60 cases where Ugandan Asians are still living in overcrowded conditions in Highfields'. The worst case that it had reported was of 17 people, made up of three families, sharing one house in Mere Road.[27] The city's Health Department agreed that there was 'still some overcrowding ... we are surveying to determine whether the situation is worsening, which we believe it is not, or easing, or altering in any way.' From April 1972 the Housing Department had a registration scheme for houses 'in multiple occupation with more than two families', and had made every effort to persuade these occupants to put their names on the housing list. But the arrival of the Ugandan Asians had 'slowed down the process of registration'.[28] For their part the Ugandan Asians did not want to be openly associated with all this. One of them related:

> I went to a meeting in the Community Centre in September 1973 about housing.
> There were more Asian landlords there than there were tenants. They were saying
> things about knowing your legal rights. But those on the platform were the landlords.
> I knew my rights: that was to keep quiet, unless I did more harm to my family
> and other people. The head of Leicester's council housing said in July 1972 there
> were 7,000 on the Council list, by June 1973 there were 12,000 but no Ugandan
> Asian had a council house. So I knew that the only way was to get a deposit for
> a place of our own.

Others too said that if they complained about overcrowding they would be told it was their own fault for coming to Leicester. The city's 'Register' of multi-occupation was seen as a threat and its real purpose was doubted: 'All we wanted was peace so that we could work and get a better place to live in. There was no need of that Register, it did nothing to help.' In any case, there are different cultural perceptions of what constitutes overcrowding. Rukshana Smith has described how one family coped in the immediate time after leaving Uganda:[29]

> The refugees slept on mattresses and settees in the living room and kitchen. This
> arrangement was perfectly acceptable to them all, as they came from a society in
> which rooms were flexible and adaptable ... Having a family sleeping in every room
> did not worry [them]. It was normal. Only English social workers and journalists
> would have been horrified.

Two years later, though, 'without knowing it they had unconsciously accepted the Western ideal of a room for each purpose'.

It was a family living in similar conditions, this time the Karsanjis of Leicester, that *The Times* (3 August 1973) used to show what life was like for some of the refugees a year after the expulsion from Uganda. The Karsanjis, it was claimed, were living in 'poor sanitation and squalor'.[30] Because of this publicity, there was a special meeting of the City Council's Sub-Committee on Immigration. The Housing Department told the Sub-Committee that *The Times* had given 'a reasonable presentation of the facts'. 'Most immigrants seem to be ensconced with relatives and friends, there are 150–200 Ugandan Asians on the waiting list for Council houses, and the situation regarding availability of houses to purchase is now easier.'[31] The Chief Public Health Inspector was more specific: '937 houses are said to be occupied by 4,363 Ugandan Asians ... the new arrivals caused at least 10% of the houses they occupied to be legally overcrowded.' He added that movement of families from one address to another was continuous, so a large number of visits and investigations could result in only approximate statistics. He estimated that '8 per cent of the 937 houses were still legally overcrowded.' The Rent Investigation Officer reported that 'the Ugandan Asian family at the centre of this controversy' were not prepared to be helped. They had refused to go to the Rent Tribunal, and there were very few tenants who would give evidence against their landlords about what was a criminal offence: 'The immigrant community has the impression that the landlord has the power of life and death over them and that he has only to tell them to quit the premises and they will be forced to do so.'[32]

Overcrowding, whether of Ugandan Asians or others, continued. In 1975 the Spinney Hill Conservative Association published their report which claimed that 67 per cent of Asians in the area were living in illegal multi-occupation.[33] This report coincided with current speculations (especially by local Tories) that another 12,000 East African Asians could come to Leicester[34] following the proposal by Alex Lyon, Minister of State at the Home Office, to allow all British passport-holders and their dependants in that area to enter the UK during the next three to four years.[35] Once again, as had happened in 1968 and 1972, there were wild guesses by local politicians about how many Kenyan Asians Leicester would have to accommodate. The chairman of the Housing Committee pointed to the 14,000 on the city's housing list and he was joined in his call for a ban on further immigration into the city by the Senior Community Relations Officer, Barry Brazier. The latter was concerned that with the closure of Imperial Typewriters and the general instability of local industry, immigrants could once again become scapegoats. In retaliation, Dr Seth (described as 'of the India League') emphasized the capacity of immigrants not to be a burden on the taxpayer, and Dr Sayeed referred back to the 'unnecessary hoo-ha over the Ugandan Asian crisis'.[36] Fortunately, the scare came to nothing.

By 1975 the Ugandan Asians had their own reasons for not revealing their housing conditions:

We let the community leaders say how nicely we were settled in. Many of us had relatives in Kenya and if they could come then we would want to share what accommodation we had ... Let me tell you no one likes to go on being called a 'refugee' forever. It makes you feel hopeless and helpless. We were still hoping to get our assets out of Uganda. Once you get a council house or complain about a landlord you draw attention to yourself. Most of us had had too much of that already, and there were those lies in the false letter.

The first Ugandan Asian family to be granted a council house had certainly had its share of attention. The mother and the eldest sons had come to Leicester before the expulsion, and had put their names on the housing list. But when the family (there were six children) were granted tenancy in one of the least desired council properties they were accused of jumping the housing waiting queue. The chairman of the Housing Committee pointed out that had they not been housed 'they would probably have been split up at the cost of £150 a week to the Social Services', but he also emphasized that no preferential treatment would be given to Ugandan Asians: 'they have to take their turn like everyone else. I have stood by the pledge.'[37] The father of the family remembered what it meant for them:

Then it all started. Not only did the people here turn their backs on us, but then came the letters telling me that I should "Get out or watch out!'. We had four attacks on us with big stones in through the windows. Then the National Front told the papers we had plenty of money because of the family allowance and we had thrown out the furniture because it was not good. We lived through that, and the Council said we had done nothing wrong. The Asian leaders didn't help me; if the government had lent me money for property I would have paid it back by now. We are still in the same house.

The 'lies in the false letter' referred to a hoax letter which was posted to indigenous householders (especially in Belgrave and Highfields) in October 1972. Printed on a forged letterhead of the Department of the Environment, and signed by a 'Third Secretary' (with an African name), the letter warned the occupier of the house: 'We understand that you have a spare room in your house, we would like you to accept a family of Ugandan Asians.' Details of how much the government would pay (£10 per week), how the family was to be met at Heathrow and the number to be billeted in the house, together with provisions required, like rice and yams, are catalogued. Other versions, with even more distasteful language, also circulated in the city. BAWS and the Community Relations Officer asked that these be handed in at the Community Relations Office.[38]

Trivial though this evidence may appear – it was repeated in 1975 and later in various other cities – it is significant that it was remembered almost a decade later. The main effect was to reinforce the conviction of Ugandan Asians that they should 'disappear' as soon as possible into the Asian community and not make any demands (especially housing) that might draw attention to them as a group.

5. FINANCE AND HOME OWNERSHIP

Not all of the Asians had owned their own homes in Uganda,[39] and many had 'lived over' (or more accurately behind) their shops. But it was for house purchase in Leicester that any recovered assets from Uganda would have been used. This was often connected with the hope of starting up businesses in the retail trade. Certainly there had been indications that a government-initiated loan scheme based on the assets would be discussed. After all, the Ugandan government had compiled a register of their property before they left.[40] One source of house purchase was through insurance companies. Many of the refugees had life insurance policies with companies whose head offices were in the UK, so they hoped for loans on the security of these. When the Asian Task Force was set up by a group of well-known Asian businessmen, an approach was made to the Pearl and Prudential companies. This was followed in July 1974 by a joint meeting of the British Life Offices Association, the CCWEU and the Community Relations Commission. Because the issue was so 'extremely complex', local Community Relations Officers were told not to give advice to Ugandan Asian clients requesting help. But the direction from the Life Offices given to the refugees was that assets could only be paid if an individual could obtain Ugandan Exchange Control authority, and this was virtually impossible.[41] Insurance companies could neither pay the benefits in the United Kingdom nor cancel the Ugandan policy and transfer the value to a UK policy issued in its place.

One refugee, previously a Kampala accountant, said that as the companies had used the money for many years, and had put some of the premiums into investments all over the world, he and others deserved a fairer deal. While he approved of the government diverting £10 million from overseas aid to Uganda, 'this should be used for house purchase and business loans, not on community centres and so on.'

Every other avenue for obtaining loans was blocked. When the Bishop of Leicester had acknowledged in the House of Lords that a special scheme for loans might lead to a white backlash, he also stated: 'If Her Majesty's Government can face that point, I think they will get a response from the nation which will surprise them.'[42] Lord Colville replied that 'the right reverend Prelate ... said that we must be careful in the field of race relations because we could do a great deal of damage if the belief gained ground that public money was being made to Ugandan Asians but not to the existing population.' The granting of loans for mortgages or any other purpose was not *prima facie* a role that the government could assume. The only source would be the refugees' own pockets – from assets left in Uganda which the Ugandan government had promised them after their properties had been sold and paid into the individuals' bank accounts. He made no suggestions as to how this should be made to come about.

In Reading and Bristol innovatory schemes for local authority mortgages were suggested, but received 'a dusty answer' from the Resettlement Board.

Leicester's Community Relations Council unsuccessfully applied for an interest-free 100 per cent loan from Central Government to buy a few large properties and make them available to some of the refugees living in the most overcrowded accommodation.[43] This received no support locally, though Alderman Philip Hartley, the leader of Brent Council, gave a similar scheme his official backing. When the Uganda Evacuees Association had its founding meeting in January 1973 at the Town Hall in Brent, its first aim was to press for cash advances from the government to help with housing. Alderman Hartley said:[44]

> If the Government made loans to one section of the community, as against another, it would be showing preference. But the Ugandan Asians here are British citizens and the assets they have left behind must be considered British assets. If the Government is able to secure these then it should advance percentage loans against them.

As for those refugees without property assets, it was suggested that interest-free or low-interest loans be advanced against their future earnings. Despite discussion with the Home Office, and a proposal to set up a British Uganda Credit Loan Trust, with the bulk of the money coming from the commercial banks, in August 1973 the Home Office said that after further consideration it was unable to help in the matter.[45] Many of Leicester's refugees reacted by pointing out that 'We have always been credit-worthy. The banks and the Government know it and ignore all our past records.'

6. 'A PARALLEL HOUSING MARKET' AND THE ROLE OF THE VOLUNTEER VISITORS

In reflecting on their housing experiences, the Ugandan families referred to two particular facts: first, that they dealt exclusively with Asian landlords and agents, and second – and in reality of minor importance – the role played by the small band of volunteer home visitors, who though they merely hoped to alleviate some of the hardships in the first year after the expulsion, incidentally provided some means of access to the indigenous housing agencies. There is no lack of evidence that what is called a 'parallel housing market' exists when, because of discrimination by indigenous house owners and estate agents, Asians deal exclusively with Asians.[46] But that exploitation can still take place, especially in the rented sector, was apparent in the case of considerable numbers of the Ugandan Asians. Very few, as has been seen, took their case to a Rent Tribunal, but Councillor Arthur Hamlin, the chairman of the General Purposes Committee of the city, is on record as saying, 'Some of the Ugandan Asian refugees now living in Leicester are being exploited by their own countrymen.'[47]

An element of this exploitation, and one which had particular effect on the Ugandan Asians in the first year or two, was the concentration of house ownership in a few hands and the charging of exhorbitant rents – not only basic house rents but also rental charges on fittings, furniture and even outhouses. There was also a conspiracy of interest between landlords, agents and financiers (with companies, families and individuals often fulfilling all roles at once),

poor conveyancing practice and little security of tenure on rented accommodation or retail establishments. In 1973 it was estimated that 63 per cent of
the refugees were paying more than a third of their wages in rent: one such
was a family of nine who received £20.45 in supplementary benefit, £10 of
which went in rent.[48] But sometimes the landlords met their equals. One refugee
related how his uncle was paying £11 a week for a house in Belgrave, with
no bathroom, no hot water and an outside toilet. He had been a businessman
and when he found out 'how the British income tax worked', he blackmailed
the landlord. He made him 'put the rent down', put the amount in the rent
book and said that 'if he didn't hand over the difference in cash then he'd
tell the Income Tax.'

There were, however, plenty of refugees who defended Leicester's Asian
landlords. For one thing it was felt that the city's Housing Department was
more ready to report malpractices than to offer alternatives. As the refugees
saw it,

> We were told not to come to Leicester. We came, and overcrowded our families
> in houses. If we reported that, we were blaming ourselves. Then we moved into
> rented accommodation, and paid a high rent, and we were still overcrowded. So
> we moved again to a bit better place. But the landlords did give us a roof when
> no one else did.

And indeed within six years a number of the refugees had not only managed
to achieve house ownership but had also bought a second property and become
landlords themselves: 'As soon as we began to work, all this family began
to save, all of us together.' Several bought a second house for relatives who
might want to, or have to, come from East Africa, especially Kenya. All these
transactions took place within the Asian housing market, except for those families who moved out into the suburbs. Becoming a landlord meant something
beyond mere monetary considerations; it meant that status was regained within
the individual's community: a landlord is 'one who knows the ropes, and can
get things done'.[49] Only one form of landlordism was universally condemned:
the large companies, the 'faceless landlords' (described as being run by Asian
estate agents) who 'kept up high prices, and employ people to collect the rents
and want to force small landlords out of business'.

The influence of the voluntary home visitors was out of all proportion to
the small size of their team. The team consisted of a few dozen women,
untrained, speaking no Asian language (though later three Asian women participated), but determined to continue the 'welcome to Leicester' message of the
railway station reception. They worked in cooperation with the Community
Relations Council. The total operation, which lasted two years (though it was
carried on by some after that), cost just £15 which was all that the volunteers
claimed for their expenses. Yet their existence was widely known among the
refugees, for these were for many the only 'Leicester people', other than officials,
that they met during their first years in the city. They were a link with the

outside world, helping with access to schools, immigration problems, lost passports and above all housing.

The role of the home visitors in housing included the assurance that if
all else failed the refugees could return to the camps, [50] advice about landlords
and rent books, help in interpreting the application forms for council housing
and the system of allocation and, above all, their sympathetic but uncondescend-
ing attitude to the conditions in which the families were living. The volunteers
were also used as confidants about landlords who refused to issue a rent book,
sometimes because they did not want to declare the rent to the Inland Revenue,
or because the house was on a mortgage and the landlord was not allowed
to sublet by the terms of the mortgage.

The visitors themselves still remember their 'letter of introduction' (printed
in English) shown on their first visit, the damp rooms, the lack of basic amenities
and yet the hospitality extended to them. One Asian woman, remembering
her visitor, explained how much the volunteers had helped them: 'I would
like to see her again to thank her, not just for the blankets she brought, but
for making me feel that the state of the rooms was not my fault.' This feeling
was in sharp contrast to the way many of the Asian women felt about officials
'doing surveys', who they found were less sensitive to just how difficult it
had been to adapt to the very different houses from those which they had
known in Uganda. This proved a deterrent to their considering council accommodation since the Housing Department sent their officers to assess a family's
suitability for particular estates, as well as the ability to make a regular payment
of rent. It was believed, however unfairly, that these officers, unlike the volunteers, were measuring the households against an idealized indigenous standard.[51]

7. THE DISTRIBUTION OF UGANDAN ASIANS IN LEICESTER

In 1976 the Leicester Community Relations Council initiated the last of three
studies concerned with the location of immigrants in Leicester. This 1976
survey gave the total number of Ugandan Asian households as 704.[52] When
these were mapped, three major areas of settlement appeared: Highfields and
some parts of Evington, Belgrave, and across the city in the Narborough Road
area (see fig. 3). The results of this 1976 survey confirmed the hypothesis
that though the distribution of Ugandan Asians in Leicester took place over
a short period of time, 'clustering or grouping has still taken place in formerly
occupied immigrant areas of relatively old and low standard housing on the
periphery of the Central Business District ... the dispersal from Leicester
to other metropolitan areas has not occurred.' The substantial number of refugee families located in the outlying suburbs was accounted for by relatives
already located there offering accommodation to the newly arrived refugees.
Also within these areas, although generally defined as middle-class zones of
occupation, there were small pockets of cheaper or rented premises which

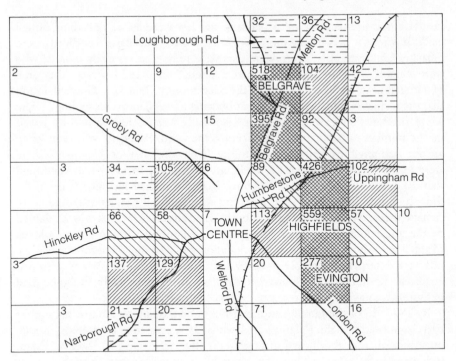

under 20 persons per sq km

—·—· 20-50

50-100

100-250

over 250

The map is divided into 1 km squares:
figures in the corner of each square indicate the
number of individuals resident in December 1973

Figure 3 Distribution of Ugandan Asians in Leicester, December 1973 (compiled from
the British Asian Welfare Society's register of new arrivals; the map does not show
those who failed to register at the BAWS office)

were made available. The emerging attraction of the Belgrave area, both on
account of its better housing stock and its potential for business enterprises,
was already becoming apparent.

Immigrants' perceptions of the Belgrave/Melton Road area seem to have
changed within a very short time. In 1973 it was 'a forgotten area with little
to offer compared to Highfields' which was already serviced by Housing Advice
Centres. Belgrave had a number of housing problems. There was lack of information on when rehousing from clearance areas would start: although information was sent by the Council to the landlord, this was not relayed to the
tenant. Above all there was lack of information about the proposed Eastern
Relief Road about which rumours were rife. People had difficulty in selling

property because of the road proposals, and few were aware that the Council could buy up the accommodation under compulsory purchase. Landlords were delaying improvements, there were excessive rents and very few tenants who were eligible for rent allowances had applied.[53] In a 1973 survey, this time of indigenous people in Belgrave, the Community Relations Council found that their chief complaints were about housing and Asian overcrowding.[54] The white residents suggested that rates (especially water rates) should be levied on the number of occupants. Significantly, the word 'Pakistani' was used when anyone had anything objectionable to say. 'Kenyan Asian' or 'Ugandan Asian' were terms used 'with at least a modicum of respect'. In 1973 a survey found that 70 per cent of houses in Belgrave lacked standard facilities.[55] By 1977, though, it was found that long-standing residents (all indigenous) wished to remain there, as did the ethnic minority householders.[56] This was explained by the attractions of the area: cheap terraced housing with an adjacent stock of small workshops provided accommodation and a labour force for small-scale business enterprises, notably in textiles. For those Ugandan Asians who had acquired the necessary resources to start up in business again, Belgrave had definite advantages.

By 1977, 13 of the families in the group of 68 studied by the present author had also moved into the Belgrave area, whilst 34 remained in Highfields, though most moved from the 'heart' of Highfields (that is, around Melbourne Road) to houses at the edge of the district, notably near to Evington or to the streets adjoining Highfields and Belgrave. Of the remaining 21 in the group, four had council accommodation and ten were living in the Narborough Road, whilst the others had property in the outer suburbs, Rushey Mead (with its new estate), Knighton or Oadby. Those who were able to buy property quickly were, naturally, the families who had managed to send assets out of Uganda before 1972. When they first came to Leicester, most of the refugee families – both those who came straight to relatives and those who went to the camps – moved frequently, on average three times in two years. The reasons were summarized by one Ugandan Asian woman: at first they had no possessions, 'then a few, now we have many and won't move again.' They moved, too, because they began to know the better districts, and how to judge 'a good house': 'Then I began to make judgments. As well as money you have to get to know about different conditions ... Would you know about buying a property in Jinja? So then we moved because we were wiser as well as having more money.'

The few who moved out to the suburbs did so because there were possibilities for furthering their business enterprises, and house buying there is seen as an investment, part of good money management policy (the fact that for a decade after 1972 house prices rose by an average of 16 per cent per annum and generally outstripped inflation was well appreciated). One of the suburbanites explained his motives:

You move into an area, open a supermarket or better still a post office business.

You open long hours, serve your customers well, get a good reputation, that's what I mean by being accepted here. It is good to be near a motorway – our people can visit us from every place, and we them.

For some families, however, government policies in relation to local authority lending had an unfortunate effect. These were families who wanted to buy older properties within the inner city, where Local Authorities had traditionally been more willing to finance mortgages than other sources. But in 1975–6 the Local Authorities were unable to do this directly; instead they had to obtain finance from building societies. In Leicester, as elsewhere, the building societies 'redlined' whole areas where they would not normally make loans. This meant that Highfields, Belgrave and parts of Evington and the Narborough Road were affected.[57] Another result was that the proportion of empty houses in Highfields was higher than in 1971,[58] yet house prices did not fall.[59] Although the end to 'redlining' was formally announced in September 1976, many of these families lost confidence in Leicester's Housing Department, and the majority turned to insurance companies for house finance. The families who did so lost out financially, because as low wage earners they received no tax relief on their interest payments.[60] But the city's Director of Housing, whilst believing that the Building Societies exaggerated the risks of lending on older properties, pointed out that funds in excess of the £1.14 million available to the City Council in 1976/77 were needed for general improvement in those older housing areas where the Ugandan Asians, along with others were concentrated.[61]

At the time when the Ugandan Asians were looking for accommodation the reduction in the supply of cheap housing caused by the Council's demolition programme was already being criticized.[62] In the early years of the 1970s Highfields was going through its worst housing and environmental period, the limbo between demolition and the first phase of the Renewal Strategy ultimately announced by the City Council in April 1976.[63] But it was also the time when the new high-rise flats and deck-access maisonettes were built on the St Peter's Estate in Highfields. In 1971 the then Conservative-controlled City Council formed a special committee which was to deal specifically with the 'social problems' of Highfields as an area 'of social evils and depravity'. But the Labour elected members claimed that the situation was exaggerated. As soon as Labour was in power, this committee was disbanded.[64] Conservative Councillor Barry Clayton later criticized 'the liquidation of the machinery, which could have dealt with the whole problem', especially at the height of the Ugandan crisis.[65] Although in October 1972 when the Ugandan Asians were moving into the area, two of the full-time social workers in Highfields were holding public meetings emphasizing to the refugees and others that the district was an area of great potential, those of the Ugandan Asians who moved into rented houses such as those around Bartholomew Street were certainly not convinced. Even more than in Belgrave, fears about the Eastern Relief Road exacerbated the housing blight.

By 1975 plans for the road were dropped, and by then there were residents' associations in Highfields which were formed to counteract the problems of prostitution, dumped rubbish and poor housing. But those of the refugees who had the means still felt the pull of Belgrave, though it was not until 1978 that the Council's Renewal Strategy began in that area. In 1975 too, when the then chairman of the city's Housing Committee was asked about a suggestion by the Race Relations Board that Local Authorities should disperse their immigrant communities, he stated that 'Leicester has no need to do so, coloured immigrants have dispersed themselves, many buy their homes and they have settled in Highfields, also immigrants are now living in Belgrave.'[66]

One of the Ugandan Asian women summed up her view of the two areas like this:

> It was in Highfields that I lived after Uganda. For two years I was afraid to go out at nights ... the Headmistress of my children's school said it was not safe for daughters. We were used to the 'kondos' [African robbers]. England was not as safe as we had thought ... Moving away was the best dowry I could give my daughters. It is a better area now ... but I would not move back.

Nevertheless, as was recently revealed, 'contrary to what people outside Highfields might think, a lot of people live in Highfields by choice.'[67] Highfields is a large area with a population the size of a small town such as Grantham. To the Ugandan Asians who still live there it is *where* in Highfields they live which is important: the streets near to Spinney Hill Park and East Park Road, for example, are seen as very desirable.

8. COUNCIL HOUSING

The Ugandan Asians continue to regard council houses as 'second best', even today, though a number of the older members and, by contrast, some of those who were schoolchildren in 1972 and are now married with young children of their own, have become council tenants. But for most, home ownership – or increasingly, Housing Association provision – is still preferred. One reason for this needs no further explanation: had council housing been allocated to them when they first arrived, then they would have readily taken up tenancies: 'We would have moved to Braunstone even, but the Council said: "No houses for Ugandans", so we did without then and now.' A second reason is the general objection to paying rent (this was before it became possible to buy council houses): 'Only a fool does so.' By the end of the 1970s some of the families had saved up to go on visits to the Indian subcontinent for family weddings and other events: 'Who wants to pay rent for an empty house? I can rent my own house to someone in my community and this will pay the rates.'

There remains also an inherent fear that to enter council housing is to encounter bureaucracy and officialdom: 'We just wanted to avoid anything like that again after Uganda.' The same misapprehensions about 'inspection' by Council officials before and after taking up council house tenure remain. Ten years after the worst overcrowding there is still misunderstanding of what this entails. One mother of a student said: 'You praise me for putting a bed in the front room for Dilip so he can study and sleep, but would this be allowed in a council property?' Now that the families are settled, they constantly host a steady stream of visitors from India, Kenya, Malawi and often from other places within the UK such as Brent, or Redbridge – sometimes for a few days, but mostly for a few months. There is in any case a shortage of large properties for single families in Leicester's council estates: certainly there would be difficulties if visiting relatives had to be accommodated. And for most Ugandan Asians here, haunted by memories of their own fate, there is still the wish to have a house where any relatives still living there could be accommodated in the event of their being forced to leave, as well as wanting to visit.

Another factor influencing perceptions of council accommodation was that the first estates that the refugees knew anything about at first hand were the least successful of those built in the post-war years. One of these, St Peter's, was opened in the year that the Ugandan Asians arrived. With its tower blocks hailed as 'the Hiltons of Highfields' and deck-access maisonettes, St Peter's has the advantage of being near to Asian places of worship and shops, but it has no large single units, and by the time the refugees had achieved the length of residence in the city necessary to qualify for council accommodation, this estate had acquired 'a far from happy reputation' – it was regarded as 'a dumping ground for problem families ... a black ghetto'.[68]

But perhaps the most important factor of all was that very soon after coming to Leicester the Ugandan Asians concluded that if they moved into council accommodation they would be the target of both verbal and increasingly actual physical attack.[69] The fate of the much publicized first Ugandan Asian family who had allegedly 'jumped the queue' in 1973 was noted and remembered. The first local election which the Ugandan Asians experienced was in June 1973, when the National Front had 26 candidates. In its election literature, housing was highlighted as of 'paramount importance': particular stress was put in its election statement that no immigrant should be allocated council accommodation while white people were still on the waiting list.[70] The man behind the Front's campaign, Graham Eustace, and the candidate for the Humberstone Ward, Terance Verity, both spoke of 'decent housing estates' being threatened by proposed allocations to Asians.[71] A pamphlet was circulated which showed Robert Carr, the Home Secretary, running with open arms towards a Ugandan Asian family, and brushing aside a pair of white old age pensioners. In 1974 the National Front issued a pamphlet to back its 'Housing Britons Before Immigrants' campaign, led by John Calver. This claimed that it had 'indisputable evidence' that by deliberate overcrowding immigrants would obtain council accommodation three or four times faster than indigenous people.[72] This campaign certainly acted as a deterrent to those contemplating joining the housing waiting list, and in personal terms was more meaningful than the counter-campaign of the Socialist Workers Party. To the SWP the blame for the problems of 30,000 Leicester families who in 1974 still lived in houses with neither their own inside lavatory, nor hot water, nor bath, lay with the Labour-controlled Council, who had granted planning permission for another 2 million square feet of office accommodation (when a million square feet was already standing empty) rather than building houses for working-class people. Their literature claimed that the Ugandan Asians were certainly not to blame: 'Now that the Ugandan Asians have been here some two years and no-one can say that their lives are very different than before.'[73]

Though Asians generally were in 1981 still under-represented on the council house waiting list, the Director of Housing saw a 'movement into the public sector which seems to be a continuing trend ... it is suggested that this was initiated to a considerable extent by the arrival of East African Asians.'[74] By the end of their first decade in Leicester, as hopes of returning to Uganda faded, Asians – especially the younger ones – seem to have been shifting in attitude and to see certain advantages in acquiring a council house.[75] One recently married couple claimed that they were typical of a new trend:

> Most of us still want a home that we own. But getting a council flat or house is
> a way of getting separate accommodation after we get married. A lot of us now
> want to live near but not with our parents-in-law. So the only way to do this, if
> you don't have the money for a mortgage, is to get into a council place.

Moreover, the more recently built inner area council accommodation, with its concentration on family houses rather than on flats and deck maisonettes, and on small developments rather than large estates, is seen as offering better value for money than the older schemes. Some Belgrave area families, who were still in rented accommodation in 1979, hoped to be rehoused in new council property near Loughborough Road. One middle-aged woman gave her reasons: 'We have waited so long to have a decent property ... This council estate has come to us and we will go there without fear.'

Chapter 8 Problems of adjustment: the women's views

1. INTRODUCTION

Little has been written on the emotional adjustment experienced by the Ugandan Asian refugees, although the effects of displacement on other groups has been the subject of comment and analysis. A survey of 20 women who, along with their families, were expelled from Uganda in 1972 and resettled in Leicester was undertaken between 1974 and 1978. Although this very selective sample cannot validly claim to reflect the general incidence of either the maladjustments of, or the coping by, women refugees experiencing the traumatic and rapid transition from one kind of life style to another, its findings can reasonably be regarded as indicative of the type of problems which faced the women refugees on and after their arrival in the UK. The survey showed that the economic problems and above all the subordination of their emotional needs to those of the culturally approved role were common ground to all.

2. THE GROUP

It must be emphasized that the group of women studied was never intended to be a properly representative sample of all Ugandan Asian women refugees. The participants were aged between 18 and 50, they all volunteered their opinions, and accounts were based on informal talks rather than firmly structured interviews; all the women spoke English with a good degree of fluency. Most were contacted through visits to their homes, but six of them were women who took part in the various group discussions about the establishment of a separate hostel for Asian girls in the city.

The women were predominantly Hindu, mostly of the Patidar and Lohana gnatis, there were four Sikhs and two Muslims. Fourteen out of the 20 were in work or at college, three were temporarily without a job and three were at home looking after their young children. Those who worked outside the home did so in factories, offices and shops. Except for three older women, all had had secondary education either in the UK or in Uganda, thirteen were married, four were betrothed, three were full-time students. In no way, then, were they typical of the vast majority of Asian women in the UK who at that time were factory shift workers, employed at the lowest end of the unskilled labour market, exploited and often socially isolated, nor did they belong to the other end of the spectrum, 'the establishment Asian women'.[1] Instead they emphasized that they were 'unspecial, except that we have all had a lot of troubles to face since we were thrown out of Uganda'. The link between them all, then, was that they had been refugees, 'having had to fight for a place again in life'. Eight of the 20 had been in Resettlement Camps and two had been separated in the period between September 1972 and the summer of 1973 from their 'stateless' husbands: one husband had been in a camp in Belgium, another in Austria. Those who had joined their relatives directly and had not stayed in the camps nevertheless spoke in varying degrees of their feelings of alienation, anomie and loss. The relocation process – both physical and psychological – followed the cross-cultural adjustment patterns of many other sojourners in strange social settings. Initially there was an elation at escaping from Amin's Uganda and a determination to start afresh and to forget the assets and the good life left behind: 'One must begin again a million times over.'[2]

But for many the process was not smooth. It was often painful, and involved unlearning as well as learning. Elation gave way to disillusionment. Fresh and daunting difficulties and complexities appear. Then the women began to have a growing insight into the harsh realities of the job market in 'prosperous Leicester', and they often did so before the male members of their families. They had to share household facilities, and the non-arrival of their packaged goods and chattels, which they had last seen freighted at Entebbe Airport, did not help their domestic situation. They felt the pressure too of being part of a community so frightened of losing its traditional values along with its material possessions that it reacted against any further change, particularly on the part of its women. Other immigrants can be sustained by the possibility, however remote it may be, of returning to their own country.[3] But within a year or two most of the women refugees recognized that even if Amin were to be deposed, life in Uganda would still be too dangerous for them, and if their husbands decided to 'take a chance' on going back, it would mean being separated. The longer compensation payments were delayed, the more remote became the possibility of receiving any lump sum of money. Emotionally, they went through experiences of 'shock-optimism-pessimism-fatalism'.[4]

3. THE NEED FOR COUNSELLING

It became clear that Ugandan Asian women together with other Asian women were articulating the need for some sort of client relationship with 'qualified counsellors'. The need of provision for 'worry relief' was constantly mentioned, and the term 'counselling' was frequently employed with a very extensive connotation. Whatever form this might take, it was agreed that this should be outside their immediate group. What made the Ugandan Asian need different from others was that when they most needed such help there was a singular lack of it. And even though they might have recovered from some of the immediate traumas of being a refugee, there were still long-term emotional scars.

Because the first generation of Asian immigrants underused the existing counselling services, it was assumed until the mid 1970s that their emotional (like other more practical) problems could be resolved within the family. But then social workers, psychiatrists and professional counsellors began to ask whether this underuse was because these services had not only failed to make themselves known, but also used Western-based therapies and made no concession to cultural differences.[5] For instance, when the Marriage Guidance Council used Leicester (among other places) in a survey which was meant to improve public relations and to show that clients had definitely benefited from the service, no mention was made of the existence in the city of a multiracial population, including several thousands of Ugandan refugees.[6] And when a short training course for Marriage Guidance Counsellors was held in Leicester in 1979, it was concluded that 'Asian problems are contained by and within the Asian community.'[7] But when a similar course took place at Southall, (a place which had also received substantial numbers of Ugandan Asians) it was resolved that 'the challenge to the M.G.C. and the Asian communities remains to discover ways in which we can effectively work to meet the particular needs of the immigrant societies within our culture.'[8] But all this took place almost a decade after the forced migration from Uganda. At the time when the refugee women most needed appropriate support there was virtually no recognition that there was any such need, or that there should be special sensitivity by existing services to the rapidly changed circumstances of the refugees. This was in contrast to the special provision made for the Vietnamese refugees when they began to come to the UK in 1979 when it was said: 'counselling the families had been a process involving support and guidance – to help them understand the changes and their own feelings ... most of the refugees ... are unaware of their own emotional health needs.'[9]

But the Ugandan Asian women were cognizant of their own needs, and they said how much they would have welcomed an agency or even just a single case worker who could have helped in the first few years after their coming to Leicester. But they did concede: 'We Indians are very good at keeping everything inside the family. When we can't do that, and only then, it is a ball of fire and the water has to be thrown on it by someone outside.'

Not only the women refugees suffered. The men, too, had problems of adjustment – though they dealt with them differently. Expectations of the accepted female role survived, but there were other more important factors. One young woman said:

Why do people always talk about us Asian girls? You are always asking about our problems. But our brothers and husbands are not asked about personal things, but about their views about jobs or the police and other changes since coming to Leicester from Uganda. There are a lot of Asian men who need personal help. It has been in the paper about some of their drinking and becoming alcoholics. And look at those advertisements for girlfriends in the Leicester Mercury – they are all men who pay to put those advertisements in.

In 1979 the newly appointed Director of the Regional Council for Alcoholism claimed that in Leicester 'first generation immigrant children are hitting the bottle.'[10] In another report a local psychiatrist said that alcoholism was 'on the increase ... what evidence there is shows that it is virtually unknown among Asian women.' Ugandan Asian men who had not been able to re-establish their former positions 'drink to narcose themselves from the reality of life and their perception of failure'.[11] But the women emphasized that outsiders frequently exaggerated conflicts within the Asian families. Marital problems did exist and were often more stressful than they had been in Uganda. But far more important were the effects of the loss of social position and of the life they had lived. Of course all these things are interrelated, they said, but being made a refugee explained the origin of most of their personal tensions.

4. PRACTICALITIES

None of the local organizations who had expertise in helping with personal emotional dysfunctioning saw the need to make any special effort – such as advertising in an Asian language – to alert the refugees to their work. In any case the organizations were understaffed and underfunded and it was this, together with their unquestioning belief that Asians could look after their own, rather than any theoretical speculation about the hazards of cross-cultural counselling that resulted in their making no overt outreach to the Ugandan refugees. Nor was there any deliberate attempt to recruit any Asians on to their volunteer teams.

Most of the women sought help from their medical practitioners. There is an indisputable tendency for physicians in medical centres to attract patients of their own ethnic group. There is no language barrier and their surgeries are conveniently situated. If symptoms of psychosis are relative to a culture, then it would seem that counselling should be located in health centres or in surgeries run by ethnic minority medical practitioners.[12] But the women indicated their reservations. The surgeries were crowded with people known to them and their families, there was no way in which they could keep their visit to themselves. There was little chance of consulting a woman doctor, for there were then very few Asian women general practitioners. And though it is true that Asian medical practitioners have insights into their own group's behaviour, they are qualified in Western medicine and like their white counterparts are generally prone to prescribe – especially for women patients – the usual psycho-therapeutic drugs. It was just because of this that two of the women decided to consult a 'vaid' (healer)[13] and spoke of him 'not just writing a prescription; he gave us a lot of time and because we paid him we did not feel helpless.'

All of the women who had contact with Health Visitors spoke highly of them, praising the tact and understanding of this service, which was then totally staffed by white women. Few of the women knew of the existence of the Marriage Guidance Council, and those who did had been told about it by their Health

Visitor. But they had been put off using this resource because when they phoned there was just a recorded message and when they did make contact they were told of the waiting period for an appointment. One woman had attended a counselling session but had not returned because she had not appreciated the client-centred counselling: 'The counsellor was gentle and quiet, but I wanted to be told what to do ... ' In Leicester the Marriage Guidance Council played no discernible part in the initial reception or later resettlement of the Ugandan Asians. At the time it had no Asian trained as a counsellor or as a receptionist. It had no resources for an immediate response to a personal crisis. The financial position of the Council makes it difficult for it to be innovatory. But 14 years after the Ugandan Asians came to Leicester, the MGC was largely responsible for setting up the separate Asian Family and Marriage Counselling Service, which has a full-time 'Asian organiser and is staffed by Asian volunteers'.

The Samaritans was the organization known to all and used by some of the women, through the visual impact of posters which convey instant messages and which are widely distributed in telephone kiosks and places like public libraries. The Samaritans and telephone calls from intending suicides are extricably twinned in people's minds.[14] The disorganizing effect of migration is known to be reflected in suicide, particularly it is claimed among women.[15] Although the Ugandan Asian women preferred to talk about themselves as having 'depression',[16] they spoke of others who had contemplated suicide (usually by overdosing with malaria tablets). But whatever the degree of desperation the Samaritans provided a round-the-clock telephone service, even though at the time when the Ugandan Asians arrived in Leicester there were no Samaritans who spoke an appropriate Asian language. Moreover, its volunteer workers are skilled in crisis counselling. One of the women accounted for the Samaritans' popularity and effectiveness when she said: 'We Asians are telephone people ... you can phone in private from a kiosk even and there is no waiting.' Several other women affirmed how important it is for anyone but especially so for refugees not to have to negotiate with receptionists or 'gate keepers', that is, people who act as filters for an organization. One woman who had actually consulted the Samaritans at their Leicester headquarters praised this service: 'The room was comfortable, it made me feel a welcomed guest, not just a Ugandan Asian who could not cope with her own life.' By the 1980s there were several Asian women's centres in Leicester, all of which offer telephone advice. But there is not yet an Asian organization parallel to the Samaritans although back in 1976 one of the women, who spoke for many others, said that there was a real need for such a service 'for everyone, not just those of us who have come from Uganda, and tried to put all that happened behind us'.

5. MIGRATION AND MENTAL HEALTH

The differences in status and 'adjustment' of refugees as compared with voluntary immigrants include the obvious one that the refugee leaves behind the material fruits of a life's work and often that of his or her ancestors too. Then there is the fact that refugees are allowed into a country because of humanitarian feelings, whereas voluntary immigrants are accorded some sort of status through being admitted on the basis of their own skills and capabilities. The particularly psychological problems of refugees should not be undervalued, either on the part of the refugee or by the receiving society.[17] Refugees are not people who make the decision to move after much thought and careful planning. Instead they suddenly find themselves in another country with little likelihood of ever returning to their homeland. Even their close kin often do not realize the true implications of forced expulsion, and that fact was referred to by all the Ugandan Asian women in the sample. Mira, who was 21 in 1972 and had just married, told how 'every day my sister-in-law would ask when our luggage would arrive ... she kept on saying about how well she had packed her dishes and clothes when she came from India to marry my brother ...' Mira went on to relate how in April 1973 she had gone to try to claim her luggage which had been delivered at the BAWS headquarters. She was excited thinking of 'sarees and other things' of her own. But despite searching through the damaged crates, she and her father found nothing, 'It was no use. It was then it hit me – I had nothing. It was really the end of Uganda and all we had possessed.'

Another trait frequently alluded to by the women was that in their own community there tended to be a great deal of initial sympathy and welcome which bolstered and encouraged the refugees at the start. But even among close kin, this compassion cannot be sustained indefinitely. Sometimes the obligations of the refugee begin to be heavily emphasized, and this falling off in support comes just at the time when the task of standing on one's own two feet, finding employment and taking up the thread of life become vital tasks for the individual. Amrit, who was 19 in 1972, related how she went to the 'sweet mart to buy barfi and jalebi'. She had been in Heathfield Camp for over two months, but had been living with her husband's cousin in Leicester for a few weeks. She still remembered: 'Some other Asian customers in the shops ... I heard one of them saying that we Ugandans had brought fortunes, were not working and were being kept by the government.' Two other women related how they had been told by close relatives that the Ugandan Asians had upset the 'peaceful race relations' in Leicester. In this context, some of the advantages of living in the camps were acknowledged. 'There in the camp we were, in a way, more independent. No one asked you to do things for them because they were giving you a roof and food.'

In one study of displaced persons – Hungarians who had a much longer time than the Ugandan Asians in camps – it was observed that the critical period of adjustment in the 'settlement Country' was between three and six months after arrival.[18] But some refugees, who did not manifest primary reactions during the critical period, had delayed reactions identical in nature to these a year or more after their arrival. There were differences in the reactionary patterns but the most fundamental and frequent was 'depression'. This, as has been mentioned, was certainly the most common term used by the Ugandan Asian women to describe their feelings. All of them, apart from the two wives separated from their stateless husbands, reported that this 'depression' seemed at its peak 12 months after leaving Uganda. Rita was a typical example. She had a job in a city office in 1973, nevertheless, she said, 'I started to cry all the time ... I could not help it, yet I had a job, new clothes and was engaged to a good man with prospects.' She added, 'perhaps there was no time for crying in 1972.'

Refugees are expected to be docile, and to show a deep sense of gratitude and obligation for the privilege of being admitted to the recipient country. But the refugee often reacts with resentment and begins to criticize and belittle all aspects of the new social milieu. This process was illustrated by Pannakumari, who was 28 when she left Uganda. She said that in Uganda she had been a secretary in her father's export–import business. Though now in Leicester she needed a job, she just 'couldn't be bothered somehow' to do anything but intermittent outwork (sewing anoraks) for very little payment. Finally she worked evenings in her uncle's shop:

> I began to think all the customers were laughing at my English ... one of them said 'this was a good shop before you Patels took over ....' I began to hate going behind the counter. I thought 'I hate this place, and the people hate us and nothing will ever be the same again.'

Another younger woman who had obtained a job and was living with her family in a house in the suburbs, explained how she had adjusted. She said this did not mean a total passive acceptance of her new situation, but at least she came to terms with her ability to live with change. But this was out of pace with some of her family, and brought difficulties. She said:

> Now my Mum, she just got on with things and was glad to be living with my brother and his wife. But my Dad, he was only 50 but he just gave up. He said he felt too ill to work ... I started having rows with him and he said I was getting like English girls ... I went to the pub and he tried to beat me and he said he'd throw me out.

People belonging to the middle classes have been shown to be more vulnerable than others when they suffered displacement.[19] Here again most studies have concentrated on the male refugees and describe how they lose their characteristic skill of rational planning for the future.[20] In simple and general terms the refugees had been 'the middle class' of Uganda. Some of the male refugees discovered that their entrepreneurial talents could find no outlet in Leicester. As a general rule the faster the tempo of change, the greater is the adaptive stress. The effects of being socially mobile downwards was felt by all the refugees, but particularly by those who faced unemployment because they sought occupations commensurate with what they had held in Uganda.[21] The women often realized the futility of this before the men did. Indira, who had three children and was pregnant when the family fled from Kampala in October

1972, described how for the first six months her husband tried to get a job as a bank cashier. 'Every week he failed, as I knew he would. The bills began to get bigger. One day my mother-in-law found a bill I had hidden. Then the rows and the hittings began.' Life for Indira 'got much better, almost like it used to be' after her husband gave up trying to get even a clerical job, but found employment as did many other Ugandan Asians at the Leicester Imperial Typewriters factory. But within a year the factory was closed and 'then it all began to go wrong again.'

Sometimes the premigratory and long-standing inter-group rivalries are perpetuated after migration,[22] and can make loss of status even more poignant. Meera, a charge-hand in a knitwear factory, described what all this had meant for her:

> All our community suffered, but some were clever and sent money out of Uganda. Some were lucky and got a job straight away. But for our family everything went very wrong. I think my husband was jealous as well as unemployed. And in our community there are always a few people who point the finger at you if you have fallen from being over some of them.

Some of the Ugandan Asian men who were in their late forties or fifties found one way of keeping their self-esteem – they opted out and took 'early retirement' which in the 1970s was much less socially acceptable generally than it was to become in the 1980s. Their wives took on a parallel role: that of premature matriarchy. But for the wives of younger unemployed, what type of new role they should play posed a dilemma. One of the women whose husband had been stateless in 1972 had been living with her 'cousin-brother' and his family and earning her own living. When her husband eventually joined her, he went through an accelerated process of optimism, pessimism and fatalism, after he found and then lost three jobs in close succession. Though they desperately needed the money she was earning, she gave her job up because she felt that she was undermining the little confidence that he still had left. Mandhuben, who remembered a similar experience, said:

> It was then I started not wanting to go out at all. It was very nice to have my husband with me again. But we just looked at the TV all day. It was better, when he got his fourth job in a warehouse, but I didn't go back to shift work at the factory for three years. I felt ill all the time.

The few studies which do deal specifically with the effect of migration on women, maintain that women experience more difficulties than men.[23] Females are reported as being specially prone to a high rate of mental illness, and they find adjustment to a new environment more difficult. Yet this group of Ugandan Asian women maintained that they had not succumbed to their own feelings, and it was the sheer practical difficulties that faced them that caused them distress. Six of the group found employment before the male members of their families, and this was work in small knitwear factories where conditions were sordid and the pay meagre. And these were women who had never set foot in a factory before. Nor were they used to doing all the domestic tasks, though these were now shared with other females in the household. There was a gulf between them and their unemployed husbands, and it was in these circumstances that they felt distressed and would have welcomed some help and 'counselling'.

The women's crash course in adjustment, their commitment to keeping the family together by bringing in a wage packet, often then led to inter-family friction and the tightening of the bonds of family authority against them. They were accused of abandoning their private roles as wives and daughters and of entering the wider society, even though this was mostly confined to that of the place of work. Faced with the inescapable necessity of deciding whether to continue in paid employment and losing this respect, four of the married women related how they had submitted and given up their jobs. It was some time before a new pattern eventually emerged: 'I can tell you of some other women from my community who gave up their work until after their husband had a job. In a short time the men began talking about buying a house and a car, and then they said that their wives could do a part-time job.' In retrospect the women realized that their happiness and sometimes their health suffered an often unperceived lowering of standard for the first year or two after their leaving Uganda. Their hard work and commitment had, however, given them insights and perspectives denied to their unemployed husbands. They came to know the white women with whom they worked. Although they emphasized that they had worked for economic survival rather than independence, they had gained in self-esteem, and going out to work had made them less introspective and nostalgic for the 'good life' of Uganda. It was hard that for some, when they most needed to work, they had then been most criticized for breaking from the convention of being full-time housewives.

There is another explanation for this. Although not all the women were Hindus, the characteristics of orthodox Hindu culture patterns were operating. This complex and highly developed socio-religious system[24] determines the personality development of its members in many ways. In family life as well as in social organization, there is a remarkably intricate system of interdependent privileges and responsibilities in which everyone is enabled to make some unique contribution. The end product is security and stability. Importantly, decision-making by individual members is strongly discouraged and a premium is put on conformity. These qualities remain, even when the family unit is undergoing severe economic and psychological strains. So though it made economic sense for the women to work, conformity demanded that they should cease to do so because of the 'shame' that their low-status work brought to their husbands. Whilst acknowledging this, similar pressures on the indigenous need to be recognized: there is a widespread belief that mothers ought not to work and this applied even in places like Leicester where traditionally women have worked outside the home. If mothers do work, it is expected that they should do all the domestic tasks done by mothers who do not.[25]

Other aspects of family life which take on particular significance after a forced migration can be traced in Urmilaben's account. She began by describing how the family had a good business (a garage) in Uganda, where she helped with the accounts: 'Yes, I got a job in Leicester, and I liked the feel of money in my hands. We have three children and my mother-in-law looks after them. She said that the women I worked with were not respectable. They were not from Africa like us.' She went on to relate how her husband joined with her mother-in-law and then 'the bickerings became loud.' She added: 'Then I was pregnant again. I think it was a way out of things. I know a lot of Ugandan women who had babies in the first year in the UK. Perhaps it was a way of saying that the family would go on and pretending nothing had changed.' (Two years later, after severe depression not alleviated by 'doctor's medicine', she found a childminder and was back on shift work.)

Among all their speculations and assessments about the stress on family life during the resettlement in Leicester, only two of the women mentioned arranged marriages as contributing a negative factor. The majority though were women who had been married in Uganda under some form of traditional arrangement, and several went out of their way actively to defend this, saying that 'love marriages' are more stressful than the traditional form. However, outward acceptance may mask the accumulation of grievances, and the projection of these on to marriage partners.[26] Traditional marriages, like every other relationship, cannot be immune from becoming dysfunctional when the marital situation has imposed on it emotional and socio-economic problems. Though the jobs that the Ugandan Asians did were of a lower status than those of the Indian professional women written about by Promilla Kapur,[27] yet they had the same problems: in times of economic necessity when the women worked their husbands resented this and felt insulted. Generally men fear failure, whilst women fear that success outside the traditional family-centred roles will be equated with 'masculinity' and detract from the traditional mould of their husband as complete provider.[28] Different cultures have different conceptions of the proper roles to be played by participants in stress situations,[29] but in most societies there is emphasis that male members should still be 'in charge'. One explanation of the consistent research findings 'that women are more likely than men to suffer from emotional problems', and are particularly prone to this in time of upheaval and change,[30] may be simply that women are generally more self-disclosing about changes in their lives and more ready to offer personal data in interview situations than men.[31] Coupled with this verbal self-revelation may be also the expectancy of reciprocity of self-disclosure from others. This can be a therapeutic device. As Fatima put it:

> My husband got a factory job on night shift: so I used to walk around with the small children so that he could sleep. I used to meet the other women. I knew some of them from back home ... Whenever anyone asked about my husband I would say he was just fine. He had been a headmaster and I pretended he had an office job. But there were times when we were just honest with each other: I remember once I just started shivering and then I was crying. I remembered all my furniture in Uganda and how there was so much space, and warm weather everyday. My

legs moved, but my head was iron and I had to go through streets that frightened me.

This idealization of a lost place, and the surfacing of both direct and displaced anger over the loss, was frequent even among those of the refugee women who had apparently adjusted to the change of location with remarkable alacrity. The whole question of the importance of spatial identity has until comparatively recently been neglected in studies of human behaviour. Now both psychologists and anthropologists acknowledge that the phenomenon of *any* relocation causes the fragmentation of comforting routines and relationships.[32] One of the older Asian women described her feelings:

> Everything was different – just everything. Though I kept saying to my husband and the children even, that we had our health and our strength and we would have nice things again, for four years I think I still didn't know where I was, only the things I didn't have. I hardly went outside Highfields – not on the bus or to London or anything. I kept on pretending that outside the door was Kamuli, and all the people and places I knew were there.

In many studies of migration, the 'cushioning' effect of a cohesive family structure in alleviating symptoms of psychological anxiety is emphasized, especially as giving a measure of relief during the early months of adjustment.[33] But the examples given in this study show that it is simplistic to think that all tensions and anxieties are invariably so contained. The need for continued supportive help was recognized in connection with the Vietnamese who came as refugees after the Ugandan Asians.[34] Of the Jewish refugees who came before it has been speculated that long-term emotional distress stems from 'disasters caused by humans rather than those caused by nature'.[35] Such a cause applies to the Ugandan Asians too. Whether suppressed anger and resentment has been passed on to those who came as children in 1972 remains a speculation. Certainly it had affected the confidence of one woman who was 15 then:

> Now that I am at College and soon I'll be married I can see how my dad was scared stiff and angry too. He took it out on me. I had changed, but he had changed more . . . I still think that life can end for us here too, and we'll be kicked out from here. Whenever I look at my passport I don't feel confident, it triggers off all sorts of memories. I hate the feel and the look of anything official with the Government stamp on it: even college entrance forms.

The traumas of the Ugandan Asians cannot be equated with those of Jewish refugee families. Nevertheless the women all knew of families where the husbands had last been seen when they were carried off by Amin's soldiers. When Wakerley School opened there were a significant group of fatherless children. When they talked about their own children the women said that adolescents seemed to react in two ways: they either became withdrawn or began to become more 'independent' or even defiant. They were particularly restless in the months when they were waiting for a school place and when, too, they felt humiliated by their parents' having to become 'the poor relations' in a shared house. The older children sometimes became impatient when there was constant talk by their parents and grandparents of what life had been like. The findings of the Institute of Social Trauma in Israel and of Counsellors of Jewish Families generally may have relevance. They report that some of the children of Jewish refugees resented the fact that, decades after the events, parents still continually spoke of their experiences and made it clear that the emotional problems of their children were unworthy and even unnecessary. In turn the children resented this, yet felt guilty about their resentment. What the Ugandan Asian mothers maintained was that 'security in the family and success at school' were the best antidotes for their childrens' instability. Indeed, in a local radio broadcast in 1977, Brian Piper of Wakerley School spoke of the first pupils as being 'severely traumatised ... they came down the school drive in refugee clothes, shuffling not walking ... coming to Wakerley was the first step back to normality.'[36]

Finally, expressing their belief that it was the expulsion from Uganda that was responsible for the stresses they had described, the women still unanimously condemned what they believed were the stereotypes of them often held by white medical and social workers. This was that 'Asian women' somehow discovered that they could be emotionally disturbed and became over-enthusiastic in their use of National Health facilities, whereas in their pre-migratory 'natural setting' where medical visits were restricted such maladjustments were virtually unknown:[37]

> We had a marvellous hospital in Uganda run by my own people ... there were Government Hospitals too ... we did not abuse them, so why should we start here? I think that one of the reasons I was depressed after coming here was that people treated me like I was primitive and stupid. The real problem was just that we had no money ...

And Fatima, who was among the first to move from a factory to an office job, summarized what others of the women refugees had said:

> We British Asians who were called the Ugandan Asian refugees are like everyone else now, but different too. Some of the women will say that it's all over now and no use looking back. They will say that they are perfectly all right, but I tell you those same people are on tranquillizers and some have trouble with their children. But they deny everything to everybody. That is their pride. Amin could not take that, though he took our possessions.

Conclusion

In the end less than 30,000 Ugandan Asians arrived in 1972, of whom one in five came to Leicester. Despite all attempts to steer them away, subsequent outcomes have proved that the Asians were correct in their belief that Leicester was the place where they could survive and begin to reinvest their skills. And they did so against a background of antagonism and even an official Council advertisement advising them not to come to the city. Remarkably, within a couple of months, certainly by the beginning of 1973, the Ugandan Asians had vanished from the headlines. They were remembered as a distinct group only in the pamphlet literature of the extreme right-wing parties or when journalists asked them for views on events happening in Uganda.

The Ugandan Asians themselves welcomed this invisibility which made them, at least as far as most outsiders were concerned, indistinguishable from other Asians in the city. After all, they had neither sought nor gained much from the public furore of 1972. They had, however, been supported by fellow Asians, particularly those from Kenya, who were already settled in Leicester and outnumbered them.

Nevertheless, the Ugandan Asians were different from other groups from the New Commonwealth. Whilst many of the latter were economic refugees, there was still a measure of voluntary choice and self-selection involved in their migration. The expulsion from Uganda was one of a total population, including a proportion of the very elderly and also many who were without any finance. Other immigrants were indirectly regulated by having been recruited to work in specific industries and services, but the Ugandan Asians were the first to have the geography of their settlement expressly dictated. While it is true that the Uganda Resettlement Board only enforced this by greeting the refugees with information about places like Leicester where they would face difficulties over accommodation and school places, there is a very delicate balance between persuasion and pressure, especially when dealing with people seeking asylum.[1]

The Board attracted plenty of criticism. Its own officials agreed that its name was a misnomer and its attempt at the actual resettlement of the refugees into homes and jobs was disappointing. This it left to the ordinary community services, both statutory and voluntary. But the refugees rated the Board's actual reception work as efficient and they did not object to the policy of the camps. What they did suggest was that less temporary accommodation should have been provided, with a greater degree of privacy, and more of the camps should have been situated within reasonable distance of Leicester. Had this been so, then they would have been convenient bases from which considered decisions about permanent settlement could have been reached by the refugees themselves. The tentative suggestion made by some Leicester officials that Beaumanor Hall (a few miles from Leicester) should be the centre of a refugee village was not as incredible as it appeared at the time. A proportion of the Ugandan Asian families would also have welcomed the opportunity of going to the smaller towns in Leicestershire. But with the exception of Loughborough, even those towns a short journey away from Leicester regarded the refugees as a problem for the city alone. Since this was two years before the local government reorganization of 1974, little could be done administratively to enforce cooperation.

The volunteer organizations, mostly merged to form an umbrella organization – the Co-ordinating Committee for the Welfare of Evacuees from Uganda – also attracted their share of criticism. Again this came not so much from the refugees as from young social work professionals who saw many of the volunteers as patronizing amateurs. But the refugee women welcomed the practical help given by women volunteers such as the WRVS. The most significant volunteer organization in Leicester was the British Asian Welfare Society. This was promoted by the national media as a model of Asian community help for operating the refugee programme. Locally, though, it was the target of censure from other Asian organizations. But even if some of this was justified, BAWS deserves to be remembered as an organization which functioned with an absolute minimum of public funding at a time when there were no professionally qualified Asian social workers in Leicester. Along with the now defunct Leicester Council for Community Relations, BAWS co-ordinated the reception at the local railway station by groups of 'ordinary citizens', who tried to disavow that Leicester was the most unwelcoming of all cities.

Leicester's politicians were also embarrassed by this reputation. In 1972 the city's leaders allowed themselves to be so overcome by the undisputed and largely unpredictable 'refugee problems' that they succumbed to psychological and political fears about a white backlash. True, until the end of the 1970s the National Front manifestos maintained that the Leicester City Council had not done enough 'to keep the Ugandan Asians away'. This theme was also prominent in the pronouncement of the English National Party (formed in 1974 when the Enoch Powell Support Group merged with 'some other City nationalists') and in those of the British Democratic Party (founded by a Leicester solicitor, Anthony Reed Herbert, in 1980). The National Front made significant inroads into Leicester's politics from 1974 to 1977 and the local branch increased its membership with the result that in 1975 it won its party's national award. But by 1977 membership had fallen to a small core of stalwarts[2] still sustained by memories of the momentum of 1972. The Labour Party in Leicester worked hard to rectify its first negative reactions to the refugees. By 1974 it was among the first of the Labour Party branches to print electoral messages in Asian languages. It opposed the decision to allow the National Front to stage marches in the city in 1974 and 1979. There was recompense too, in that Leicester's first Asian councillor, Krishnalal Shah, was a Kenyan Asian who had first come to prominence in working for the reception of the

Ugandan Asians. But the refugees themselves did not become politically active until they had re-established themselves economically. By the 1980s they had joined all three major parties, and one Manzoor Moghal had been selected as an Alliance candidate in the 1987 parliamentary election in Bradford. When Keith Vaz won Leicester East for Labour in 1987 he made history by being the first Asian to be elected to Parliament for decades, though his background is Goan, not East African.

The silent majority of Leicester's citizens also had an opportunity to reverse the tarnished reputation of the city. For five years from 1977 the 'non-party political ecumenical organisation', Unity Against Racism, functioned and in its heyday was able to attract 3,000 in one procession through the city's main streets. In 1977 the *Leicester Mercury* (30 April) published Unity's manifesto which attracted 500 signatories of whom the former Labour leader Edward Marston was one. The *Leicester Mercury*, which like other evening papers has a great impact on local opinion,[3] maintained in 1972 that it spoke for the 'silent majority' who were definitely less than welcoming to the Ugandan Asians. But with a change in editor and a conscious reaction against its previous stance on race-related matters, by 1980 the paper was being described as 'The Leicester Mockery' by the British Movement: 'a paper that hides the inevitable results of lunatic multi-racial policies'.

The Ugandan Asians were different from other groups in another way: they were the first non-European refugees to arrive in considerable numbers, and this arrival marked the shift of the world refugee problem from Europe to Africa (and later to Asia). The Ugandan Asians themselves preferred to be described as 'expellees' or 'evacuees', mainly because they believed that these terms were in line with their legal right to be admitted as British citizens. But regardless of citizen status, all Ugandan Asians, not only those who were stateless, fell within the definition of a refugee by the United Nations Convention of 1951.[4] Had this refugee status been fully acknowledged, then the Ugandan Asians might have been more successful in their campaign for compensation for their abandoned assets and property. Although there remains little optimism, the issue of compensation was still being raised in the parliamentary election campaign in Leicester East in 1987, despite the broken promises of Idi Amin, Milton Obote and Yoweni Museri, and the refusal in 1983 of the Foreign Office to press for block compensation.[5] Significantly in 1972 it was the *Economist* which was the most outspoken about the need for initial payments for these lost assets, and also for a commercial loan scheme so that Ugandan businessmen should have their confidence as well as their fortunes restored. Both of these schemes were shelved.

Some of the Asians believed that one day the Ugandan authorities would ask them to return. So in 1979 when Amin was overthrown by Yusufu Lule, the 'forgotten Ugandan Asians' of Leicester were sought out by the *Leicester Mercury*. The vast majority of 'the City's exiles' said that a war-torn Uganda did not attract them.[6] Two years later, this time when Milton Obote was back in power and trying to restore Uganda's economy, an 'exile' who had succeeded in building up a thriving business told the *Mercury* that 'Asians have gone back ... the majority never will, but they are those who did not lose a lot when they were expelled.' And then in 1982, to mark the tenth anniversary of their expulsion, Ugandan Asians were newsworthy. Like other papers, the *Mercury*[7] reported a series of interviews about the fate of the '5,000 to 8,000 who came to Leicester'. The general consensus was that they were 'now back on their feet, using the skills that helped them regain their former careers and life-styles'. But most of those interviewed were the successes of the exile, although the very rich never came to Leicester. The multi-millionaires of Uganda settled in London. It is also true that Canada 'skimmed the cream of the Ugandan Asian refugees', tending in general to select the professional and managerial class members whilst the less skilled workers and operators of small retail stores came to the UK.[8] Those then in middle and lower middle occupations came to Leicester. But even among those who were rated as successes in Leicester by the *Mercury*, there was one who said 'there used to be bricks through our windows, cards telling us to go home, even a few months ago eggs were thrown ...' The Asians had learnt how to endure unpopularity in Uganda, and they had transferred to Leicester their psychological skills for dealing with this. The *Mercury* did not interview those who had not prospered, apart from one man who had lost his job when the Imperial Typewriters factory had closed down in 1974. Neither did it explore the most significant indicator of resettlement – the substantial number of Ugandan Asians who came as children and had succeeded at school and also in higher education. However, the *Mercury* in 1982 did conclude that the time had come for dropping the label 'Ugandan Asian': the group was now part of the community, with the same problems and achievements as everyone else.

There had been other changes since 1972. The British Refugee Council was set up in 1981 to coordinate activities of voluntary agencies and to press the Home Office for adequate investment in resettlement.[9] Perhaps this organization will build up a store of knowledge, so that the lessons learnt with one group of refugees will not be lost for the next. The expertise built up through the Ugandan Asian experience had been effectively lost by the time the Vietnamese arrived a few years after them.[10] Locally, the Leicester Council for Community Relations, torn by internal disputes, effectively ceased to function by 1983 when its funding bodies refused to continue support. Its place has been taken by advisory committees whose members are all from the ethnic minorities and who work at local government level. BAWS has been replaced by numbers of professionally qualified Asian social and welfare rights workers. Had the Ugandan Asians arrived in 1982, there would have been far less talk of the refugees 'not being a burden on the rates'. Instead those Asians running the reception programme would have looked for and found support from Leicester's Asian councillors. These young Asian professionals, too, would have been much more aware that answers to the refugee predicament were to be found from the statutory agencies and from such sources as the Housing Corporation. But the arrival of any non-white refugees would still be met with suspicion and anxiety, despite the evidence that the Ugandan Asians have contributed to the economic life in the city.[11] But perhaps some lessons have been learnt by the politicians since that time in 1972 when Leicester's Community Relations Officer wrote to the city's leaders:

> It seems ironic that at the same time as the great resources of the City were being proclaimed in 'Expo 72', the City Council was pleading poverty in the face of a human crisis and advertising that poverty in Uganda and the world at large. Perhaps in the end, our community may benefit from the implied admission that the quality of life for many people in this City is far from satisfactory . . . We urge the Civic leadership to redeem the public image of the City . . .'[12]

Notes

Note Places of publication are given only for works published outside the United Kingdom. In abbreviating less frequently cited periodicals the commonly accepted usage of *Soc.* for *Society*, *J.* for *Journal*, *Rev.* for *Review* etc. has been followed. Other abbreviations are listed below.

EAS	*East African Standard*
LM	*Leicester Mercury*
NC	*New Community*
NS	*New Society*
RT	*Race Today*
TES	*Times Educational Supplement*
THES	*Times Higher Education Supplement*
UA	*Ugandan Argus*

INTRODUCTION

1 N. Pye (ed.), *Leicester and its Region* (1972). This volume was published to coincide with the Annual Meeting of the British Association for the Advancement of Science held at Leicester University, September 1972.

2 'The Golden Triangle on Trent Side', *Sunday Times*, 20 Aug. 1967.

3 D. Phillips, 'Social and spatial segregation of an ethnic minority: the case of Asians in Leicester', paper given at the Conference on Current Research in Social Geography, Oxford, 1980.

4 B. Troyna, *Public Awareness and the Media: A Study in Reporting on Race* (Commission for Racial Equality, 1981).

5 J. Rex and S. Tomlinson, *Colonial Immigrants in a British City* (1979).

6 I. Katznelson, *Black Men, White Cities* (1973); D. Lawrence, *Black Migrants, White Natives: A Study of Race Relations in Nottingham* (1974).

7 P. Harrison, 'The life of cities', *NS*, 5 Dec. 1974, 599–604. It was E. Burgess, in *The Growth of the City* (Chicago, 1925), who analysed the reasons why the newcomers (Jews, Italians, Poles) first take up these locations. He described the 'zone of transition' in terms of competition for land use. In the next generation immigrants move on outwards into the next ecological zone. This interpretation of the ecology of the city was modified and put into a British context by J. Rex and R. Moore in *Race, Community and Conflict* (1973). The authors outline a threefold process: competition for use of sites, competition for buildings vacated by previous occupants and general competition for scarce material resources. This model was applied to the settlement of Muslims in Leicester by D. Henderson and P. Smith, 'The Islamic environment in a British city – a case study of Leicester', paper given at the International Symposium, King Faisal University, Saudi Arabia, 1979.

8 S. Kapur, 'Black ethnic minorities of Leicester with special reference to education' (M. Ed. thesis, University of Nottingham, 1983). Kapur repeats the tradition that the first Indian immigrant to Leicester was a Muslim from the Punjab, M. Alam, who set up as a herbalist in The Newarke in the 1920s.

9 *Health of the City of Leicester* 1970 (Leicester City Corporation). Dr Moss defended his findings by stating that 'one of the basic techniques of epidemiology is to divide communities into groups' (p. 91). But he admitted that his estimates of immigrant maternity rates were based on birth certificates and were approximate figures only.

10 *1966 Sample Census: County Report Leicester*.

11 *Health of the City of Leicester* 1966 (Leicester City Corporation).

12 O. Pool, 'The needs of immigrant communities in Leicester' (M. Phil. thesis, University of Nottingham, 1973).

13 The 1971 Census based its statistics on questions asked about birthplace or parents' birthplace, thus excluding those born in the UK, or who had parents born in the UK, who might have been of a particular ethnic origin.

14 *Health of the City of Leicester* 1970, 41.

15 *Health of the City of Leicester* 1971, 54.

16 Leicester Council for Community Relations, 1978. The Council used a combination of the Electoral Registers and the 1971 Census Returns. It stressed that its figures were

estimates and had not been corroborated by other research.

17 Press release: *The Survey of Leicester* (Leicester City and County Council, Sept. 1984). The authors of the survey state that the figures were estimates rather than absolute numbers. The apparent equal divide between Asians in Leicester who were born in the Indian subcontinent and those born in East Africa does not take into consideration the fact that many who were born in the subcontinent had subsequently emigrated to East Africa – especially at the end of the Second World War when controls were lifted. Neither does the survey give the individual island of origin of Leicester's Afro-Caribbeans. In 1979 the Leicester United Caribbean Association estimated that there were 7,000 from the West Indies, the majority of whom were from Jamaica but with significant numbers from Barbados, Trinidad, Antigua and the small island of Barbuda.

   Other demographic details are given by A. Sills, M. Tarpey and P. Golding in *Inner Area Research Project: Social Survey. First Report* (Centre for Mass Communications Research, University of Leicester, 1981)

18 H. Tambs-Lynche, *London Patidars: A Case in Urban Ethnicity* (1971).

19 This description is taken from a pamphlet issued for an Exhibition of Indian Art, Craft and Culture held at the Trade Hall, Leicester in June 1973. The organizer was the Indian National Club (UK).

20 Harrison, 'The life of cities'.

21 R. Pritchard, *Housing and the Spatial Structure of the City* (1976).

22 *LM*, 29 Dec. 1973.

23 'Suburbia and the Asians next door', *Guardian*, 12 Sept. 1972.

24 A. Sills, G. Taylor and P. Golding, *Housing and the Inner City* (Centre for Mass Communications Research, Unversity of Leicester, 1982).

25 Henderson and Smith, 'The Islamic environment', 9.

26 *Ibid.*, 3.

27 Harrison, 'The life of cities'.

28 Indian National Club pamphlet.

29 *Financial Times*, 25 Apr. 1983.

30 D. Don Nanjira, *Aliens in East Africa* (New York, 1976), 193.

31 'Queue now, stay later', *Guardian*, 25 Nov. 1970.

32 R. Boston, 'How the Immigrants Act was passed', *NS*, 25 Mar. 1976, 448–52.

33 *Weekly Hansard*, House of Commons, Session 1967–8, vol. 759, col. 1345, 27 Feb. 1968.

34 *Ibid.*, col. 1578, 28 Feb. 1968 (statement by the Solicitor General).

35 When Sean Lalor, who was the Commonwealth Citizens Liaison Officer, stressed the need for Leicester to extend a welcome to the Kenyan Asians, Page Four of the *Leicester Mercury* contained response from readers such as: 'This exodus is the result of Africanization of employment . . . it would appear that when colour discriminates against colour it is not worthy of comment' (28 Feb. 1968); '275,000 Asians have decided to go back to their motherland, but this country is a socialist paradise', (14 Feb. 1968).

36 *LM*, 5 Mar. 1968.

37 'Citizens – second class', 17 Apr. 1972.

38 'Students to stage protest march to *Mercury*', *LM*, 26 Apr. 1968.

39 Interview with Mr John Peel, MP, *LM*, 3 Mar. 1968.

40 Interview with Surgit Mann, *LM*, 26 Feb. 1968. This estimate was based on advance notices of arrival from airport authorities which gave the number of 1,067 adults and 454 children as 'making for Leicester'. The figures did not of course include others who might have moved into Leicester after temporary settlement in London, Birmingham or elsewhere in the UK.

41 *LM*, 7 June 1968.

42 'A.I.M.S. could harm City race relations', *LM*, 8 June 1968.

43 'School building axed in stupid cuts protest', *LM*, 21 June 1968.

44 'Immigrants could cause massive education expense', *LM*, 26 June 1968.

45 Pye (ed.), *Leicester and its Region*, 307.

46 *Ibid.*, 280.

47 *LM*, 26 Aug. 1972.

48 *The Times*, 7 Feb. 1975. In 1974 the JCWI was reported as collecting data on individual cases of hardship caused by the wait for entry vouchers. This survey was conducted 'as a contingency against any sudden mass expulsion of 90,000 Kenyan Asians similar to that ordered by General Amin in 1972 . . . in the present situation it would be foolish to be complacent . . . the Asians could be kicked out almost overnight' ('Pressure on Britain to open doors to the Asians', *The Times*, 29 Aug. 1974).

49 *Report on U.K. Passport Holders in Uganda* (JCWI, Dec. 1970).

50 'A plain matter of duty', *Spectator*, 12 Aug. 1972, 248. M. Dines, 'The implications of Uganda', *RT*, *4*, no. 9 (Sept. 1972), 293.

CHAPTER 1. THE EXPULSION FROM UGANDA: BACKGROUND AND CAUSES

1 Details of the Asians' role in Uganda are contained in: M. Twaddle (ed.), *The Expulsion of a Minority. Essays on Ugandan Asians* (1975); Y. Ghai and D. Ghai, *The Asian Minorities in East and Central Africa* (Minority Rights Group, 1971); Y. Tandon, *Problems of a Displaced Minority: The New Position of East Africa's Asians* (Minority Rights Group, 1973); M. Mamdani, *Politics and Class Formation in Uganda* (1976); R. Ramchandani, *Ugandan Asians. The End of an Enterprise* (Bombay, 1976); P. Theroux, 'Hating the Asians', *Transition*, 7, no. 2 (Oct./Nov. 1967), 46–51. Also: D. Don Nanjira, *The Status of Aliens in East Africa* (New York, 1976); F. Woolridge and A. Sharma, 'The expulsion of the Ugandan Asians', *International and Comparative Law Quarterly*, 23, pt 2 (1974), 397–425; N. Montani, 'Uganda's Asian refugees: their historical background and resettlement in Canada and the U.S.A.', *Kenya Historical Rev.*, *13*, no. 1 (1975), 27–46. Montani stresses that the Europeans take their profit discreetly in the board rooms and the stock exchanges, whilst the Asians as retailers were much more visible.
2 B. Adams, 'A look at Uganda and expulsion through ex-Ugandan eyes', *Kroniek Van Afrika*, 3 (1975), 237–49.
3 *Sunday Mirror*, 3 Sept. 1972.
4 D. Martin, *General Amin* (1974), 246.
5 H. Kyemba, *State of Blood. The Inside Story of Idi Amin's Reign of Terror* (1977). Kyemba was a minister in the Ugandan government from 1972–1977.
6 T. Mudzingwa, 'Uganda at the cross roads', *African Clarion*, *1*, no. 5 (1972).
7 'Amin film misses the point', *Guardian*, 14 Sept. 1980. The film was made in Kenya by Sharad Patel.
8 'Iago disguised as Othello', *The Times*, 28 June 1974. This film was made by Barbet Schraeder with a French crew. When it was screened by the India Film Society at Leicester's ABC cinema there was a disturbance by some youths ('The night the cinema had a general disturbance', *LM*, 26 Nov. 1974). There was an appetite for accounts of Amin's atrocities. This was illustrated by such sales as that of a book called *Lust to Kill*. This sold 100,000 copies when it appeared in 1979 and sales were particularly high in Kenya.
9 K. Mulemba, 'An unfair press', *Africa*, *19* (March 1973), 46.
10 S. Meisler, 'From dreams to brutality', *The Nation*, *215* (13 Nov. 1972), 463–6.
11 P. Enahoro, 'Amin and the Asians', *Africa*, *14* (Oct. 1972), 13–18.
12 T. Sathyamurthy, 'Ugandan politics', *Economic and Political Weekly*, *7*, pt 42 (1972), 2122–8.
13 I. Wamala, 'Amin and the Asians', *Third World*, *1* (1972), 5–8.
14 J. O'Brien, *Brown Britons* (Runnymede Trust, 1982).
15 H. Patel, 'General Amin and the Indian exodus from Uganda', *Issue*, Winter 1972, 12–22.
16 F. Edmead, 'Industrious minorities', *The Friend*, 25 Aug. 1972, 1041–2.
17 E. Bonacich, 'A theory of middleman minorities', *American Sociological Review*, *38* (IOC 1973), 505–94; see also H. Blalock, *Towards a Theory of Minority group Relations* (New York, 1967), 81.
18 T. Kabwegyre, 'The Asian question in Uganda', *East African Journal*, June 1972, 13.
19 P. Berghe Van Den, 'Asian Africans before Independence', *Kroniek Van Africa*, *6* (Special Issue on Asian Minorities in Africa) (1975), 193–7.
20 C. Davies, 'Asians of East Africa', *Quest*, *77* (July–Aug. 1979), 37.
21 R. Mukherjee, *The Problem of Uganda: A Study in Acculturation* (Berlin, 1956).
22 Ronald Watts and Stanley Meisler, 'Amin ploy to divert domestic criticism', *Guardian*, 7 Aug. 1972.
23 J. Jorgensen, *Uganda, a Modern History* (1981), 438.
24 H. Chattopadhyaya, *Indians in Africa: A Socio-Economic History* (Calcutta, 1970), 285.
25 J. Zarwan, 'Indian businessmen in Kenya in the twentieth century (Ph.D. thesis, Yale University, 1976).
26 M. Twaddle, 'Was the expulsion inevitable?', in *The Expulsion of a Minority*, 2.
27 N. Kasfir, 'Review of *The Expulsion of a Minority*', *American Political Science Rev.*, *72* (1978), 345–6.
28 A. Mazrui, 'The de-Indianisation of Uganda', paper delivered at the East African Social Science Conference, Nairobi, December 1972.
29 H. Johnson, 'The role of the Indians', Foreign Office, Outward File, A38, vol. 1, item 1, 26 Oct. 1900.
30 D. Apter, *The Political Kingdom of Uganda* (Princeton, NJ, 1967), 181–93.
31 V. Jamal, 'Asians in Uganda, 1880–1972, inequality and expulsion', *Economic History Rev.*, *29*, no. 4 (1976), 270–302.

32 A. Mazrui, *Cultural Engineering and Nation-Building in East Africa* (Evanston, Ill., 1972).

33 A. Gupta, 'The Asians in East Africa: problems and prospects', *International Studies, 10*, (1969), 270–302.

34 Y. Ghai, 'The Asian dilemma in East Africa', *East African Journal*, March 1965, 6–21; A. Gupta, 'Uganda Asians: Britain, India and the Commonwealth', *African Affairs, 73*, (1972), 312–43; W. Ocaya-Lakidi, 'Black attitudes to the brown and white colonies of East Africa', in Twaddle (ed.), *The Expulsion of a Minority*, 81–7.

35 Mamdani, *Politics and Class Formation*, 307.

36 R. Ramchandani, 'The Asians of Uganda', *Economic and Political Weekly*, 9 Dec. 1972. The paper was given at a Bombay University Conference attended by members of the Jambo Club which was responsible for looking after the welfare of Ugandan Asians in India.

37 R. Deshai, *The Family and Business Enterprise among the Asians in East Africa* (undated mimeo).

38 Details of the social and religious groups among the Asians are contained in: C. Soper, 'Some aspects of race relations in an East African township' (Ph.D. thesis, University of London, 1953); D. Pocock, 'Difference in East Africa', *South Western J. of Anthropology, 13* (1957), 289–300; B. Ward, 'East Africa', *International Social Science Bulletin, 10* (1958), 372–81; A. Bharati, 'A social survey', in *Portrait of a Minority*, ed. D. Ghai (University of Nairobi, 1965), 15; H. Morris, *The Indians in Uganda, Caste and Sect in a Plural Society* (1968); J. Mangat, *A History of Asians in East Africa* (1969); A. Bharati, *The Asians in East Africa, Jahind and Uhuru* (Chicago, 1972); D. Nelson, 'Problems of power in a plural society: Asians in Kenya', *South Western J. of Anthropology, 28* (1972), 255–64; R. Barot, 'Varna, Nat-Jat and Atak among Kampala Hindus', *New Community, 3*, no. 1/2 (1974), 59–67; H. Tinker, *The Banyan Tree* (1977).

39 Tandon, *Problems of a Displaced Minority*.

40 Ghai, 'The Asian dilemma', 20.

41 J. Parsons, 'Africanising trade in Uganda: the final solution', *Africa Today, 20* (Winter 1973), 59–62.

42 M. Michaelson, 'The relevance of caste among East African Gujaratis in Britain', *NC, 7*, no. 3 (1979), 350–61.

43 'Assembly's only Asian Member', *Guardian*, 8 June 1981. Krishna Cantama was elected to Kenya's National Asembly in 1979. He was described as 'constantly having to reply to the criticism that he represents only the interests of his own community'.

44 Ramchandani, *Ugandan Asians*, 247.

45 Evidence of this is contained in *Report of the Ugandan Cotton Commission* (Chairman Mr Whitley) (Ugandan Government Publications, Entebbe, 1948), 17: 'Most of the growers who appeared before us were emphatic that African buyers also cheat ... but whereas the Indian buyer cheats systematically and cleverly, the African ... is less experienced and is more easy detected ... his money stays in this country, whilst in the case of the Indian "it goes to Bombay".' In the *Preface to the Report* it was noted that 'dishonest practices and fraudulent transactions are prevalent throughout Uganda today.' However, Mamdani (*Politics and Class Formation*, 261) and Mukherjee (*The Problem of Uganda*, 260) look for an explanation in terms of colonial exploitation. They assert that the hunt for 'easy money' practised by the colonial government and therefore under official protection was emulated by the intermediaries whether African or Asian.

46 'Asian romance', *Africa, 7* (1972).

47 'Jobs for the faithful', *Guardian*, 15 Jan. 1973. 'Much has been made by Amin's European detractors of the frequency with which the names Abdue Mohammed and the like, have occurred in the lists of successful applications ... a random breakdown of allocations in of Kampala and Jinja ... that about 50 per cent of businesses have gone to people indicating that they are Muslims': report by Martin Walker.

48 *The Times*, 30 Dec. 1972.

49 'The Immigration Bill', *Law Society Gazette, 9* (8 Mar. 1972), 1.

50 J. Kramer, 'Profiles: the Ugandan Asians', *New Yorker, 50* (8 Apr. 1974), 47–93.

51 D. Don Nanjira, *The Status of Aliens in East Africa* (New York, 1976), 171. The clause giving anyone born in Uganda citizenship by right was cancelled in December 1971.

52 John Fairhall, 'Queue now, stay later', *Guardian*, 25 Nov. 1970.

53 'East African Asians' plight worsening', *Sunday Times*, 2 July 1972.

54 'House of Commons Report' *The Times*, 8 Aug. 1972. (Statement by Sir Alec Douglas-Home on 7 Aug. 1972.)

55 'British government firm on immigrant control', *The Times*, 8 Aug. 1972.

56 Don Nanjira, *The Status of Aliens*, 11.

57 'Ugandan Asians who lived in fear for six years', *Guardian*, 8 Aug. 1968.

58 M. Howard, *The Greatest Claim* (Bow Group, 1970); P. Mason, *The Crisis for the British Asians in Uganda* (British Council of Churches, 1970); D. Tilbe, *East African Asians*, (Race Relations Committee, Society

of Friends, 1970); P. Luff, 'Passport to nowhere', *The Internationalist, 3* (May–Aug. 1971), 11–17; K. Couper and H. Lakhani, *Stet – the Unemployed, Homeless and Destitute: A Report on the British Asians in Uganda* (JCWI, 1971).

59 'Asian flight denied', *Guardian*, 4 Jan. 1971.

60 Luff, 'Passport to nowhere', 11. During the last part of July 1972 it was reported that the Home Office was changing its policy in one respect. East African Asians possessing no entry visa but only a British passport were no longer being put on a transit flight with a round-the-world air ticket, in the hope that some country would accept them. These 'migronauts' were too costly. Instead they were placed on a transit flight back to the point of departure. 'Where humanity had failed to move the Home Office, expense provoked action' ('Shuttlecocks and migronauts', *Guardian*, 4 Aug. 1972).

61 'No Rosy Vision of the U.K.', *Guardian*, 21 Aug. 1972.

CHAPTER 2. THE NINETY DAYS: 5 AUGUST–7 NOVEMBER 1972

1 *UA*, 8 July 1972. This carried an advertisement for the Madhvani Sugar Works Limited prefaced by: 'Because of further expansion, in order to continue the process of Ugandanising personnel, there are vacancies for qualified Ugandan citizens.' The Madhvani sugar group employed only 450 Asians out of a workforce of 13,000. Many of the Asians were, however, in key positions and when they were expelled the sugar shortage became acute.

2 Arnold Raphael, 'The Asian issue. The situation gets worse', *UA*, 26 July 1972.

3 'Pressure mounts over Indians', *UA*, 4 Aug. 1972.

4 *UA*, 31 July 1972.

5 W. Kuepper, L. Lackey and E. Nelson Swinerton, *Ugandan Asians in Great Britain* (1975), 37.

6 'The future of Asians in Uganda', *UA*, 5 Aug. 1972.

7 'Asians milked the cow: they did not feed it – General Amin', *UA*, 7 Aug. 1972.

8 'Some will stay, some will go', *UA*, 19 Aug. 1972.

9 'Domination ends', *UA*, 7 Nov. 1972.

10 M. Mamdani, *From Citizen to Refugee* (1973).

11 E. Markham and A. Kingston, *Merely a Matter of Colour* (1973), 51, 88.

12 T. Melady and M. Melady, 'The expulsion of Asians from Uganda', *Orbis, 19*, no. 4 (1976), 160–200.

13 M. Meisler, 'Uganda', *Atlantic, 230* (Dec.

1972); W. Kibedi, 'Kibedi speaks out', *Africa Report*, July–Aug. 1974, 45–8.

14 Evidence that there was physical brutality against the Asians is to be found in observations made by commentators such as: S. Bandali, 'Small accidents', in *Our Lives: Young People's Autobiographies* (ILEA English Centre, 1979), 53–93; B. Jackson, *Starting School* (1979), 60; B. Kidman, *A Handful of Tears* (BBC, 1975), 54; T. Melady and M. Melady, *Uganda: The Asian Exiles* (New Delhi, 1976), 14.

15 B. Adams and M. Bristow, 'Ugandan Asian expulsion experiences: rumour and reality', *J. of Asian and African Studies, 14*, no 3/4 (1979), 191–203. The authors analyse the situation by relating it to the findings of T. Shibutani, *Improvised News: A Sociological Study of Rumour* (New York, 1966). Richard West writing in the *New Statesman* stressed the over-reaction by those who relied on second-hand reports of events in Uganda (8 Sept. 1972, 318).

16 Cf. 'Statement concerning the status of Asians in Uganda', *J. of International Law and Politics, 5* (New York University, Winter 1972), 603–5.

17 'Ugandan crisis grows', *African Digest, 19*, no. 57 (1972), 95.

18 '*All* Asians must GO', *UA*, 21 Aug. 1972. Yet in early September, Asian teachers with British passports were instructed by the Ministry of Education that they should apply for exemption so that schools could be staffed at the beginning of term.

19 'The miguided policies of Nyerere', *UA*, 23 Aug. 1972.

20 'The man who decided that only black was beautiful', *Economist*, 12 Aug. 1972.

21 Report by John Fairhall, 'Asians likely to be allowed £50 a family', *Daily Telegraph*, 26 Aug. 1972.

22 *Guardian*, 25 Aug. 1972.

23 'Airlift posing huge problems in Whitehall', *Guardian*, 25 Aug. 1972.

24 'Britain all set for Asians', *UA*, 6 Sept. 1972. On the same day an advertisement appeared in the *Argus* carrying the advice that all those intending to go to Leicester should contact the Leicester 'Sangit Kala Kandra'. The author has not been able to trace the originators of this notice.

25 'Asians are urged to settle in new areas', *UA*, 30 Aug. 1972.

26 'No dual citizenship', *EAS*, 7 Sept. 1972.

27 'Britain is accused', *UA*, 6 Sept. 1972. (See ch. 5 for the alleged 'Leicester connection' with this threat.)

28 *African Digest, 19*, no. 6 (1972), 122. Manubhai Madhvani was released on 8

November and went to Bombay. The Madhvani enterprises also extended to textiles, steel and secondary industry.

29 S. Meisler, 'From dreams to brutality', *The Nation*, *215* (13 Nov. 1972), 463–6.

30 '107 Asians at Mombasa', *EAS*, 20 Sept. 1972.

31 'Uganda against delaying tactics', *EAS*, 20 Sept. 1972; 'General Amin gives more than 8,000 British Asians two days to leave Uganda', *The Times*, 23 Sept. 1972.

32 'Cut the red tape plea to Britain', *UA*, 27 Sept. 1972. A plea for his 'fellow Asians' to obey the rule of first come, first served was made by a 'Jinja Asian' in the *Ugandan Argus* on 9 October. In particular he blamed the 'intellectuals' of being the worse queue jumpers. He reminded them that all Asians 'are in the same boat or aircraft'.

33 'New ultimatum by Amin – 8,000 Asians to get out in 48 hours', *EAS*, 25 Sept. 1972.

34 'Nyerere asked', *UA*, 3 Oct. 1972.

35 'General Amin serves stern warning to students', *UA*, 6 Oct. 1972.

36 'I.C.E.M. notice', *UA*, 9 Oct. 1972. This stated that a mission was established in Kampala. It offered opportunities to the Asians to start a new life in developing countries, such as Argentina, Bolivia, Brazil, all of which had a shortage of skilled technicians.

37 'Stateless Asians may go to European camps', *UA*, 11 Oct. 1972.

38 *UA*, 28 Oct. 1972.

39 'Tanzania, Kenya and Zambia Asians to quit', *UA*, 20 Oct. 1972.

40 'General Amin briefs Kenyatta', *UA*, 17 Oct. 1972.

41 'No need for money', *UA*, 19 Oct. 1972.

42 Mamdani, *Politics and Class Formation*, 40.

43 'Asians prefer the cosy British camps', *UA*, 30 Oct. 1972.

44 'Domination ends', *UA*, 7 Nov. 1972.

45 'Asians to work in fields', *UA*, 13 Nov. 1972.

46 'Confident of winning the economic war'. *EAS*, 23 Nov. 1972.

47 'Businesses to be Allocated', *UA*, 30 Nov. 1972.

48 Fred Mpanga, 'They call it "according to plan"', *LM*, 8 Feb. 1973.

49 'A reader's comment', *EAS*, 23 Aug. 1972: 'President Amin is in the habit of getting too many dreams and relying on them. Nixon's dream is of God who ordered him to utilise all atomic weapons to destroy evil minded people.'

50 Hella Pick, 'The sad silence', *Guardian*, 5 Sept. 1972.

51 *Keesing's Contemporary Archives*, 6–12 Jan. 1975, col. 26817. The International Commission of Jurists also accused the Amin government of lawlessness and brutality. In 1975 it submitted a highly critical 63-page report to Dr Kurt Waldheim, requesting that its findings be considered by the UN Commission on Human Rights. In this document the expulsion of non-citizen Asians was condemned as 'overtly racist' and 'a gross violation of human rights'. The report included many eyewitness accounts of ill treatment of Asians. It also emphasized that the Ugandan government had shown no signs of fulfilling its promise to pay compensation.

52 V. Sharma and G. Woolridge, 'The expulsion of the Ugandan Asians', *International and Comparative Law Quarterly*, *23*, pt 2 (1974), 397–425. (Sharma and Woolridge point to the general paucity of international arbitral awards concerning collective as compared to individual cases); V. Iyer, 'Mass expulsions as violation of human rights', *Indian J. of International Law*, *13* (1973), 169–75. Other legal experts also demonstrated the duty of the UK government to admit the Ugandan Asians, for example: G. Schwarzenberger (Professor of International Law, University of London), 'Mass expulsion in international law', *The Times*, 19 Aug. 1972; Sir Peter Rawlinson (the Attorney-General), 'Britain is bound by law to admit Ugandans', *The Times*, 31 Aug. 1972; R. Plender, 'The exodus of Asians from East and Central Africa', *Target, 4* (Easter 1970).

53 Letter from Michael Twaddle, *The Times*, 25 Aug. 1972; *Daily Express*, 8 Aug. 1972; letter from Professor A. L. Goodhart, QC, 'U.N. and Uganda's expulsion of the Asians', *The Times*, 28 Aug. 1972.

54 'Asians' plight put to the U.N.', *Guardian*, 28 Sept. 1972.

55 Gupta, 'Ugandan Asians'.

56 J. Critchley, 1972 'The Ugandan refugees: a world problem', *Crisis Paper* no. 24 (Other Atlantic Publications, 1972).

CHAPTER 3. THE PRESS AND THE POLITICIANS: NATIONAL AND LOCAL REACTIONS

1 'Colouring the news', *Sunday Times*, 3 Sept. 1972.

2 'Between the lines–thanks for the media', *Race Today*, *4*, no. 10 (Oct. 1972) 320–1; 'Ugandan Asians and the Press', *New Statesman*, 8 Sept. 1972, 310; 'The new arrivals', *New Society*, 14 Sept. 1972, 490.

3 B. Troyna and R. Ward, 'Racial antipathy and local opinion leaders', *NC*, *10*, no. 3

(1982), 454–66; B. Troyna, *Public Awareness and the Media: A Study in Reporting on Race* (Commission for Racial Equality, 1981); D. Kohler, 'Public opinion and the Ugandan Asians', *NC 2*, no. 2 (1973), 194–7.

4 M. Dines, 'Uganda. A gamble with men's lives', *RT 4*, no. 10 (Oct. 1972), 323.

5 *Financial Times*, 21 Aug. 1972.

6 'Humanity at the War Office', *Guardian*, 9 Sept. 1972.

7 D. Schoen, *Enoch Powell and the Powellites* (1977), 92. Letter from Mr Enoch Powell, MP, *The Times*, 8 Aug. 1972; 'Mr Powell says talk of passports is spoof', *The Times*, 17 Aug. 1972. Dipak Nandy, Director of the Runnymede Trust, denied that the entry of Ugandan Asians provided a precedent for the influx from elsewhere. He argued that these latter passports had been given by colonial administrations and therefore their right of entry was restricted by the Immigration Act of 1962. In the event of a forced expulsion, there would be an international refugee problem. Similarly E. J. B. Rose (*The Times*, 9 Feb. 1973) argued that 'our obligation to U.K. passport holders throughout the world is not the same as the East African Asians.' The crucial point was that the East African Asians were given the option of having a UK citizenship which would give them exemption from the 1962 Immigration Act: 'They are in a different category from the dual citizens of Malaysia, and the colonial citizens of Hong Kong.' However in the *Daily Express*, 25 Aug. 1972, the reporter Chapman Pincher argued that he could reveal 'the astonishing facts . . . there is no need to allow the Ugandan Asians in.' He alleged that the Foreign Office admitted that Enoch Powell was correct: 'passports were not enough in themselves . . . but the Government was taking the view that in international law it was right to allow the Asians in . . . customary international law does not normally apply to U.K. citizens without right of abode here.' A similar view was expressed by Mr Robert Clements, formerly a prominent member of Leicester City Council and Conservative candidate for Derby South ('We bowed to Amin, what next?', *LM*, 14 Sept. 1972).

8 *Sunday Times*, 3 Sept. 1972.

9 *Sunday Telegraph*, 20 Aug. 1972.

10 *Guardian*, 9 Sept. 1972.

11 *Financial Times*, 5 Sept. 1972.

12 *Guardian*, 9 Sept. 1972.

13 'T.U.C. ready to help over Ugandan Asians but government must act', *The Times*, 9 Sept. 1972.

14 *Economist*, 16 Dec. 1972.

15 *LM*, 31 Aug. 1972.

16 'City to advertise in Uganda "Don't come to Leicester"', *LM*, 7 Sept. 1972. 'Don't go to Leicester plea in Asian Board ads', *LM*, 4 Sept. 1972.

17 'Edward Heath at Leicester: Ugandan Asian problem could be worse', *LM*, 27 Sept. 1972.

18 'City advertises Asian problem', *Guardian*, 16 Sept. 1972; 'Stay away call by Leicester', *Daily Telegraph*, 16 Sept. 1972.

19 *Financial Times*, 16 Sept. 1972.

20 'New brooms clash with the Old Guard', *LM*, 23 Sept. 1972; *Guardian*, 16 Sept. 1972. The nine councillors were led by Rev A. Billings, who was already in the process of moving to Sheffield. The others were J. Hale, Dorothy Davis, J. Longman, B. Briant, H. Dunphy, D. Corrall, P. Kind and J. Marshall. (Marshall became leader of the City Council in 1974 and MP for Leicester South in October 1974.)

21 Letter from Mr Paul Rose, MP, *Guardian*, 20 Sept. 1972.

22 No mention was made in any Council debate that the city's Finance Committee had cut the rates in the current year from 76.5p to 73.5p in the pound. This was in spite of the fact that the social services were under strain in dealing with the continual arrival of immigrants into the city (sources: Leicester's Finance: Annual Report 1972).

23 *LM*, 27 Sept. 1972.

24 'The Tide Turns', *LM*, 2 Sept. 1972.

25 *LM*, 3 May 1972.

26 *LM*, 5 Sept. 1972.
    In 1972 the three Leicester Parliamentary Constituencies were: Leicester North East (T. Bradley, Labour); Leicester North West (G. Janner, Labour) and Leicester South East (J. Peel, Conservative). By 1974 the Boundary Commission had made substantial changes and the constituencies were renamed Leicester East (T. Bradley); Leicester West (G. Janner) and Leicester South (T. Boardman, Conservative). In the October 1974 elections J. Marshall gained Leicester South.

27 'Anti-Immigration March in Leicester', *LM*, 11 Sept. 1972.

28 *LM*, 7 Sept. 1972.

29 *LM*, 19 Oct. 1972.

30 'Powell's Position', 12 Sept. 1972.

31 *LM*, 28 Sept. 1972.

32 *The Times*, 22 Sept. 1972.

33 'Sez Leicester', *New Statesman*, 8 Dec. 1972, 863–4.

34 '"Stress" of Asian influx', *Guardian*, 12 Sept. 1972.

35 Personal interview, June 1974.

36 *Weekly Hansard*, House of Commons Oral

Answers to Questions, vol 851, cols 1256–7, 27 Feb. 1973.

37 *Sunday Telegraph*, 3 Sept. 1972.

38 R. Miles and A. Phizacklea, 'Racism and capitalist decline', in *Urban Change and Conflict*, ed. M. Harlow (1981), 80–100.

39 C. Critcher, M. Parker and R. Sondhi, 'Race in the provincial press. A study of five West Midland newspapers', in *Ethnicity and the Media* (UNESCO, 1977), 25–192.

40 B. Troyna, *Public Awareness and the Media: A Study of Reporting on Race* (Commission for Racial Equality, 1981), 61.

41 'Asians. What do most people believe?', *LM*, 9 Sept. 1972.

42 'No time for marching', *LM*, 28 Aug. 197.

43 The term 'agenda setting' is explained as the power to set the context within which a topic is presented: C. Seymour-Ure, *The Political Impact of the Mass Media* (1974).

44 In the *Guardian* (2 June 1981) Michael McNay commented that cartoonists operate at their best when they have 'a guaranteed slot and a total licence to jest', and that particular cartoonists because of their own personal convictions tend to reinforce the prejudices of their readers. This may well apply to the series of cartoons ('Rab') which appeared on Page Four of the *Leicester Mercury* in 1972.

45 *The Guardian*, 11 April 1973.

46 'Leicester may get more aid to settle Asians', *The Times*, 2 Feb. 1973.

47 *LM*, 4 April 1973.

48 *LM*, 13 April 1973.

49 'Leicester told the Asians don't come here, but they did, and this is what happened', *Sunday Times*, 12 Feb. 1978.

50 *Equality* (Inter-Racial Solidarity Campaign Newsletter), Spring 1978: Votes per National Front candidate in Leicester.

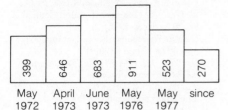

399	646	683	911	523	270
May 1972	April 1973	June 1973	May 1976	May 1977	since

51 *Financial Times*, 26 Aug. 1972; *The Times*, 25 Aug. 1972; *Telegraph and Argus*, 5 Sept. 1972.

52 'Between the lines – thanks for the media', *RT*, *4*, no. 10 (Oct. 1972), 320.

53 '"House full" in an affluent society', *Municipal J.*, 8 Sept. 1972, 1173.

54 'Archbishop's suggestion is not practical', *The Times*, 9 Sept. 1972; *Daily Telegraph*, 2 Sept. 1972.

55 *Sunday Times*, 17 Sept. 1972. In 1972 Councillor Charles Swift, the Labour leader of Peterborough, stressed that there were no protests when houses were allocated to Italians and Germans, 'who may have fought against us in the war'. Writing in *Focus* he said: 'It would have been easy for me to jump on the anti-Asian band wagon ... this would make me the most popular person in Peterborough.' In 1979 it was reported that Peterborough, which had provided 120 homes for refugees from Vietnam, would take no more until the government took direct control of the resettlement programme. Charles Swift (now deputy leader of the Labour-controlled Council) said that the authority had no confidence in the British Council for Aid to Refugees who were running the scheme. 'We have been absorbing ethnic minorities for 35 years with remarkable success. We've got 13,000 now – Poles, Latvians, Italians, West Indians, Pakistanis and Ugandan Asians. All these people have worked hard to make their lives a success ... but the boat people don't want to start by getting their hands dirty' (*Guardian*, 12 Oct. 1979).

56 *Daily Telegraph*, 22 Sept. 1972; *Financial Times*, 5 Sept. 1972.

57 D. Humphrey and M. Ward, 'Where does charity begin?', ch. 9 of *Passports and Politics* (1974).

58 'Avoid Asian influx – M.P.s', *Guardian*, 16 Aug. 1972; *Birmingham Post*, 26 Sept. 1972.

59 *Guardian*, 9 Sept. 1972; 'Sieg Heil cries over Jordan's council speech', *LM*, 1 Sept. 1972.

60 'Settlement picture is not so bleak', *The Times*, 1 Sept. 1972; 'Use for Asian skills', *Guardian*, 18 Aug. 1972.

61 'Survey casts doubts on town's case', *The Times*, 29 Sept. 1972. D. Nandy and R. Briant, the authors of the survey, had both lectured at Leicester University. Briant was one of the 'rebel councillors' who had protested against his own Labour leadership over the Ugandan Asians being told that they should not come to Leicester. But the authors ignored the fact that Nottingham Corporation decided to warn the Resettlement Board that Nottingham's social services were 'already stretched almost to breaking point'. Councillor John Carroll, acting leader of the controlling Labour group, said: 'If Asians have friends in Nottingham and they want to live here, then we have no power to prevent them. But they must realise that they are putting even more strain on a tense situation' (*Guardian*, 9 Sept. 1972).

62 A. Marsh, 'Race, community and anxiety, *NS*, 22 Feb. 1973, 406–8.

63 *LM*, 15 Nov. 1956.

CHAPTER 4. RECEPTION,
NOT RESETTLEMENT:
STRATEGIES FOR SETTLING
THE REFUGEES

1 *Weekly Hansard*, House of Lords, Session 1972–3, vol. 338, col. 266, 6 Dec. 1972.
2 The race relations expert Christopher Bagley also praised the Dutch for peacefully absorbing 150,000 coloured immigrants from Indonesia in the 1950s (*Guardian*, 12 Sept. 1972). But street riots in Rotterdam against Turkish migrant workers coincided with the Ugandan Asian 'crisis' in the UK. There was also hostility towards the Surinamese from the Dutch colonies in the West Indies. Bagley sought to explain this by pointing to the emphasis that the Dutch put on 'conformity to certain external standards of behaviour . . . once these are learnt the group is readily accepted . . . this is in sharp contrast to Britain' (*The Times*, 12 Aug. 1972).
3 Nandy's observations were reported in *LM*, 12 Jan. 1974. Jackson wrote in *NS*, 10 October 1973 (p. 165) that 'the Ugandan Resettlement Board is just about to wind up, but surely the board should be doubled in strength . . . nearly 30,000 refugees came, it was treated like a mini-Dunkirk . . . the illusion was thinking it was a twelve month job.'
4 'View from the Home Office', *RT*, 4, no. 2 (Nov. 1972), 356.
5 A review by Gillian Reynolds of the Radio 4 documentary 'From Riches to Rags' appeared in the *Guardian*, 1 Sept. 1973. The BBC documentary 'The Promised Land' was shown on 7 Sept. 1973.
6 Eyewitness accounts are contained in: 'I used to live in Uganda', *NS*, 1 Nov. 1973; R. Smith, *Sumitra's Story* (1982); J. Salveston, *Uprooted* (1977); B. Kidman, *A Handful of Years* (BBC, 1975). A catalogue of the insults is to be found in M. Mamdani, *From Citizen to Refugee* (1973), e.g. pp. 88–9.
7 W. Kuepper, L. Lackey and N. Swinerton, *Ugandan Asians in Britain: Forced Migration and Social Absorption* (1975), 110; 'One in four Ugandan Asians still jobless', *Guardian*, 4 Nov. 1975.
8 Praful Patel was by 1975 Secretary of the British Government backed Ugandan Evacuees Resettlement Advisory Board [Trust], whose Chairman was Sir Walter Coutts, a former Governor General of Uganda. Patel said that by the time the second Wisconsin study was published it was out of date. 'The survey gives a totally false picture. The situation was certainly difficult when the Asians were expelled in 1972 . . .

The situation is very different today and the great majority of the Asians have settled in remarkably well' (*Africa Diary*, 15–21 Jan. 1976, 7763).
9 Various facts on the resettlement of the refugees both in the UK and elsewhere are analysed in: M. Bristow, B. Adams and C. Pereira, 'Ugandan Asians in Britain, Canada and India: some characteristics and resources', *NC*, 4, no. 5 (1975), 155–166; M. Bristow, 'Britain's response to the Uganda Asian crisis: government myths against political and resettlement realities', *NC*, 5, no. 3 (1976), 350–64; C. Pereira, B. Adams and M. Bristow, 'Canadian beliefs and policy regarding the admission of Uganda Asians to Canada', *Ethnic and Racial Studies*, 1, no. 3 (1978), 350–64; R. Ward, 'What future for the Ugandan Asians?', *NC*, 2, no. 4 (1973), 372–78; D. Pollard and E. Parsloe, *The Ugandan Asians: The Reality of Resettlement*: Report published jointly by the Co-ordinating Committee for the Welfare of Evacuees from Uganda and International Voluntary Service (1972).
10 *Ugandan Asians in Wandsworth*: Report by Wandsworth Council for Community Relations for the Chairman of the Resettlement Board (1973).
11 H. Middleweek and M. Ward, *A Job Well Done?*: Report prepared for the Co-ordinating Committee for the Welfare of Evacuees from Uganda (1973), 10, 27.
12 S. Weir, 'Your rights', *RT*, 5, no. 4 (May 1973), 148–9; S. Weir, 'Supplementary benefits – discrimination', *NC*, 2, no. 4 (1973), 379–83; N. Ardill, *Interim Report of the Development Office* (London Council of Social Services, Ugandan Asian Unit, 1976); 'How happy?', *Economist*, 29 Sept. 1973, 3.
13 J. Romijin, *Tabu – Ugandan Asians, the Old, the Weak, the Vulnerable* (London Council of Social Services, 1976), 2.
14 Uganda Resettlement Board, *Interim Report*, May 1973, Cmnd 5296, 18.
15 *One Year On: A Report on the Resettlement of the Refugees from Uganda in Britain* (Community Relations Commission, 1974). The report points out that the 'Ugandan Asians evacuees are referred to on occasion as refugees', and this was because it was a term 'synonymous with forced migrants'. But the CRC claimed that 'British citizens from East Africa do not have the status of refugees in International Law' (p. 5).
16 *Refuge or Home? A Policy Statement on the Resettlement of Refugees* (Community Relations Commission, 1976).
17 'Ugandan Asians who lack support', *Guardian*, 26 Feb. 1976.

18 'More than half the Uganda refugees lack jobs and homes', *The Times*, 13 Apr. 1973. The Uganda Evacuees Association functioned independently of the Ugandan Evacuees Resettlement Advisory Trust (see note 8). An account of the Association, which was set up before the Trust, is to be found in *NS*, 18 Jan. 1973, 132. The Advisory Trust is described in *The Runnymede Trust Bulletin*, no. 53 (1974). Both organizations hoped to help businessmen re-establish themselves and sought bank loans for this. The Advisory Trust, like the Association, was not directly involved in giving loans but received applications which were then put before the clearing banks. Both organizations worked for the compensation of lost assets from Uganda.

19 *Ugandan Asians: An Assessment of the Situation from the January Survey*: Statement by Navnit Dholakia, Senior Development Officer, Community Relations Commission (28 Feb. 1973).

20 'Newest Britons in safe hands', *Sunday Telegraph*, 27 Aug. 1972.

21 'Man with 42,000 futures on his shoulders', *The Times*, 21 Aug. 1972.

22 The additional members of the Board were: Sir Ronald Oliver (the Labour leader of Sheffield City Council); Sir Frank Marshall (a Conservative alderman of Leeds City Council); Lord Thorneycroft (a former Chancellor of the Exchequer); and Sir Walter Coutts (a former Governor General of Uganda). The exclusion of Mary Dines or any other representative of the Joint Council for the Welfare of Immigrants was surprising. But Michael Levin, in *What Welcome?* (Acton Society Trust, 1982), points out that the campaigning stance of the JCWI was politically out of step with others on the Board. The absence of any staff of the United Kingdom Immigrants Advisory Service was attributed to the fact that in 1972 the organization was currently going through an internal dispute.

The Board had many of the characteristics of the already existing Community Relations Commission, the government's own agency, which had built up expertise and contacts in the race relations field since the race relations legislation of 1968. Yet the government chose not to give the resettlement task to the Commission, despite the fact that it had offices in more than 80 centres of immigration. On the other hand, the CRC itself throughout its history never wished to take on the role of welfare agency. When on 23 August the Home Office announced that the Chairman of the Board was to be Sir Charles Cunningham, Mr Mark Bonham-Carter, the Chairman of the Commission, was among those named as members. He wrote to the Chairmen of the local Community Relations Councils and Community Relations Officers: 'I am sure you will agree that in accepting this invitation I took the right decision ... The whole matter [of the expulsion] is essentially a short-term problem.' He went on to point out analogous situations in the past (the Canvey Island and east coast flooding in 1954, and the absorption of the Hungarian refugees in 1956) where there had been evidence of 'similar *short-term problems*' (own emphasis).

23 'Resettlement Board still working in the dark', *Guardian*, 31 Aug. 1972; 'The Asian refugee crisis', *The Times*, 31 Aug. 1972.

24 'Computer fails to fit in', *Guardian*, 9 Sept. 1972. The essential advance information about the first arrivals from Uganda (giving such details as ages and breakdown of family and types of jobs needed) which a special team of immigration officers analysed in Kampala, was planned to be processed by computer in London. Sir Charles Cunningham had said that 'this would enable us to guide the people to the best areas.' The original plan was to put individual skills into a Whitehall computer, along with jobs supplied by the Department of the Employment. But the information was in a form incompatible with the computer programme and had to be broken down manually. Help came from one of the bigger computer firms who sent some of its trainee managers both to the Home Office and later on to work in one of the Reception Centres. (Information from personal communication from the Community Programmes Adviser of IBM.)

25 'Skill as our lever', *Guardian*, 15 Aug. 1972; 'The middle class exodus', *Guardian*, 17 Aug. 1972; 'Figures behind the flood', *The Times*, 30 Aug. 1972; A. Little and J. Toynbee, 'The Asians: threat or asset?', *NS*, 26 Oct. 1972, 206.

The *Guardian*, 18 Aug. 1972, claimed that 'East Africans in the past have fitted in very well. There has been a dispersal pattern, they have gravitated to boroughs (for example on the outskirts of London) which have not been traditional areas of working class immigrant settlement.' Similar comments were made in E. Krausz, *Ethnic Minorities in Britain* (1972), 317. The determining factor, according to Krausz, was their 'urbanism' the possession of skills and attitudes necessary for life in an urban industrial society. The UKIAS also estimated that at least two-thirds of the refugees could be accommodated in the homes of fellow East Africans already in the UK and had skills that would prove useful in British society. Louis Kushnick in the editorial of *Race Today*, *4*, no. 10 (Oct. 1972), even hinted that their arrival would result in the withdrawal of attention away from other sections of the black community: 'Their likely success, measured by the number of Ugandan business and professional men ... and the high standard of living achieved, at least by the visible position of the group ... will seem to give the lie to the charges of racism ...'

26 'Taking the highroad to kinship', *Guardian*, 15 Sept. 1973.

27 S. Wallis, 'The Asians' arrival', *NS*, 27 May 1976, 472–3.

28 S. Goldenberg, 'Kinship and ethnicity viewed as adaptive resources to location in opportunity structure', *J. of Comparative Studies*, *8*, no. 2 (1977), 149–63; T. Drabeck, 'The impact of disaster on kin relationships', *J. of Marriage and the Family*, *37*, no. 3 (1975), 481–93.

29 F. Hawkins, 'Ugandan Asians in Canada', *NC*, *2* no. 3 (1973), 268–75; G. Dirks, 'Behind the headlines, the plight of the homeless: the refugee phenomenon', *Canadian Inst. of International Affairs*, *38*, no. 3 (1980), 16–17; M. Fisher, 'Asian Indians in New York City', *Urban Anthropology*, *7*, no. 3, 271–85; B. Adams, 'Ugandan Asians in exile: household and kinship in the resettlement crisis', *J. of Comparative Studies*, *8*, no. 3 (1977), 167–78.

30 'Board lists areas where Asians to be discouraged', *Guardian*, 18 Sept. 1972. The failure of the dispersal policy was admitted in the final report of the Resettlement Board. The face-saving proviso was that those who had been persuaded to disperse might serve as a magnet for others 'as they experience the strain of life in places where we counselled them not to go'. (p. 19). Mr Reg Freeson, the Minister for Housing, admitted that with hindsight the whole steering operation was unrealistic and did not allow for the inevitable pull of existing communities (*Equals*, CRC, June/July 1976).

31 Reproduced in full in D. Humphrey and M. Ward, *Passport and Politics* (1974), 55–7.

32 'Plans for reception', *The Times*, 19 Aug. 1972; 'There is still a refugee problem', *The Times*, 11 Nov. 1972.

33 Sir Charles Cunningham, 'The Ugandan Resettlement Board and hiving-off: some possibilities for future research', *Public Administration*, *51* (1973), 251–60.

34 'Carr promises cash for migrants', *Daily*

Telegraph, 21 Sept. 1972; 'Asian refund in full was promised', *LM*, 7 Nov. 1972.

35 'Uganda refugee camps regretted', *Guardian*, 17 Aug. 1972. John Ennals, the Director of the UKIAS, seems to have envisaged a rapid and efficient reception process such as the Canadian government ran at Longue Point.

36 'Uganda: next question', *Guardian*, 2 Sept. 1972.

37 'Local bodies advocated for settling Asians', *The Times*, 28 Aug. 1972.

38 *Annual Report 1973*, Womens Voluntary Service; *Progress Report No. 3* (CCWEU, 1972); K. Bentley Beauman, *Greensleeves: The Story of the W.V.S./W.R.V.S.* (1977), 163.

39 'Too many cooks', *Sunday Telegraph*, 1 Oct. 1973.

40 *Guardian*, 11 Oct. 1972; *The Times*, 1 Jan. 1974. Gwen Cashmore, one of the three Directors of CCWEU, circulated a memorandum to all members on 30 March 1973. She pointed out: 'We need member organisations' assistance in working with difficulties at *every* level, from that of a national pressure group which compels statutory bodies to do their duty to the immediate but equally necessary response to individual need.'

41 Letter from Helen Bush, Secretary of the Association of Volunteers in Social Work, *The Times*, 17 Oct. 1972.

42 J. Hamilton-Preston, 'Camp on John Bull Island', *Nova*, April 1973, 68–72.

43 M. Mamdani, *From Citizen to Refugee* (1973), 96, 124.

44 *NS*, 22 Feb. 1973, 403.

45 R. Littlewood and M. Lipsedge, *Aliens and Alienists: Ethnic Minorities and Psychiatry* (1982), 127.

46 Various accounts of how the Ugandan Asians reacted to life in the camps can be found in: P. Martin, 'Reluctant exiles' *Sunday Times*, 8 Dec. 1972; *Sunday Times*, 1 Oct. 1972; *Guardian*, 8 Nov. 1972.

47 J. Bourne, 'Resettlement blues; *RT*, *2*, no. 4 (1972), 357; *Guardian*, 5 Sept. 1972.

48 S. Naipaul, 'We always knew that one day we should have to come', *Sunday Times*, 31 Dec. 1972.

49 *Ibid.*

50 'Villages protest on Asians', *Daily Telegraph*, 8 Oct. 1972.

51 *Progress Report No. 4* (CCWEU, 1972).

52 *Guardian*, 4 Dec. 1972 (own emphasis). Other comments on the Asians' life in a rural community and the reactions by the local population are made by Peter Watson, 'The new outgroup', *NS*, 23 Nov. 1972, 444.

53 S. Hunt, 'Adaptations and nutritional

applications of food habits among Ugandan Asians settling in Britain' (Ph.D. thesis, University of London, 1977).

54 R. Bourne, 'The last Asians', *NS*, 31 May 1973, 484–85.

55 *Daily Mirror*, 2 Nov. 1972; *The Times*, November 1972.

56 J. Kramer, 'Profiles: Ugandan Asians', *New Yorker*, 4 Apr. 1974, 47–93.

57 'Army camps urged as a stop-gap', *Daily Telegraph*, 26 Aug. 1972.

58 R. Glyn Jones, *A Report on the Experiences of Ugandan Asian Families Settled in Blackburn* (Community Relations Council, Blackburn, 1973), 13.

59 *The Times*, 8 Nov. 1972.

60 B. Jackson, *NS*, 18 Oct. 1973, 165. In his contribution to the 'readers letters', Jackson suggested 'that a Migrant Resettlement Service should be set up to take over from the Uganda Resettlement Board and also suggested that these next three years are the time when the Ugandan Asians and the areas where they live ... need fluid supporting services' (see also *NS*, 1 Nov. 1973, 293).

61 'Service with a smile is back in Britain and it's all thanks to Amin', *Daily Mail*, 11 Feb. 1976; 'Amin's Asian refugees back in business', *Daily Telegraph*, 5 July 1978.

62 Statement by Leicester Department of Employment, 14 Sept. 1973.

63 P. Cole, *Ugandan Asians and Employment* (Runnymede Trust, 1973), 19.

CHAPTER 5. THE ROLE OF THE VOLUNTARY ASSOCIATIONS

1. Letter from S. Barraclough, Secretary to the Uganda Resettlement Board, to Directors of Social Services, 15 Mar. 1973.

2 Letter from BAWS to Leicester Council for Community Relations, 15 Aug. 1972. The associations listed as being represented on BAWS were 'the Pakistani Association; the Islamic Centre; the Indian League; the Hindu Union; Dr Shivader (representing the Hindu Temple); the Brahma Samaj (N.B. Gujarati); the Commonwealth Community Centre and the British Asian Welfare Council'. BAWS wished to emphasise the Gujarati members and hence the East African Asian representation.

3 'No refuge in Kenya for Ugandan Asians', *LM*, 8 Aug. 1972. See also 'Immigrants move in Ugandan crisis', *LM*, 9 Aug. 1972; 'Asians are offered 1,000 homes', *LM*, 16 Aug. 1972.

4 R. Parsons, 'Now you see them, now you don't', *NC*, 7, no. 1 (1978), 92–7; C. Husband, 'News media, language and race

relations', in H. Giles (ed.), *Lanugage, Ethnicity and Intergroup Relations*, 223.

5 'Leicester in Asian talks', *Guardian*, 31 Aug. 1972.

6 'No room of our own', 'Airlift us out of it', *LM*, 25 Aug. 1972.

7 'The people who wanted the best of both worlds', *LM*, 19 Aug. 1972.

8 'Scaremongers', *LM*, 15 Aug. 1972; '"Asians: we have done all we can", says Council', *LM*, 31 Aug. 1972.

9 'The Council' here referred to was the Leicester Council For Community Relations.

10 IWA (GB), Leicester Branch, *Long Live the Indian Revolution* (mimeo, 1973).

11 'Welcome Asians appeal', *LM*, 1 Sept. 1972. The India Film Society's President was Mr Tara Mukherjee, who then lived in Leicester. He was also prominent in other organisations, for example he was President, Confederation of Indian Organizations (UK): see *Asian Directory and Who's Who 1977–1978* (Asian Observer Publication).

12 'Society plans to help the refugees', *LM*, 11 Sept. 1972.

13 Accounts of the Board's visit include: 'A city waiting for Asians', *Financial Times*, 4 Sept. 1972; 'Board tours overcrowded city', *The Times*, 6 Sept. 1972; 'Asians: city will ask government for £300,000', *LM*, 8 Sept. 1972. The City's Council General Purposes Committee produced this assessment at the request of the Home Office. Alderman E. Marston announced that in addition the city would ask for an extra £200 a year for each immigrant child who would have to be bussed to a county school. The *Mercury* (8 Sept.) also headlined the fact that the 'City's Immigration Policy Leader Goes Abroad Indefinitely': Councillor Maurice Tracy, the chairman of the city's General Purposes Committee which was 'charged with implementing the Corporation's policy on Ugandan Asian immigration', had taken up a legal appointment in Hong Kong. He was a Labour member and represented Spinney Hill Ward.

14 'What Asians Face: Goodwill but Snags', *Sunday Telegraph*, 3 Sept. 1972.

15 'City to advertise in Uganda "Don't come to Leicester"', *LM*, 7 Sept, 1972; '"Don't go to Leicester Asian Board ads"', *LM*, 14 Sept. 1972. The insertion of the advertisement was recommended to the General Purposes Committee by both Labour and Conservative party leaders. They argued that they were following the lead of the Uganda Asian Resettlement Board. Alderman Marston told the *Mercury* on 7 September: 'We hope the advertisement will impress people in Uganda

... this will show the people of Leicester that we are doing everything to get their point of view across.' On 14 September there was an account of complaints by workers at County Hall about a document from the local NALGO branch. They had received a pamphlet which came from NALGO officials headed 'Sensational Bargain Offer'. It contained such offensive material as: 'Stocks will not last ... You can have a Ugandan Asian in your home free. All you have to do is throw the rubbish off the bed in your spare room' ('"Aid Asians" appeal was too flippant – complaints', *LM*, 14 Sept. 1972).

16 'City has 350 Asians already, 1,000 expelled', *LM*, 4 Oct. 1972.

17 Details of the part played by Jani are contained in: '"Kill Amin" plot claim started after man's letter', *LM*, 8 Sept. 1972. See also 'It's Irresponsible to form a Fight Uganda group, say Asians' *LM*, 23 Oct. 1972; 'Appeal to Carr over city's Asian leaders', *LM*, 26 Oct. 1972.

18 'Asians in Leicester need association says new arrival', *LM*, 6 June 1973; 'Asian hits at call for new association', *LM*, 7 June 1973. The Boarders Association consists of ex-students who had lived together in various school hostels in Kampala. It aims to do charitable work for both indigenous and Asian groups. A second association, The Friends of Uganda, organized a dinner in March 1982 at Leicester's Centre Hotel when the Ugandan High Commissioner promised compensation for assets in Uganda (*LM*, 16 Mar. 1982). The venue for the dinner was criticized by Ranesh Jani who spoke as a founder member of the separate 'The Friends of Uganda Society'. Jani said that the dinner was too expensive for many who wished to attend (*LM*, 15 March. 1982). Mr M. Moghal, who was the convenor of the Friends of Uganda, said that the demand for the £10 tickets was so great that people had to be turned away, and that 'Mr Jani was not a member of Friends of Uganda.'

19 'Count the Asians riddle', *LM*, 6 Nov. 1972.

20 'How Asians fare', *Sunday Telegraph*, 7 Jan. 1973.

21 N. Bosanquet and P. Doeringer, *Race and Employment in Britain* (Runnymede Trust, 1973).

22 'Walkabout at Highfields off to a rowdy start', *LM*, 7 Feb. 1973.

23 'Let in stateless Asians', *LM*, 18 Feb. 1973.

24 Memo from Deputy Director of Social Services, 10 Dec. 1972.

25 Circular from Lord Sainsbury, Chairman of the Trustees of the Ugandan Asian Relief Trust, to all Local Authorities and Managers

of New Town Development Corporations, 13 Nov. 1972.

26 Letter from Lord Lanesborough to the Director of Social Services, 22 Jan. 1973.

27 Letter from Uganda Resettlement Board (Grants Section) to the Town Clerk, 22 Jan. 1973.

28 Letter from the Director of Social Services to the Town Clerk, 2 Feb. 1973.

29 Progress Report by Dr Seth to the Director of Social Services, 18 Apr. 1973.

30 Letter from BAWS to the Executive Members of LCCR, October 1973.

31 Minutes of Special Sub-Committee on Immigrants, 3 Sept. 1973.

32 J. Rex and S. Tomlinson, *Colonial Immigrants in a British City* (1979), 244; A. Jansari, 'Social work with ethnic minorities: A review of literature', *Multi-Racial Social Work, 1* (1980), 17–34.

33 M. Dines, 'Immigrants and the Social Services', *Social Services Quarterly, 43*, no. 2 (1969), 57–60.

34 'A *chamcha* is a humble, everyday object. It is in fact a spoon. The word is Urdu; and it also has a second meaning. Colloquially, a *chamcha* is a person who sucks up to important people, a yes-man, a sycophant. The British Empire would not have lasted a week without such collaborators amongst its colonised peoples' (Salman Rushdie, 'The Empire writes back', *The Times*, 3 July 1972). In April 1977 the Newsletter of the Leicester Council for Community Relations featured an article by an anonymous 'young Asian' in which the leaders of Leicester's 90 Asian organizations were described as the '*Chamchas* of the Establishment'. The close links of these 'executive committee Asians' with local MPs, the Lord Mayor and the Editor of the *Leicester Mercury* were derided.

Other accounts of the challenge to the older leaders of the Asian community are illustrated in: D. Hiro and I. Mather, '"We won't be sheep any longer" say young Asians', *Observer*, 13 June 1976; A. Brah, 'Age, race and power relations: the case of South Asian youth in Britain', in *Black Kids, White Kids, What Hope?*, ed. M. Day and D. Marsland (Brunel University Publications, 1978), 31–40.

35 The concept of 'brokerage' is discussed by D. Brooks and K. Singh, 'Asian brokers in British foundries', in S. Wallman, (ed.), *Ethnicity at Work* (1979), 93–112. Its function in the USA is analysed in: J. Higham, (ed.), *Ethnic Leadership in America* (Baltimore, Md, 1978); V. Greene, 'Becoming American: the role of ethnic leaders', in M. Holli and P.

Jones, (eds), *The Ethnic Frontier* (Grand Rapids, Mich., 1977), 145.

36 R. Paine, 'What is gossip about? An alternative hypothesis', *Man, 2* (1967), 278–85.

37 Letter from the Rev. B. Taylor to the Town Clerk and the Director of Social Services, 17 Aug. 1972.

38 'Prepare now to help Asians', *LM*, 22 Aug. 1972.

39 Letter from the Director of Social Services to the Social Services Committee, 4 Sept. 1972.

40 Letter from the Rev. J. Taylor to the *Leicester Mercury*, 17 Aug. 1972.

41 Memo from the Leicester Council for Community Relations and the Leicester Council of Social Service, *Ugandan Asians – A Summary of Issues*, 21 Sept. 1972. The Gujarati Welfare Society also offered to keep a register of accommodation. But they were informed that 'Any information will be channelled to Mr Singh who has been appointed by the Social Services Department. He is stationed partly at the Commonwealth Community Centre (B.A.W.S.) and the Department of Social Services at Thames Tower' (Letter from the Community Relations Officer, 21 Sept. 1972).

42 Report, British Federation of University Women (Leicester Branch), Dec. 1972.

43 Personal interviews, 1981, with Mrs P. Emmet, SRN, and Mrs J. Smith.

CHAPTER 6. UGANDAN ASIANS AND EDUCATION

1 'Refugee children in Leicester schools'; *The Times*, 20 Oct. 1972.

2 'Asians: school chief hits back', *LM*, 3 Oct. 1972.

3 J. Mander, *Leicester Schools 1944–1974* (Leicester City Council, 1980), 43–50.

4 A. Hill, 'The fertility of the Asian community in East Africa', *Population Studies, 29*, no. 3 (1975), 335–72. Hill calculated that the total Asian population in Kenya and Uganda stood at 249,000 in 1969. The figures for immigrant children in Leicester schools are detailed in J. Mander, 'Freedom and restraint in a Local Education Authority' (Ph.D. thesis, University of Leicester, 1975) (see note 10 below). This source does not attempt a count of those immigrant students who were attending the local Further Education Colleges and who were following 'O' and 'A' level courses. In Leicester's submission to the *Select Committee on Race Relations and Immigration: Education (1972–1973)* (1973), III, 451, it was said that the number of immigrant students in one college alone totalled 19 per cent (924 out of a total of 4,902 students). The tenacity and persistence of these students and the response of the colleges was the subject of: V. Marett, 'East African Asian students in Further Education Colleges (M.Ed. thesis, University of Leicester, 1976).

5 'How Asians Fare', *Sunday Times*, 7 Jan. 1973. An interesting item in regard to this special fund is to be found in a note by the Director of Education to the Finance and General Purposes Sub-Committee on 30 November 1972: 'The Committee will realise that the year 1972–73 is one when Education costs in Leicester are bound to rise – quite apart from inflationary elements. The raising of the school leaving age is fully effective in July 1973 ... Under Primary Education, delete Immigration Fund £2,500, increase Development Fund by £1,000, thus saving £1,500.'

6 *Select Committee (1973)*, 495.

7 *LM*, 15 Nov. 1968, 17 Jan. 1970 and 24 Jan. 1972.

8 'Secondary school for immigrants planned', *LM*, 10 July 1971.

9 Report to the Leicester Council for Community Relations (Education Sub-Committee), 20 Dec. 1974.

10 The figures are taken from those given by Mander, 'Freedom and restraint', 270. Mander was a senior member of Leicester's Education Department and was able to compile the data from the returns made by Leicester's schools on Form 7(1). These were 'locally collated and the main headings confirmed in the Department of Education and Science Statistics Return 63 for the years stated'.

11 'City Revolt over Migrant Count', *LM*, 25 Nov. 1973.

12 *LM*, 10 Dec. 1973 (own emphasis).

13 'Figures back the case for aid', *LM*, 9 Feb. 1973; also 'City heads provincial pupil chart', *LM*, 9 Feb. 1973.

14 T. Wilkinson, 'Ugandan Asians in Leicester: initial resettlement', *NC, 3*, nos. 1–2 (1974), 147–59.

15 *One Year On* (Community Relations Commission, 1974), 73.

16 'All Asians now at school: but Leicester disagrees', *The Times*, 4 May 1973.

17 *Progress Report No. 5* (CCWEU, 1972).

18 J. Wintour, *Press Release: Waiting List for School Places in Leicester*, 11 Jan. 1974. Wintour used the following data to support his case:

'The numbers of children in maintained

schools has not increased unexpectedly, as the following figures show:

Date	Numbers	Change from previous year
January 1967	48410	—
January 1968	49207	797
January 1969	50297	1090
January 1970	51020	723
January 1971	51970	950
January 1972	53418	1448
January 1973	54672	1254
January 1974	58156	1339

Note: Part-time pupils are included as half of a full-time pupil. An allowance of 2145 is made for the raising of the school leaving age and excluded from the change January 1973 to January 1974.
Sources: Leicester Education Committee, *Report 1972*, p. 62 and information from Mr Hill, Leicester Education Department.
The staffing ratio of pupils to full-time and full-time equivalent teachers is improving as the following figures show:

Date	Staffing ratio
January 1970	22.74
January 1971	22.59
January 1972	22.10
January 1973	21.24

Source: Leicester Education Committee, *Report 1972*, p. 65.

Mr Wearing of Leicester Education Department told J. Wintour in a telephone conversation on 7 January, 1974, that the staffing ratio was still "improving".'
19 'School Place Delays Denied by Education Director', *LM*, 11 Jan. 1974; 'Places row at Leicester', *TES*, 18 Jan. 1974.
20 Report by Richard Bourne, 'Schools prepare for 19,000 Asian schoolchildren', *TES*, 15 Aug. 1972.
21 Minutes of the Finance and General Purposes Committee, City of Leicester, 28 Sept. 1972 (Minute 123).
22 'Ugandan Asians: authorities get ready to do their best', *Education*, 1 Sept. 1972. A special appeal to the DES was made in 1968 by Wolverhampton when faced with an influx of Kenyan Asians.
23 'How much money the L.E.A.s can expect', *Education*, 29 Sept. 1972. In addition, grant aid for the salaries of extra temporary staff to all LEAs receiving the refugees was promised. This was to be on a separate basis from the existent Section XI teachers under the 1966 Local Government Act, whose salaries were funded again up to 75 per cent to LEAs with large numbers of immigrant

children. The grants were to be administered directly by the Resettlement Board although it was left to the LEAs to apply either directly to the Board or to channel their requests through the DES: 'It is understood that the Department will be pretty flexible over grant arrangements ... the main thing that L.E.A.s have to do, it seems, is to convince the D.E.S. that they have a case of need.'
24 'L.E.A.s get go ahead on Asian spending', *TES*, 3 Nov. 1972. The Chief Education Officer of Newham supported Councillor Davis in her criticism of the lack of clarity over what money spent by the LEAs would be refundable: 'The Circular of the Resettlement Board of September 18 offered help, but did not tell us how much we could spend. We still do not know what allocations there will be for any new schools to be put up.'
25 'Councils protest over spending on Asians', *TES*, 10 Nov. 1972.
26 *Report: Uganda Resettlement Board Grants* by the City Treasurer to the City Council, 1973. The final expenditure and grant in respect to the two 'emergency schools' was shown as:

Education	Actual 1972–73 Expenditure £	Grant £
Hugh Latimer Primary School		
Capital Cost*	3,200	2,400
Running expenses	7,000	7,000
Wakerley Secondary School		
Capital costs*	37,000	28,000
Running expenses	—	—
Other costs (including awards to students)	4,500	4,500
Social Services	2,000	2,000
	£53,700	£43,900
	Estimate 1973–74	
Hugh Latimer Primary School		
Capital Cost*	21,000	15,800
Running expenses	29,000	29,000
Wakerley Secondary School		
Capital costs*	57,000	43,000
Running expenses	56,000	56,000
Other costs (including awards to students)	8,000	8,000
Social Services	1,500	1,500
	£172,500	£153,300

* Subject to 75% grant

27 Minutes of the Finance and General Purposes Committee, City of Leicester, 28 Sept. 1972 (Minute 123). Further details about the finances are to be found in: Minutes of the Finance and General Purposes Committee, 2 Nov. 1972 (Minute 129); 'Report on extra cost', *LM*, 26 Jan. 1973. By January 1973 a detailed statement on financing had been made by the Resettlement Board which made it clear that the spending on running expenses and equipment would be met by a 100 per cent grant for one year, from the date on which any part of the spending was incurred. Thus the running and equipment costs would be reimbursed for the period up to 3 December 1973, that is, one year after the opening of the school. For the following year, 1973/4, the cost to the rates was estimated at £12,000.

28 'Old school to be opened for Asian children', *LM*, 10 Oct. 1972.

29 'Refugee pupils settle in at English school', *LM*, 6 Feb. 1972.

30 'Re-opened school may be used more', *LM*, 8 May 1974.

31 'Report calls for school closure', *LM*, 1 Sept. 1980.

32 *LM*, 10 June and 8 Dec. 1980.

33 Personal interview with Miss A. E. Watson, 9 Apr. 1982.

34 'Ex-city school may be Hindu H.Q.', *LM*, 23 July 1982.

35 'Site earmarked for a new school for immigrants', *LM*, 11 Nov. 1972.

36 'Make-shift schools for Asians not the answer', *LM*, 29 Nov. 1972. The Hillcrest site was, a few years later, chosen for the site of Moat Community College, the first purpose-built community college in the city.

37 'Mobile classrooms for Ugandan Asians will cost £93,000', *LM*, 15 Nov. 1972.

38 'Emergency school delayed', *LM*, 8 May 1972. The school was scheduled to be opened in the first week of May, but the positioning of the mobile classrooms and 'the national shortage of bricks' caused the delay. The controversy over the school's continued existence is to be found in 'National Front agrees with Race Relations Board', *LM*, 15 Dec. 1973. The local branch of the National Front continued to urge for school segregation. Its press officer, John Ryde, issued a statement in answer to the reported findings of the Select Committee on Race Relations and Immigration: Education. 'Possibly the greatest fear expressed by white parents in Leicester is that of the development of their children being arrested by the necessary need for special treatment for immigrant children. The sensible solution is separate classes or separate schools' (*LM*, 31 Aug. 1974).

39 'It's thrilling to get back to school', *LM*, 24 Aug. 1973 (own emphasis).

40 *Teaching Scheme at Leicester College of Education, Scraptoft* (undated mimeo): 'In view of the fact that many Ugandan Asian children do not yet have places in schools, members of the Students Union of Leicester College of Education have volunteered to set up a teaching scheme in their spare time. This is not intended as a substitute for schooling, but to occupy some of the children awaiting school places ... On Monday 13 November, 27 children of primary age were collected from their homes and taken to Scraptoft ... the teaching seems to have been profitable for all involved, both students and children.'

41 Details of this St Peter's school are to be found in: 'Choir vestry a school room for Ugandan Asians', *LM*, 2 Feb. 1972; letter from the Rev E. Carlile, Chairman Leicester Council for Community Relations to Mr Bonham-Carter, 15 Dec. 1972.

42 Additional details of the schemes run by Leicester University students and other volunteers are to be seen in: 'Student volunteers to teach English', *LM*, 16 Dec. 1973; 'School in the holidays', *LM*, 7 July 1973.

43 *TES*, 19 Sept. 1975.

44 Commentaries on the concepts and logistics involved in 'bussing' include: K. Kogan, *Dispersal in the Ealing Local Authority:* Report prepared for the Race Relations Board (1975); L. Killan, 'School bussing in Britain', *Harvard Education Rev.*, 49, no. 2 (1979), 185–206; D. Kirp, *'Doing Good By Doing Little':* *Race and Schooling in Britain* (Berkeley, Cal., 1980); 'Separate schools for immigrant pupils': Statement by S. C. Kapur, *Select Committee* (1973), 518.

45 'Leicester: whites are bussed too', *TES*, 19 Sept. 1975, p. 15.

46 'School bussing condemned by parents', *LM*, 4 Apr. 1975.

47 'Racial bussing out of court', *The Times*, 1 June 1975.

48 *Select Committee* (1973), 519.

49 Minute Books, City of Leicester, Primary Schools Committee, 19 Apr. 1973 (Minute 198).

50 *Select Committee* (1973), 487.

51 Colin Vann, 'View from the blackboard', *LM*, 10 Dec. 1968.

52 Minute Books, Primary Schools Committee, 483.

53 Attitudes of Asians in East Africa to schooling

are described by: J. Hunter, *Education for a Developing Region* (1963); E. Stabler, *Education since Uhuru* (New Haven, Conn., 1969); J. Cameron, *The Development of Education in East Africa* (New York, 1970); J. Olson, 'Secondary schools and elites in Kenya 1961–1965', *Comparative Education Rev.*, *16*, no. 1 (1973), 44–53.

54 L. Byers, 'Exams every term, tests every week', *Where*, Dec. 1972, 343–4; 'The losers as the Asians quit Uganda', *Daily Telegraph*, 21 Sept. 1972.

55 The series of leaflets ('*Welcome*') was prepared by Brian Jackson, Beryl McAlhone, Julia McGawley, Stella Hatton and Luise Byers of the Advisory Centre for Education (ACE) Cambridge and published by the Advisory Centre for Education and the Co-ordinating Committee for the Welfare of Evacuees from Uganda. They were based on discussions with the first families to arrive in Britain. The four leaflets were:
1. *Have You a Child under Five Years Old?*
2. *Have You a Child between Five and Eleven?*
3. *Have You a Child over Twelve?*: information on getting the main educational qualifications in Britain
4. *Basic Facts about Education in Britain*
Among the information was:

Mr Osman: Play is very pleasant. We all like to play. But play is play and education is education. We are asking you about education.

Brian Jackson: In Britain our education system begins with play . . .

Mr Osman: But is this teaching, Mr Jackson? Is this teaching really?

(*Welcome: Have You a Child under Five Years Old?*)

HOW LONG SHOULD I EXPECT TO STUDY?
As long as possible. For example, if you want to take a secretarial course you can take one after O-level, after A-level, or after getting a degree. The more academic qualifications you collect first, the more opportunities you will have for a good career later on.
(*WELCOME: Have you a Child over Twelve?*)

56 C. Davies, 'Ugandan Asians in Britain. A burden or a boon?', *Education*, 8 Sept. 1972, 166.

57 D. Mason, *The Crisis for British Asians in Uganda:* Report for the British Council of Churches (1970), 5–6.

58 *Leicester Schoolmaster*, *7*, no. 2 (published by the Leicester and Leicestershire Schoolmasters Association).

59 'Exodus from Uganda', *TES*, 18 Aug. 1972.

60 '30 Asian Teachers Doing Menial Jobs', *LM*, 18 June 1972.

61 The case for the teachers was argued in: 'Ugandan Students to Replace Asian Teachers', *The Times*, 14 Dec. 1972; letter from Urmila Patel and Elizabeth Bray, *Guardian*, 8 Oct. 1973; 'Into the Cold', *Observer*, 30 Oct. 1973.

62 'Head Hunters from Africa', *TES*, 28 Dec. 1973.

63 Letter from Professor J. A. Bright, *Guardian*, 8 Oct. 1973. Bright stressed the high professional competence and the dedication among Asian teachers. He pointed out that it was wasteful not to use them to remedy teacher shortages, particularly where they were caused by an influx of Asian children from Uganda. Yet he also saw that both the DES and the National Union of Teachers were right to insist on the appropriate qualifications and a non-dilution of standards. In the absence of any special arrangements, he argued that the Ugandan Asian teachers should be classed as 'mature students' and as such should be considered for entry to one- or two-year courses and given sympathetic consideration for grants.

64 Details are to be found in: 'Let Asian Teachers Take Jobs', *The Times*, 6 Oct. 1972; 'Ugandans Shy Away from Training', *TES*, 12 Oct. 1972; 'Flying Squads Needed', *TES*, 3 Nov. 1972; 'Teaching Refugee Children', *TES*, 1 Dec. 1972.

65 'City out ahead on ideas in migrant education', *LM*, 2 Mar. 1974. Among other policies was the decision made in November 1973 not to drop the collection of statistics of immigrant children attending Leicester's schools. This went against the national decision by Mrs Margaret Thatcher, the Education and Science Secretary. She accepted the recommendation of the Select Committee on Race Relations and Immigration: Education, that the collection should cease (see note 11). *LM*, 25 Nov. 1973.

66 Accounts of the experiences of the Vietnamese teachers are: 'Fighting on alien soil', *THES*, 28 Aug. 1981; C. Daglish, 'Re-orientation for teachers from Vietnam', *NC*, *10*, no. 1 (1982), 127–31.

67 *Grants for British Asian Students*, Press notice no. 7, Uganda Resettlement Board (1972).

68 'Ugandan Asian students face money crisis', *Guardian*, 29 Sept. 1972.

69 The *Leicester Mercury* ran a series of reports on local students: 'Ugandan Asians apply for

aid', 7 Oct. 1972; 'Asians rely on fellow students', 27 Oct. 1972; 'Interview with Shoki', 2 Feb. 1973.

70 *Northampton Chronicle and Echo*, 2 July 1973.

71 When in 1985 the Resettlement Board ceased to subsidize expenditure on student grants, Leicester took a more lenient view than did Brent or Newham. Their policies prompted the suggestion in *New Society* ('Discretion file', 17 Apr. 1975, 124) that since 'Amin Dada' had offered to pay for the Prime Minister Harold Wilson to go to Uganda to discuss compensation for Britain on confiscated property, some of the money should be spent on these students. In September 1980 refugees living in the UK became entitled to the equivalent award benefits as home students for degree or equivalent courses in further or higher education. The amending regulation went before Parliament on 11 September 1980. This followed 'many years of campaigning by refugee agencies' (*Guardian*, 15 Sept. 1980). But this ruling applies only to official refugees (defined as within the meaning of the United Nations Convention). It does not apply to Asians from East Africa driven out because of 'Africanization' policies. Thus Jay Thakkar of the Asian Community Action Group was quoted as saying: 'A student of 17 who comes from Malawi with his family is not counted as a refugee. Yet because of the political situation in Malawi he has no choice but to leave with his family. In many cases, the family has come over with little or no money and is not credit worthy. Such students still have to pay the much higher overseas student rates for their fees ('Higher fees block East African students', *TES*, 3 Oct. 1980).

72 'Help Asians gain skills', *TES*, 15 Sept. 1972.

73 Details of the responses of the universities are contained in: 'Universities will help with Ugandan Asians', *TES*, 22 Sept. 1972; 'St Andrews offers places to Ugandan students', *THES*, 29 Sept. 1972; 'Keele places for Ugandan Asian students', *THES*, 6 Oct. 1972.

74 Report of the Education Sub-Committee, CCWEU, 14 Sept. 1972.

75 'Instant school for Asians', *TES*, 13 Oct. 1972; 'Exodus from Uganda', *TES*, 8 Aug. 1972.

76 'Report of Public Schools Headmasters Conference', *Guardian*, 2 Sept. 1972. The Chairman, Mr Frank Shaw, Head of King's College School, Wimbledon, suggested that the public schools could take up to 400 refugee children.

77 V. Marett, 'The resettlement of Ugandan

Asians in Leicester 1972–80' (Ph.D. thesis, University of Leicester, 1983).

78 K. Gershon (ed.), *We Came As Children* (1966), 121.

79 *LM*, 7 Sept. 1973 (own emphasis).

CHAPTER 7. THE HOUSING QUESTION

1 J. Rex and R. Moore, *'Race, Community and Conflict. A Study of Sparkbrook* (1967); C. Bell, 'On housing classes', *Australian and New Zealand J. of Sociology, 13*, no. 1 (1977), 26–40. A different perspective is advanced by other writers such as: J. Davis and J. Taylor, 'Race, community and no conflict', *NS*, 9 July 1970, 67–9.

2 P. Werbner, 'Avoiding the ghetto: Pakistani migrants and settlement shifts in Manchester', *NC, 7*, no. 3 (1979), 376–9; R. Pritchard, *Housing and the Spatial Structure of the City* (1976) (Pritchard analysed residential mobility in Leicester but makes no specific reference to ethnic minorities).

3 B. Dahya, 'The nature of Pakistani ethnicity in industrial cities in Britain', in *Ethnicity and Cities*, ed. A. Cohen (1974), 77–118.

4 T. Jones and D. McEvoy, 'Race and space in Cloud-Cuckoo Land', *Area, 10*, no. 3 (1978), 162–5.

5 Among the researches into the private sector in Leicester are: G. Lomas and E. Monck, *The Coloured Population of Great Britain. A Comparative Study of Coloured Households in Four County Boroughs* (Runnymede Trust, 1975) (this survey was based on the Ward Library Census tabulations for four separate county boroughs – Manchester, Bradford, Wolverhampton and Leicester; in Leicester rather larger proportions of ethnic minority families lived in better housing compared with Bradford and Manchester); *Housing Choice and Ethnic Concentration: An Attitude Study* (Community Relations Commission, 1977); R. Ward, 'Ugandan Asians in Britain: some local variations in the potential for resettlement', paper presented at the Seminar on Ugandan Asians, London, 2 December 1976 (Ward stresses the shortage of private rented accommodation in Leicester).

6 The lack of really accurate information about the numbers of refugees who had arrived in Leicester is reflected in a report in *LM*, 1 March 1973 ('City Ugandan population disputed'). In a House of Commons debate on February 1973, Mr Greville Janner 'shouted out 3,900' in reply to Mr Dudley Smith, Under-Secretary of State for Employment, who said that 2,200 had gone to Leicester. Mr Janner explained that he was

basing his figure on information received from the Department of Health and Social Security in Leicester rather than on the figures from the Resettlement Board. See also the *Leicester Chronicle*, 15 Aug. 1973.

7 D. Phillips, 'Social and spatial segregation of an ethnic minority: the case of Asians in Leicester', paper given at the Conference on Research in Social Geography, Oxford, 1980.

8 *UA*, 9 Oct. 1972. D. Humphry and M. Ward *Passports and Politics* (1974), 97–125, claim that the greatest frustration experienced by the Uganda Resettlement Board was the lack of response from the Local Authorities in the sphere of housing. They examine in detail the 'interesting tussle' at Basildon New Town, Essex. The authors based their findings on reports which appeared in the two local papers – the *Echo* and the *Standard Recorder*. There were many arguments against allocation of development corporation housing to the refugees. As in Leicester this caused a split in the Labour Party on the local Council. One councillor resigned over the allocation of five houses to the handful of refugees who settled in the area. There was a division between Labour's 'old guard' and the younger members over the reception of the refugees.

9 'What Asians face: goodwill but snags', *Sunday Telegraph*, 3 Sept. 1972.

10 'Suburbia and the Asians next door', 9 Sept. 1972.

11 *LM*, 6 Sept. 1972. Overcrowding was the subject of a debate in the General Purposes Committee of the Leicester City Council on 1 September. Alderman S. Bridges spoke against putting the refugees into sub-standard housing ('It is not kind to take people from a fish and chip atmosphere and dump them in the Grand Hotel or vice-versa').

12 'City facing nightmare housing programme', *LM*, 8 Nov. 1972. A full explanation of the explosion in house prices in 1970–3 lies outside the scope of this study. There were two important contributory factors. First, there was the demographic factor, the post-war baby-boom, which meant that there were 30 per cent more prospective buyers than there had been in 1961. The second factor was the acceleration in the volume of mortgage lending. These two trends contributed to a dramatic inflation in house prices that has become 'firmly established in national mythology' ('The house price rollercoaster', *NS*, 28 Jan. 1982).

13 P. Graddon and E. Barthorpe, 'The housing service in Leicester', paper presented to the Institute of Housing Managers. The role of the Housing Advisory Service is related primarily to the private sector tenant rather than those already in council accommodation. Although the situation was to change subsequently, one of the concerns when the service first began was the small numbers of immigrants who used it. During the first six months of the Highfields Centre's operation in 1972, of the 3,126 enquiries dealt with only 367 were from immigrants.

14 Minutes of the Housing Sub-Committee, Leicester Council for Community Relations, 18 Oct. 1972. Malpractices by Asian landlords had not been unknown in Uganda. M. Mamdani, (*From Citizen to Refugee* (1973), blamed the exorbitant rents imposed on Asian tenants on the 'Colonial Uganda laws', which stipulated that 'non-Asians' could only buy within urban areas. Demand therefore always outstripped the supply (p. 35).

15 'Authorities offer housing to immigrants', *Local Government Chronicle*, 8 Sept. 1972, 1509.

16 V. Marett, 'East African Asian students in Further Education Colleges' (M.Ed. thesis, University of Leicester, 1976). In particular Loughborough, Kettering and Wellingborough were popular.

17 *Progress Report no. 5* (CCWEU, 29 Nov. 1972).

18 'No room at Oadby', *LM*, 1 Sept. 1972, *passim*; 'Barrow takes another look at housing Ugandan Asians', *Loughborough Echo*, 27 Oct. 1972.

19 'County View on Asians Sought', *LM*, 28 Sept. 1972. 'Asians influx could have serious effect on Structure Plan', *LM*, 20 Sept. 1972.

20 'The wrong kind of help', *LM*, 22 Sept. 1972.

21 'House granted to Asian family causes protest', *LM*, 2 Feb. 1973.

22 'Grants muddle stops Asian housing plans', *Guardian*, 23 Nov. 1972. The authorities had based their decision on a circular from the Resettlement Board which was dated 18 October. This was interpreted 'that 75 per cent grants would be given on the provision of facilities likely to have a life extending beyond the present emergency' if the expenditure was directly attributable to the arrival of the refugees. But then a second circular appeared on 19 October, which said that grants would be payable on the provision of permanent housing. But on 20 October this was cancelled. Then on 1 November, a third circular again stated that permanent housing would not qualify for grants. The Board explained all this by pointing out that the first circular had merely stated that applications for the 75 per cent grants would

be 'considered' and that grants for housing would have to be approved by the Board before any project was begun. In Loughborough the cost of the houses was borne by the General Rate Fund with some small support from the Housing Revenue Repairs Account.

23 *Weekly Hansard*, House of Lords, Session 1972–3, vol. 338, col. 258, 6 Dec. 1972.

24 *LM*, 8 Nov. 1972.

25 *Housing Conditions in Leicester (1961–1971)* (Shelter Research Group, 1973). It was reported that in 1971 there was a housing shortage in Leicester of some 1,800 dwellings and that in terms of both multiple occupation and overcrowding, conditions had worsened since 1961. The housing shortage was most severe in the rented sector, particularly in the unfurnished sector. Highfields and Spinney Hill, with 50.3 per cent of their persons (16,586) being immigrants, had a recorded proportion of overcrowding – defined at a density of more than 1.5 persons per room – of 17.5 per cent. The increase in the decade on which they focused was more marked in these districts than elsewhere in the city. It was on this that both the Vice-Chairman of the city's Housing Committee and the *Leicester Mercury* commented, and both did so in relation to the influx of immigrants to the area.

26 Letter from Paul Herrington, Research Officer, Leicester Shelter Group, 'Overcrowding not the fault of immigrants', *LM*, 4 Oct. 1973.

27 'Asian Leaders Are Fighting Overcrowding', *LM*, 1 May 1973.

28 Report by the Public Health Department, City of Leicester, 14 Feb. 1973.

29 R. Smith, *Sumitra's Story* (1982), 26–7.

30 Report by Christopher Walker, 'Life on the edge of disaster for refugees', *The Times*, 3 Aug. 1973.

31 Report from the Housing Manager to the Special Committee on Immigration, Leicester City Council, 29 Aug. 1973.

32 Report by Rent Investigation Officer, 6 Sept. 1973. In this it was suggested that provided there was the appropriate information then it would be possible for the Local Authority to take a case to the Rent Tribunal without the tenant's consent. If this brought trouble for the tenant from his landlord then any offences committed could be investigated with a view to prosecution.

33 Report issued by the Spinney Hill Conservative Association, 1975 (the report was from the Secretary, B. Lockley).

34 '12,000 Immigrants May Head for City, Tory Group Warning', *LM*, 4 Apr. 1975.

35 'British Asians', *NS*, 13 Feb. 1975, 392; 'Britain's pledge on race', *Guardian*, 6 Apr. 1975.

36 'Leicester cannot take any more immigrants – Housing Chairman', *LM*, 11 Feb. 1975.

37 *LM*, 15 Aug. 1973 (the family had been given furniture by a local voluntary organization called The People Next Door). In its circular ('Financial Aid to Local Authorities', 1 Nov. 1972) the Resettlement Board had included the advice that basic necessities for a household could be 'from either charitable or voluntary sources . . . The Board recognises the fact that, at least in some instances, some furniture will be required by newcomers when they first move into dwellings. They understand that while housing authorities have powers under Section 94 of the Housing Act 1957 to provide such, the practice of relying on the voluntary sources should be followed.'

38 'Take in Asian letter – just a hoax', *LM*, 6 Oct. 1972; 'The great Homes for Asians hoax', *Evening Post*, 31 Aug. 1972; *Manchester Evening News*, 28 Sept. 1972.

Variations of the hoax surface at regular intervals. All these letters appear to the unsuspecting recipient as genuine and official in origin. One version thanked the householder to whom it was sent for 'offering to help our Pakistani and Indian friends in distress . . . there will be 2 grandmothers, 4 mountain goats . . . 3 holy cows.' One such was sent to a Hinckley housewife in 1981 (*LM*, 19 Dec. 1981). As the *Mancunian Indian*, Sept. 1972 ('A kind of hoax'), pointed out, the cumulative effect of these hoax letters has to be put alongside the effect of 'the group of anti-immigrant MP's' in creating fear in 'the silent majority' especially at a time such as the middle of 'the Ugandan Asian crisis'.

39 S. Hunt, 'Adaptation and Nutritional Applications of Food Habits among Ugandan Asians' (Ph.D. thesis, University of London, 1977). Hunt comments that salaried workers (including many Goans) tended to have company houses and that renting was common in the urban areas in Uganda.

40 'Asian property to be registered by High Commission', *Guardian*, 1 Sept. 1972. This was a report of the Foreign Office's statement that the British High Commission had opened a register in Kampala of assets left by the expellees. It was noted by Praful Patel, as the 'Ugandan member of the Resettlement Board', that the British government did not have any obligation to settle any of the claims, but the register, along with photostats of deeds and bank statements and documents

attested by magistrates, would help in any negotiations over compensation.

41 *Information to all Persons now residing in the U.K. who hold Ugandan Currency Policies:* Memo from CRC to all local Community Relations Officer, 30 July 1974. Though the insurance companies had in the past remitted premiums from Uganda, in 1967 by Ugandan law, all companies which had invested abroad assets from Ugandan currency policies had to transfer such assets back to Uganda.

42 *Weekly Hansard*, House of Lords, Session 1972–3, vol. 338, cols 283–6, 6 Dec. 1972. Details of the proposed schemes at Reading and Bristol are given in the Minutes of the Regional Committees of the CCWEU, 22 and 27 Nov. 1972.

43 *Temporary Accommodation Scheme to meet the Housing Shortage in Leicester* (Leicester Council for Community Relations, 1972).

44 'What the Asians want', *New Society*, 18 Jan. 1973.

45 'Homeless, but still full of the desire to make business succeed', *Guardian*, 7 Aug. 1973.

46 Phillips, 'Social and spatial segregation'. It is to be remarked that there has been definite change since 1980. There has been a very marked increase in the number of Asians buying properties in the suburban areas of Leicester. This has resulted in their negotiating with the major indigenous estate agents.

47 Minutes of the General Purposes Committee, City of Leicester, Sept. 1973.

48 'Ugandan Asians: How Happy?', *Economist*, 29 Sept. 1973, 32.

49 B. Elliot and D. McCrone, *Landlords as Urban Managers: A Dissenting Opinion* (Centre for Environmental Studies, 1975).

50 'Asians are banned from second chance camps', *Guardian*, 7 Nov. 1972. Following the pronouncements made by two national Asian leaders that some refugees were becoming too reliant on the camps, it was ruled that Asians who had moved out of the camps would not be allowed readmission, nor should admission to the camps be allowed to the 5,000 refugees who had arrived in the UK and had managed without going to the centres. The Secretary of the Resettlement Board had sent a telex about all this to the Reception Camp administrators but had not intended that it should be made public.

51 'New Guidelines Help Migrants Get better Deal Over Housing', *LM*, 10 July 1976.

52 D. Pole, *The Distribution of Ugandan Asians in Leicester* (Leicester Council for Community Relations, 1976). The other reports were: C. Cullingford, *Belgrave: The Forgotten Area* (1973); G. West, *Maps of the*

Distribution of Asians in Leicester (1974). (Both Pole and West used the Register kept by the British Asian Welfare Society for their data. The Register covered the period from September 1972 to December 1973.)

53 Cullingford, *Belgrave*.

54 C. Cullingford, *A Collection of Rumours* (Leicester Council for Community Relations, 1973).

55 S. Cowgill, *Survey of the Belgrave Area:* Report to CCWEU. Cowgill was later instrumental in setting up the Melton Road Self Help Centre which was funded out of government funds diverted from Uganda. She had previously worked with BAWS.

56 C. Tylee, 'Planning for areas of mixed development in the inner city' (diss. for the Diploma in Town Planning, Central London Polytechnic, 1977).

57 S. Weir, 'Red line districts', *Roof*, July 1976, 109–14.

58 *Wasted Assets:* Research Paper (Leicester Shelter Group, 1976).

59 Weir, 'Red line districts', attributes this to the linked interests existing between estate agents, solicitors and fringe banks.

60 V. Karn, 'Housing policies that handicap inner cities', *NS*, 11 May 1987, 301–3.

61 Personal communication from Mr E. Hadfield, Director of Housing, 10 Feb. 1976.

62 *Bartholemew Street* (Leicester Shelter Group, 1975).

63 Leicester was among the first cities to start a Renewal Programme aimed at the refurbishing of older properties. It also received extra funds from Central Government under the Inner Area Programme announced in November 1977. This allowed additional expenditure by public authorities for tackling 'the problems of urban poverty'.

64 'Highfields: We are amazed say Spinney Hill Conservatives', *LM*, 15 May 1972 (Labour elected members claimed that those who called for a clean up of Highfields 'wanted a Fascist state').

65 'Highfields No. 1 on Clean Up agenda – Tories', *LM*, 4 June 1973.

66 'No need for Leicester to disperse immigrants', *LM*, 26 Jan. 1975.

67 *Highfields Voice*, Aug. 1981. (The *Highfields Voice* was a community newspaper. Here it was commentating on the findings made by A. Sills *et al* in the *Inner Area Research Project*, Centre for Mass Communications, University of Leicester, 1981.)

68 H. Baker, *St. Peter's Estate: Some Problems of an Inner City Housing Estate* (unpublished report, 1977). Councillor Baker reported that 75 per cent of the problems with which he

had to deal were about housing. There were 1,500 people housed on the estate.

69 It is to be noted that racial harassment on local authority housing estates was already a reality by 1974 when the Ugandan Asians began to be given council houses. This was some time before this harassment was officially acknowledged in reports published by the Home Office and the Commission for Racial Equality. As the *Runnymede Trust Bulletin* (no. 149, Nov. 1982) pointed out: 'The [official] reports confirmed what many in the black community ... had been saying for some time' (p. 5).

70 'Election special', *LM*, 4 June 1973.

71 *Guardian*, 11 Apr. 1973.

72 'Housing going to immigrants – N.F.', *LM*, 27 Feb. 1974.

73 'Why you should march against the National Front in Leicester', *Socialist Worker*, 24 Aug. 1974.

74 *Ethnic Minority Access to Council Housing in Leicester:* Paper considered by the Housing Committee of Leicester City Council, 1981 (Agenda B, 3 Aug.). In this the Director of Housing noted that on average a large family 'will have to wait approximately 2–3 times as long on average as a smaller family ... Insomuch that they form almost half the large family waiting list population in housing need, the Asians are particularly disadvantaged by overall shortage of large accommodation. This disadvantage is exacerbated by voluntary limitation of choice', that is, their wish to remain near to Highfields or Belgrave. The Director did not expand on his statement that 'East African Asians have initiated the move into council housing.'

In Blackburn it has also been seen that Ugandan Asians are more likely to seek council accommodation. One of the explanations offered is that since they had no hope of returning to Uganda, unlike other immigrants they never saw investment in housing as a source of ready capital to be encashed when and if they returned 'home' (V. Robinson, 'Asians in council housing', *Urban Studies, 17, 1980*, 323–31). Further information on Ugandan Asians and council housing is to be found in: M. Bristow and B. Adams, 'Ugandan Asians and the housing market in Britain', *NC, 6*, no. 1/2 (1978), 65–77; M. Bristow, 'Ugandan Asians' racial disadvantage in Manchester and Birmingham', *NC, 8*, no. 2 (1979), 203–16. No data is available at present on the numbers of Ugandan Asians and other immigrant groups who have exercised their right to buy their council houses under the recent legislation.

75 In the late 1970s when it became apparent that Amin's power was at last on the wane, the Ugandan Asian families known to the author began to discuss the possibility of going back to Uganda. In 1981 Obote had overthrown Amin and there was some hope that he would restore normality and welcome the Asians' help in this task. Then the Leicester families made such observations as: 'Not all the family would leave Leicester, but perhaps one of our sons will go to see how much is left of our former businesses and whether there is any hope of employment for a graduate engineer.' Four men from the families did in fact go on a visit, but only one remained in Kampala. The British government also believed that Obote would restore normality and provided Uganda with £7 million a year in aid. But the true picture was revealed when in May 1985 Amnesty International published details of the Luwero Massacres. Rumours of what life was really like in Uganda had already been relayed to Leicester's Ugandan Asians by their families in Kenya. Then came the overthrow of Obote by General Tito Okello in July 1985. His regime appeared no better than those which had gone before. He appointed two army officers who had served under Amin to serve on his Military Council. The National Resistance Army led by Towei Museveni refused to cooperate with the new government. The British government, 'realising it might be backing the wrong side', dispatched Major-General Anthony Pollard to Nairobi to court Museveni. (Major-General Pollard is a member of a prominent Leicester family and his mother has been mayor of the city.) Museveni did become President of Uganda. He made a state visit to London in November 1986. He met a group of Asians and promised them a new start on compensation and told them that Uganda needed their skills. But the majority of the families are still to be convinced that these promises will be translated into reality.

CHAPTER 8. PROBLEMS OF ADJUSTMENT: THE WOMEN'S VIEWS

1 A. Wilson, *Finding a Voice: Asian Women in Britain* (1978), 48–9.

2 P. Clarke, 'The Ismaili Khojas: a sociological study of an Ismaili sect in London (M.Phil. thesis, University of London, 1977).

3 J. Gullahorn, 'An extension of the U-curve hypothesis', *J. of Social Issues, 19*, no. 3 (1963), 33–47.

4 J. Hill, *The Social and Psychological Impact of Unemployment* (Tavistock Institute of Human Relations, 1977).

5 'Cross cultural counselling', *Counselling News, 32* (May 1980). This issue was devoted to recording the transactions of the British Association for Counselling Conference which was held in 1979. A series of seminars discussed the relevance of Western-based therapies in a cross-cultural context.

6 J. Heisler, 'Client–counsellor interaction', *Marriage Guidance Quarterly J., 17*, pt 1 (1978), 233–8; J. Heisler, 'The client writes', *Marriage Guidance Quarterly J., 19, 3*, (1980), 115–25.

7 H. Hay, in *Level Crossing*, ed. W. Blair (mimeo, Commission for Racial Equality, 1979), 23.

8 D. Fitch, 'How do we counsel in Gujerati?', *Marriage Guidance Quarterly J., 19, 4* (1980), 177–84.

9 E. Lam, 'Health visiting Vietnamese refugees in Britain', *Health Visitor, 53* (July 1980), 254–5.

10 'First generation children hit the bottle', *Leicester Trader*, 25 July 1979.

11 'Alcoholism on the increase amongst Asians', *LM*, 5 Nov. 1980.

12 S. Lieberson, 'Ethnic groups and the practice of medicine', *American Sociological Rev., 23* (1958), 542–9.

13 *Guardian*, 20 Oct. 1980. Professor Stanley Davis of Nottingham University commented on the 'counselling' services provided by 'hakims' (Muslim) and 'vaids' (Hindu): 'The Hakims start with the assumption that many illnesses are psychological. Their approach is quite different and they happily spend thirty minutes trying to understand their patients' problems. How often do you get half an hour with your G.P.?'

Other accounts are contained in: H. Salim, 'An Islamic approach to healing' (unpublished paper, Leicester). Salim opened a Leicester clinic based on the philosophies and principles of 'Tibb' (Islamic medicine) and had numbers of Ugandan Asians amongst his patients. 'Prescribing Correctly for the Hakims', *Guardian*, 5 Mar. 1979.

14 O. Surridge, 'Dialling out of despair', *TES*, 14 Nov. 1980.

15 W. Breed, 'Suicide, migration and race', *J. of Social Issues, 22* (Jan. 1966), 30–4.

16 Cf. S. Field, *Resettling Refugees: The Lessons of Research* (Home Office Research Study, 45: 1985), 'it is worth distinguishing between, on the one hand, widespread psychological problems experienced by refugees . . .

including depression, and, on the other hand, severe conditions in smaller numbers of individuals requiring psychiatric care.'

17 E. Koryani, A. Kerenyi and G. Sarwer-Foner, 'Adaptive difficulties of some Hungarian immigrants', *Medical Services J., 14* (1958), 383–405; R. Taft and D. Doczy, 'The assimilation of intellectual refugees in Western Australia', *R.E.M.P. Bulletin, 9–10*, no. 4 (1962), 1–2; T. Cnossen, 'Integration of refugees: some observations of Hungarians in Canada', *International Migration, 2* (1964), 135–53; C. Schou, 'To cope with a crisis: a medical report on Hungarian experience', *International Migration, 16* (1968), 129–31.

18 H. Lehmann, 'Socio-psychiatric observations on displaced persons', *Psychiatry Quarterly, 2* (1953), 245–56.

19 *Ibid.*

20 J. Kosa, A. Antonousky and I. Zola, *Poverty and Health* (Cambridge, Mass., 1969); S. Kasl and S. Cobb, 'Some physical and mental health effects of job loss', *Pakistan Medical Forum, 6* (1971), 95–106; V. Shanthamani, 'Unemployment and neuroticism', *Indian J. of Social Work, 34* (1973), 43–5.

21 S. Gregory and J. Tilling, *Tug-of-War* (1978). This is a fictitious account of the effects of the expulsion from Uganda on them as experienced by school students who had come with their families to Leicester.

22 J. Chaudri, *The Emigration of the Sikh Jats from the Punjab to England* (Social Science Research Project, School of Oriental and African Studies, University of London, 1972).

23 The effects of migration on females is described in: B. Malzberg and E. Lee, *Migration and Mental Disorder* (Social Science Research Council, New York, 1956); cf. Breed, 'Suicide, migration and race'.

24 W. Taylor, 'Basic patterns in Orthodox Hindu culture', *J. of Abnormal and Social Psychology, 43* (1948), 3–12.

25 The expectations of women's roles is discussed by: M. Warnock, 'Back to the thirties times', *TES*, 10 Oct. 1980. This is to be compared with the account of Asian women in R. Littlewood and M. Lipsedge, *Aliens and Alienists: Ethnic Minorities and Psychiatry* (1982), 161. The authors emphasize that the stereotype of 'the traditionally passive Asian woman' needs to be redressed. It was the East African Asian women who were those who led the strike at

Imperial Typewriters in Leicester in 1974 (p. 101). Two of the women who are discussed in the present chapter took part in this protest.

26 A. Agarwal, 'Patterns of marital disharmonies', *Indian J. of Psychology, 13* (1971), 185–93.

27 P. Kapur, *Marriage and the Working Women of India* (Ghaziabad, 1970).

28 N. Schlossberg, 'A framework for counselling women', *Personnel and Guidance J.*, *51*, Pt 2 (1972), 137–43.

29 M. Clark, *Health in Mexican American Culture* (Berkeley, Cal., 1970).

30 K. Clancy and W. Grove, 'Sex differences in mental illness', *American J. of Sociology, 80*, no. 1 (1974), 205–16.

31 S. Journard, *The Transparent Self* (New York, 1971).

32 E. Erickson, 'Group identity', *American Psychoanalytic Association, 4* (1956), 56–121; L. Duhl and J. Powell, *The Urban Conditions: People and Policy in the Metropolis* (Boston, Mass., 1963), 153.

33 M. Stopes-Roe and R. Cochrane, 'Mental health and integration: a comparison of Indian, Pakistani and Irish immigrants to England', *Ethnic and Racial Studies, 3* (July 1980), 316–41; R. Cochrane and M. Stopes-Roe, 'The mental health of immigrants', *NC, 8*, nos. 1–2 (1980), 123–8. Leicester was one of the areas surveyed by the authors. They found that Indians as a whole showed 'fewer psychological symptoms than natives'. When Indians were compared with Pakistanis, there were positive psychological advantages which the researchers traced to the 'upward social mobility' of the Indian group.

34 Lam, 'Health visiting Vietnamese refugees'.

35 J. Melville, 'The scars of the survivors', *NS*, 18 Oct. 1979, 124–6.

36 'In perspective', Radio Leicester, April 1977.

37 G. Carstairs and R. Kapur, *The Great Universe of Kota: Stress, Change and Disorder in an Indian Village* (1976). This study shows the range of psychiatric problems in a rural setting in India.

CONCLUSION

1 'Thumbs Down', *Economist*, 2 Sept. 1972.

2 R. Thurlow, *Fascism in Britain* (1986), 291; M. Anwar, *Votes and Policies: Ethnic Minorities and the General Election 1979* (Commission for Racial Equality, 1980), 70.

3 Evidence based on research in 79 major

towns by the Evening Newspaper Advertising Bureau, 1975. Ray Hill, a 'mole' working inside the British Movement, has explained that this accusation about the *Leicester Mercury* was made in a leaflet which was never in fact circulated. Nevertheless the *Mercury* was tricked into devoting an entire editorial to defend its position. Thus the British Movement reached a 'far wider public' than it would have had otherwise. (R. Hill and A. Bell, *The Other Face of Terror* (1988), 130–1).

4 A refugee is defined as a person who 'owns a well founded fear of being persecuted for reasons of race, religion and nationality'.

5 In 1984 three elderly Ugandan Asians unsuccessfully challenged the Foreign Office in the High Court. In 1983 C. S. Amin, V. J. Vasant and K. Pirbhai were given leave to do so. All were in their seventies. They sought to quash the decision made by the former Foreign Secretary, Francis Pym, that the claims should be pursued through the Ugandan courts. Their counsel, Mr Ian MacDonald, said that the point at issue was whether their claims for compensation were on the basis that they were British citizens and entitled to the protection of the British government. MacDonald admitted that though the Foreign Secretary did not have a duty enforceable in law, he was exercising a discretion according to the published Foreign Office rules applying to international claims: 'In applying those rules the Secretary of State has misdirected himself both as a matter of fact and of law as to the availability of legal remedies in Uganda.' The claims were supported by the Uganda Evacuees Association. Praful Patel, its spokesman, told the *Asian Post* (5 Nov. 1983) that the Ugandan government had agreed to compensation, but after the murder of Dora Block at the time of Israel's 1976 raid on Entebbe, diplomatic relations with the UK had been broken off. They were restored in 1979 and compensation talks were resumed. But in October 1985 Master of the Rolls Sir John Donaldson dismissed the appeal ('Uganda Claims Ruling Rapped', *LM*, 18 Oct. 1985).

6 *LM*, 4 Apr. 1979.

7 *LM*, 7 Aug., 3 Sept. 1982.

8 'Canada skimmed the cream of the Asian refugees', *Globe and Mail*, Toronto, 5 July 1975. Because Canada was quick to send its immigration team to Kampala it was able to 'bid for the cream'. Ross Henderson, the

Globe's correspondent, commented that 'Afro-Asian journalists in London see Canada as a hypocritical opportunist in its immigration policies'.

9 *Settling For the Future* (British Refugee Council, 1981).

10 P. Jones, *Vietnamese Refugees* (The Home Office, 1982); S. Field, *Resettling Refugees: The Lessons of Research* (1985).

11 B. Vyas (ed.), *Dharatina Khapparma Abh* (Admedabad, 1979).

12 Letter from the Leicester Council for Community Relations to Alderman E. Marston and Alderman K. Bowden, dated 27 Oct. 1972. The 'Expo Leicester 1972' aimed to exhibit the city's thriving industries and technological developments in 'the fun-packed Abbey Park' (*Guardian*, 2 Sept. 1972).

Select bibliography

OFFICIAL SOURCES

COMMUNITY RELATIONS COMMISSION

Employment Transfer Scheme: Information to all Secretaries and Community Relations Officers from Baljit Roa, Assistant Officer, Ugandan Asians (1973).
Ugandan Asians: An Assessment of the Situation from the January Survey: Statement by Navnit Dholakia, Senior Development Officer (1973).
Ugandan Asians – Unclaimed Luggage: Circular to all Community Relations Officers from Diana Christian, Assistant Development Officer (1973).
Information to all Persons now residing in the UK who hold Ugandan Currency Policies (1974).
One Year On: A Report on the Resettlement of the Refugees from Uganda in Britain (1974).
Housing in Multi-Racial Areas: Prepared by a Working Party of Housing Directors (1976).
Refuge or Home? A Policy Statement on the Resettlement of Refugees (1976).

UGANDA RESETTLEMENT BOARD

Communications to Clerks of Local Authorities in England, Wales and Scotland, 31 August, 18 September, 1 November and 8 November 1972.
News Bulletins, September 1972 to April 1973 (nos. 1–15).
Ugandan Asians: Financial Aid to Local Authorities: Press notice, 2 November 1972.

Grants for British Asian Students, Press notice no. 7, 3 October 1972.

Letters from T. Critchley (Grants Secretary) to the Town Clerk of Leicester, 17 January, 2 April 1973.
Letter from S. Barraclough (Secretary to the Board) to Directors of Social Services, 15 March 1973.
Interim Report, May 1973, Cmnd 5296.

Final Report, April 1974, Cmnd 5594.

UGANDA ASIAN RELIEF TRUST

Circular from Lord Sainsbury (Chairman) to all Local Authorities and Managers of New Town Development Corporations, 13 November 1972.
Index of Officers nominated by Local Authorities, 30 January, 8 March, 9 July 1973 (circulars from N. Whitton, Secretary).

CO-ORDINATING COMMITTEE FOR THE WELFARE OF EVACUEES FROM UGANDA

Progress Reports 1–6, September–December 1972.
Ugandan Asians – How Can I Help?: leaflet published on behalf of CCWEU by the British Council of Churches Community and Race Relations Unit, September 1972.
Report of the Education Sub-Committee, 14 September and 2 October 1972.
Minutes of the Housing Sub-Committee, 7 November 1972.
Minutes of Representatives of Regional Co-ordinating Committees, 22 and 27 November and 12 December 1972.
Memorandum to All Organisations of C.C.W.E.U., 31 March 1973, from Gwen Cashmore (Director).
Memorandum to All Members, 31 May 1973, from Helene Middleweek (Director).

DEPARTMENT OF EMPLOYMENT

Employment of Asian Immigrants: Information for Employers on the Educational and Social Background of the Ugandan Asians, October 1972.

PARLIAMENTARY PAPERS

Weekly Hansard, House of Commons, Session 1967–8, vol. 759, col. 1345–6, 27 February 1968.
1578, 28 February 1968.
Weekly Hansard, House of Lords, Session 1972–3, vol. 338, cols. 283–6, 6 December 1972.
Weekly Hansard, House of Commons, Oral Answers to Questions, vol. 847, cols. 1657–8, 7 December 1972.

Weekly Hansard, House of Commons, Oral
Answers to Questions, vol. 851, cols. 1256–7,
27 February 1973.

LEICESTER COUNCIL FOR COMMUNITY RELATIONS

Annual Reports, 1972–9.
Minutes of Executive Committee, Housing and
Education Sub-Committees, 1972–9.

UNPUBLISHED REPORTS:

*Temporary Accommodation Scheme to meet the
Housing Shortage in Leicester* (1972).
Belgrave: A Collection of Rumours (1973).
Belgrave: The Forgotten Area (1973).
Maps of the Distribution of Asians in Leicester
(1976).
The Distribution of Ugandan Asians in Leicester
(1974).
Ethnic Minorities in Council Accommodation (1981).

CITY OF LEICESTER COUNCIL RECORDS

Health of the City of Leicester, 1968–72.
Leicester Finances: Annual Reports, 1968–72.
Report of the Education Committee, 1971–3.
Minutes of the Finance and General Purposes
Committee, 1972.
Minutes of the Housing Committee, 1972–3.
Minutes of the Social Services Committee,
1972–3.
Minutes of the Special Sub-Committee on
Immigration, August 1973.
Ethnic Minority Access to Council Housing 1981:
Paper considered by Housing Committee of
the City Council, 3 August 1981.
Renewal Stategy 1981 (Fifth Annual Review),
Leicester City Council.

LOCAL (LEICESTER AND LEICESTERSHIRE) VOLUNTARY AGENCIES

Leicestershire Branch, Red Cross Society,
Newsletter, September 1972.
Leicester Society of Friends (Quakers),
Statement, September 1972.
Petition by Miss C. Tauber and others to the
Town Clerk: The Ugandan Asians and
Leicester, 15 September 1972.
Leicester Branch, British Federation of
University Women, Report, October 1972.
Leicester Progressive Jewish Congregation,
Newsletter, October 1972.
British Asian Welfare Society, correspondence to
Leicester Council for Community Relations,
1972–3.

Gujarati Welfare Society, correspondence to
Leicester Council for Community Relations,
1972–3.
Leicester Spinney Hill Conservative Association,
Overcrowding: The Housing Situation (1975).

LEICESTER SHELTER GROUP:

Housing Conditions in Leicester (1961–1971)
(1973).
A Housing Policy for Leicester (1974).
Bartholemew Street (1975).
Wasted Assets (1977).

OTHER LEICESTER SOURCE DOCUMENTS

The Survey of Leicester.
Wakerley School: Report to Governors 1977.
Sills, A., Tarpley, M. and Golding, P., *Inner
Area Research Project: Social Survey* (Centre for
Mass Communications Research, University
of Leicester, 1981).

JOURNALS AND DIRECTORIES

Africa
Africa Diary
Africa Today
African Affairs
African Clarion
African Digest
American Sociological Review
The Asian Who's Who 1977–1978 (2nd edn),
Asian Observer Publications
Atlantic
East African Journal
Economist
Equality (Inter-Racial Solidarity Campaign,
Leicester)
Equals
Ethnic and Racial Studies
Focus (Peterborough)
Indian Journal of International Law
Indian Weekly
International and Comparative Law Quarterly
International Migration
Internationalist
Issue
Journal of African and Asian Studies
Kenya Historical Review
Kroniek Van Africa
Listener
Local Government Chronicle
Mancunian Indian
Municipal Journal
New Community
New Society
New Statesman

Orbis
Private Eye
Race Today
Runnymede Trust Bulletin
Socialist Worker
Spectator
Tanzania Notes and Records
Third World
Times Educational Supplement
Times Higher Education Supplement
Transition

NEWSPAPERS

Birmingham Post
Daily Express
Daily Mirror
Daily Telegraph
Dawn (Pakistan)
East African Standard
Financial Times
Globe and Mail (Toronto)
Guardian
Highfields Voice (1976–9)
Leicester Chronicle
Leicester Mercury
Leicester Trader
Loughborough Echo
Manchester Evening News
Observer
Sunday Mirror
Sunday Telegraph
Sunday Times
Telegraph and Argus (Bradford)
The Times
Ugandan Argus

BACKGROUND TO THE EXPULSION OF THE ASIANS FROM UGANDA

Adams, B., 'A look at Uganda and the expulsion through ex-Ugandan eyes', *Kroniek Van Africa*, 3 (1975), 237–49.

Apter, D., *The Political Kingdom of Uganda* (Princeton, NJ, 1967).

Berghe, Van Den, P., 'Asian Africans before Independence', *Kroniek Van Africa*, 6 (Special Issue on Asian Minorities in Africa) (1975), 193–7.

Bharati, A., *The Asians in East Africa, Jayhind and Uhuru* (Chicago, 1972).

Chattopadhyaya, H., *Indians in Africa: A Socio-Economic History* (Calcutta, 1970).

Couper, K. and Lakhani, H., *'Stet' – the Unemployed, Homeless and Destitute: A report on the British Asians in Uganda* (Joint Council for the Welfare of Immigrants, 1971).

Nanjira, D., *The Status of Aliens in East Africa* (New York, 1976).

Enharo, P. 'Amin and the Asians', *Africa, 14* (Oct. 1972), 13–18.

Ghai, Y. and Ghai, D., *The Asian Minorities in East and Central Africa* (Minority Rights Group, 1971).

Howard, M., *The Greatest Claim* (Bow Group, 1970).

Kibedi, W., 'Kibedi speaks out', *Africa Report*, July–Aug. 1974, 45–8.

Kyemba, H., *State of Blood* (1977).

Luff, P., 'Passport to nowhere', *Internationalist*, 3 (May–Aug. 1971), 11–17.

Mamdani, M., *Politics and Class Formation in Uganda* (1976).

Mangat, J., *A History of Africans in East Africa* (1969).

Martin, D., *General Amin* (1974).

Mason, P., *The Crisis for the British Asians in Uganda* (British Council of Churches, 1970).

Meisler, S., 'Uganda', *Atlantic, 230* (Dec. 1972), 27–38.

Melady, T. and Melady, M., 'The expulsion of the Asians from Uganda', *Orbis, 19*, no. 4 (1976), 160–200.

Melady, T. and Melady, M., *Uganda: The Asian Exiles* (New Delhi, 1976).

Mukherjee, R., *The Problem of Uganda: A Study in Acculturation* (Berlin, 1956).

Mulemba, K., 'An unfair press', *Africa, 19* (1978), 46.

Nazareth, J., *Brown Man, Black Country. On the Foothills of Uhuru* (privately printed, Nairobi, 1975).

O'Brien, J., *Brown Britons: The Crisis of the Ugandan Asians* (Runnymede Trust, 1972).

Parsons, J., 'Africanising trade in Uganda: the final solution', *Africa Today, 20* (Winter 1970), 59–62.

Ramchandani, R., *Ugandan Asians. The End of an Enterprise* (Bombay, 1976).

Sathyamurthy, T., 'Ugandan politics', *Economic and Political Weekly, 7*, pt 42 (1972), 2122–8.

Sheriff, A., 'Indians in East Africa', *Tanzania Notes and Records, 77* (1973), 75–80.

Tandon, Y., *Problems of a Displaced Minority. The New Position of East African Asians* (Minority Rights Group, 1973).

Theroux, P., 'Hating the Asians', *Transition, 7*, no. 2 (Oct./Nov. 1967), 46–51.

Tilbe, D., *East African Asians* (Race Relations Committee, Society of Friends, 1970).

Twaddle, M. (ed.), *The Expulsion of a Minority. Essays on Ugandan Asians* (1975).

Wamala, I., 'Amin and the Asians', *Third World, 1* (1972), 5–8.

Woolridge, F. and Sharma, A., 'The expulsion of the Ugandan Asians', *International and Comparative Law Quarterly, 23*, pt 2 (1974), 397–425.

THE RECEPTION AND RESETTLEMENT OF THE UGANDAN ASIANS

Adams, B., 'Ugandan Asians in exile: household and kinship in the resettlement crisis', *Journal of Comparative Studies, 8*, no. 3 (1977), 167–78.

Adams, B. and Bristow, M., 'Ugandan Asians, expulsion experiences: rumour and reality', *J. of Asian and African Studies, 14*, no. 314 (1979), 191–203.

Ardill, N., *Interim Report of the Development Office* London Council of Social Services, Ugandan Asian Unit, 1976).

Aziz, K., 'In Britain Now', *Listener*, 20 May 1976, 635.

Bandali, S., 'Small accidents', in *Our Lives*, ed. P. Ashton and M. Simmonds (ILEA English Centre, 1979).

Bourne, J., 'Resettlement blues', *Race Today, 14*, no. 11 (Nov. 1972), 357.

Bristow, M., Britain's response to the Ugandan Asian crisis. Government myths against political and resettlement realities', *New Community, 5*, no. 3 (1976), 265–79.

Bristow, M., Adam, B. and Pereira, C., 'Ugandan Asians in Britain, Canada and India: some characteristics and resources', *New Community, 4*, no. 2 (1975) 155–66.

Cole, P., *Ugandan Asians and Employment* (Runnymede Trust, 1973).

Critchley, J., *The Ugandan Asians: A World Problem*, Crisis Paper no. 24, Other Atlantic Publications (1972).

Cunningham, Sir Charles, 'The work of the Uganda Resettlement Board and hiving off: some possibilities for research', *Public Administration, 51* (Autumn 1973), 251–60.

Cunningham, Sir Charles, 'The work of the Uganda Resettlement Board', *New Community, 2*, no. 3 (1973), 265–79.

Cunningham, Sir Charles, 'The work of the Uganda Resettlement Board', *Contemporary Review, 222* (May 1973), 225–30.

Fisher, M., 'Asian Indians in New York City', *Urban Athropology, 7*, no. 3 (1979), 261–7.

Gladwin, M., 'Ugandan Asians in Britain', in *The Year Book of Social Policy*, ed. K. Jones (1972), 107–33.

Glyn-Jones, R., *A Report on the Experiences of Ugandan Asian Families Settled in Blackburn* (Community Relations Council, Blackburn, 1973).

Gregory, S. and Tilling, J., *Tug-of-War* (1978).

Hamilton-Preston, J., 'Camp on John Bull Island', *Nova*, April 1973, 68–72.

Hawkins, F., 'Ugandan Asians in Canada', *New Community, 2*, no. 3 (1973), 268–75.

Humphrey, D. and Ward, M., *Passports and Politics* (1974).

Hunt, S., 'Adaptation and nutritional applications of food habits among Ugandan Asians settling in Britain' (Ph.D. thesis, University of London, 1977).

Jackson, B., *Starting School* (1979).

Kidman, B., *A Handful of Tears* (BBC, 1975).

Kramer, J., 'Profiles: the Ugandan Asians', *New Yorker, 50* (8 Apr. 1974), 47–93.

Kuepper, W., Lackey, L. and Swinerton, N., *Ugandan Asians in Great Britain: Forced Migration and Social Absorption* (1975).

Mamdani, M., *From Citizen to Refugee* (1973).

Markham, E. and Kingston, A. (eds.), *Merely a Matter of Colour* (1973).

Martin, P., 'Reluctant exiles', *Sunday Times*, 8 Dec. 1974.

Middleweek, H. and Ward, M., *A Job Well Done?*: Report prepared for the Co-ordinating Committee for the Welfare of Evacuees from Uganda (1973).

Naipaul, S., 'We always knew that one day we should have to come', *Sunday Times*, 31 Dec. 1972.

Naipaul, S., 'Passports to dependence', in *Beyond the Dragon's Mouth* (1984), 221–9.

Nandy, D. and Briant, R., 'Survey casts doubts on town's case', *The Times*, 29 Sept. 1972.

Pereira, C., Adams, B. and Bristow, M., 'Canadian beliefs and policy regarding the admission of Ugandan Asians to Canada', *Ethnic and Racial Studies, 1*, no. 3 (1978), 350–64.

Pollard, D. and Parsloe, E., *The Ugandan Asians: The Reality of Resettlement* (Co-ordinating Committee for the Welfare of Evacuees from Uganda and International Voluntary Service, 1972).

Romijin, J., *Tabu – Ugandan Asians, the Old, the Weak, the Vulnerable* (London Council of Social Services, 1976).

Salveston, J., *Uprooted* (1977).

Shakir, M., 'Leicester lurches right', *Race Today, 4*, no. 10 (Oct. 1972), 321.

Smith, R., *Sumitra's Story* (1982).

Troyna, B., *Public Awareness and the Media: A Study in Reporting on Race*, (Commission for Racial Equality, 1981).

Vyas, B. (ed.), *Dharatina Khapparma Abh* (Ahmedabad, 1979).

Walker, C., 'Life on the edge of disaster for refugees', *The Times*, 3 Aug. 1973.

Wallis, S., 'The Asians' arrival', *New Society*, 27 May 1978, 472–3.

Ward, R., 'What future for the Ugandan Asians?', *New Community, 2*, no. 4 (1973), 372–8.

Weir, S., 'Supplementary benefits – Discrimination', *New Community, 2*, no. 4 (1973), 379–83.

Wilkins, T., 'Asian immigrants settle in', *Guardian*, 26 Mar. 1974.

York Committee for the Welfare of British Asians from Uganda, *Green For Come* (1973).

EDUCATION

Bourne, R., 'Schools prepare for 19,000 Asian schoolchildren', *Times Educational Supplement*, 15 Aug. 1972.

Byers, L., 'Exams every term, tests every week', *Where*, Dec. 1972, 343–4.

Cameron, J., *The Development of Education in East Africa* (New York, 1970).

Hunter, J. *Education For a Developing Region*, (1963).

Davis, C., 'Ugandan Asians in Britain – a burden or boon?', *Education*, *140*, no. 11 (8 Sept. 1972).

Leicester Schoolmaster, 7, no. 2 (Leicester and Leicestershire Schoolmasters Association, 1968).

Mander, J., *Leicester Schools 1944–1974* (Leicester City Council, 1980).

Olson, J., 'Secondary schools and elites in Kenya 1961–1965, *Comparative Education Review*, *16*, no. 1 (1973), 44–53.

Select Committee on Race Relations and Immigration: Education (1972–1973) (1973), III, 477–523.

Stabler, E., *Education since Uhuru* (Newhaven, Conn., 1969).

HOUSING

Baker, H., *St Peter's Leicester, Some Problems of an Inner Area City Estate* (mimeo, 1977).

Bristow, M., 'Ugandan Asians' racial disadvantage in Manchester and Birmingham', *New Community*, 7, no. 2 (1979), 203–16.

Bristow, M. and Adams, B., 'Ugandan Asians and the housing market in Britain', *New Community*, 6, nos. 1 and 2 (1977–8), 65–77.

Community Relations Commission, *Housing Choice and Ethnic Concentration: An Attitude Study* (1977).

Cowgill, S., *A Survey of the Belgrave Area*: Report to the Co-ordinating Committee for the Welfare of Evacuees from Uganda (1973).

Dahya, B., The nature of Pakistani ethnicity in industrial cities in Britain', in A. Cohen (ed.), *Ethnicity in Cities* (1974), 77–118.

Davis, J. and Taylor, J., 'Race, community and no conflict', *New Society*, 9 July 1976, 67–9.

Graddon, P. and Barthorpe, E., 'The Housing Service in Leicester', paper presented at the Institute of Housing Managers (mimeo).

Henderson, D. and Smith, P., 'The Islamic environment in a British city – a case study of Leicester', paper given at the International Symposium, King Feisal University, Saudi Arabia (Leicester Polytechnic, School of Architecture, 1979).

Jones, T. and McEvoy, D., 'Race and space in cloud-cuckoo land', *Area*, *10*, no. 3 (1978), 162–5.

Leicester City Council, *Ethnic Minority Access to Council Housing*, paper considered by the Housing Committee, 3 Aug. 1981.

Phillips, D., 'The social and spatial segregation of Asians in Leicester', in *Social Integration and Ethnic Segregation*, ed. P. Jackson and S. Smith (1981), 101–121.

WOMEN: MENTAL HEALTH AND MIGRATION

Agarwal, A., 'Patterns of marital disharmonies', *Indian Journal of Psychology*, *13* (1971), 185–93.

Blair, W. (ed.), *Level Crossing* (Commission for Racial Equality, mimeo, 1971).

Carstairs, G. and Kapur, R., *The Great Universe of Kota: Stress and Change and Mental Disorder in an Indian Village* (1976).

Cochrane, R. and Stopes-Roe, M., 'Mental health and immigrants', *New Community*, *111*, no. 1/2 (1980), 123–8.

'Cross-cultural counselling', *Counselling News*, *32* (May 1980).

Fitch, D., 'How do we counsel in Gujerati?', *Marriage Guidance Quarterly Journal*, Dec. 1980, 177–84.

Gullahorn, J., 'An extension of the U-curve hypothesis', *Journal of Social Issues*, *19*, no. 3 (1963), 33–47.

Kapur, P., *Marriage and the Working Women in India* (Ghaziabad, 1970).

Lang, E., 'Health visiting Vietnamese refugees in Britain', *Health Visitor*, *53* (July 1980), 254–5.

Littlewood, R. and Lipsedge, M., *Aliens and Alienists: Ethnic Minorities and Psychiatry* (1982).

Malzberg, B. and Lee, E., *Migration and Mental Disorder* (Social Science Research Council, New York, 1956).

Melville, J., 'The scars of the survivors', *New Society*, 18 Oct. 1979, 124–6.

Shanthamanti, V., 'Unemployment and neuroticism', *Indian Journal of Social Work*, *34* (1973), 43–5.

Stopes-Roe, M. and Cochrane, R., 'Mental health and integration: a comparison of Indian, Pakistani and Irish immigrants to England', *Ethnic and Racial Studies*, *3* (July 1980), 316–41.

Taylor, W., 'Basic personality in Orthodox Hindu culture patterns', *Journal of Abnormal and Social Psychology*, *43* (1948), 3–12.

Wilson, A., *Finding a Voice: Asian Women in Britain* (1978).

ADDITIONAL INFORMATION ON REFUGEES

British Refugee Council, *Settling for a Future. Proposals for a British Policy on Refugees* (1987).

D'Souza, F., *The Refugee Dilemma: International Recognition and Acceptance* (Minority Rights Group, 1980).

Field, S., *Resettling Refugees: The Lessons of Research* (Home Office Research Study no. 87, 1985).

Goodwin-Gill, G., *The Refugee in International Law* (1983).

Jones, P., *Vietnamese Refugees. A Study of their Reception and Resettlement in the U.K.* (Research and Planning Unit Paper 13, Home Office, 1982).

Levin, M., *What Welcome? Reception and Resettlement of Refugees in Britain* (Acton Society Trust, 1981).

Index